Paris and Oxford Universities in the Thirteenth and Fourteenth Centuries

PARIS AND OXFORD UNIVERSITIES IN THE THIRTEENTH AND FOURTEENTH CENTURIES

An Institutional and Intellectual History

GORDON LEFF

ROBERT E. KRIEGER PUBLISHING COMPANY
HUNTINGTON, NEW YORK
1975

Original Edition 1968
Reprint 1975

Printed and Published by
ROBERT E. KRIEGER PUBLISHING CO., INC.
645 NEW YORK AVENUE
HUNTINGTON, NEW YORK 11743

Printed in the United States of America

Library of Congress Cataloging in Publication Data

Leff, Gordon.
    Paris and Oxford Universities in the thirteenth and fourteenth centuries.

    Reprint of the ed. published by Wiley, New York.
    1. Education, Medieval. 2. Paris. Université--History. 3. Oxford. University--History. I. Title.
[LA91.L4 1975]   378.425'74   75-12725
ISBN 0-88275-297-9

PREFACE

This book is an account of the universities of Paris and Oxford during the thirteenth and fourteenth centuries. It is at once more and less than a history of their respective cities: more in being concerned with their position in the intellectual life of Western Europe, less in focusing attention upon those aspects of Paris and Oxford that were germane to the development of their universities. Nevertheless, as I hope will become apparent, both universities were what they were by virtue of belonging to a city; their nature and standing were directly related to the nature and standing of Paris and Oxford as towns. I have sought to keep this to the forefront without, however, attempting to minimize those features that were distinctive to a university and transcended local considerations. If little of what I have written is novel, there is not, to my knowledge, any recent study that treats the main intellectual and doctrinal developments at Paris and Oxford within context of their universities. I have been particularly concerned, on the one hand, to show the connection between the academic structure—faculties, syllabuses, teaching methods, and so on—and the intellectual activities that took place within it and, on the other, to assess what was distinctive to each university within a common urban, institutional, and doctrinal framework. This has entailed including a more general background in the earlier part of Chapter 3; but neither there nor in the last two chapters have I attemped to write an intellectual history along the lines of my *Medieval Thought from St. Augustine to Ockham*. Although in Part One I have cited all the more relevant events and their sources, in Part Two I have had to be rigorously selective, confining myself to those topics that were central to the two universities. I hope, nevertheless, that by giving the disputes over Aristotle and poverty some content and sketching the nature of Grosseteste's outlook the living characteristics of each university may have emerged as well as its wider role.

I should like to thank Mrs. Arlen Sue Fox and Miss Nancy Unger for their work on the book, and Mrs. V. Liversidge and Miss H. Pickett for so willingly and skilfully typing the manuscript.

GORDON LEFF

York, England
November, 1967

CONTENTS

LIST OF ILLUSTRATIONS

Paris and Oxford Universities in the Thirteenth and Fourteenth Centuries

Introduction

For the greater part of the thirteenth and fourteenth centuries Paris and, to a lesser extent, Oxford were the foci of speculative thought in the West. They were associated with all the main thinkers and issues of the epoch. This gave them—especially Paris—a unique significance. Not only were they, like Bologna in law and Montpellier in medicine, of international standing that went far beyond their importance as mere towns, or even, in the case of Paris, as a capital. Unlike the centers of law and medicine, whose disciplines were predominantly practical, Paris and Oxford had in addition the well-being of the Christian faith in their care. Philosophy and theology dealt with matters that directly impinged on the foundations of belief. Questions such as the existence of God or the eternity of the world had a doctrinal import that put them in another category from most issues raised by the study of law or medicine. Hence the close oversight that Paris especially received from the papacy and the ecclesiastical authorities throughout these two centuries. The debates had a wider significance, which was always likely to and frequently did erupt beyond the milieu of the schools. For that reason much of the intellectual and doctrinal development of the thirteenth and fourteenth centuries is mirrored in the history of Paris and Oxford universities.

This was not confined to its more abstract facets. Both universities, especially Paris, reflected the tensions between the demands of their own corporate life and the demands of higher—principally papal and ecclesiastical—authority. They occurred at a number of levels. There was the antinomy between theology and the pagan knowledge (mainly Aristotelian) taught in the arts faculty: it was one that was never resolved, and it led to repeated condemnations of Aristotle's works and Aristotelian notions, culminating in 1277. There was the hostility of the secular masters to the religious orders, above all the Dominicans and Franciscans. Beginning as resentment against the mendicants' autonomy and exemption from many of the obligations to which the seculars were subject, this hostility became at Paris during the middle decades of the thirteenth century a wholesale attack on the friars' *raison d'être*. Finally, there was the paradox of an autonomous body, a corporation, being judged by spiritual criteria. For the university, whether in the civic setting of the Italian towns or in the predominantly ecclesiastical ambiance of northern Europe, was essentially a self-governing community with an independent juridical standing. Unlike the monastic and cathedral schools of the preceding epoch, learning, not the cultivation of religious understanding, was its purpose; the university professionalized knowledge. It consisted of masters whose function was to teach the different subjects and students concerned to qualify themselves for a career, the majority in secular professions: teaching, medicine, and law and the vast array of notarial occupations associated with it. Theology was never more than the pursuit of a minority even at Oxford and Paris—one among the three higher faculties—whereas in the lower faculty of arts Aristotle's word was supreme. The organization no less than the content of learning was orientated to this world. Like any other corporation the university was concerned with regulating rights and privileges both among its members and in relation to the outside world. This gave rise to frequent conflict and almost continuing friction. Indeed, whatever the role of the church in controlling their activities, both Paris and Oxford universities owed their survival to the protection of the successive kings of France and England. Their repeated interventions saved both universities from dissolution on more than one occasion. Without them, physical destruction at the hands of the local citizens and dispersion in times of crisis would have meant the certain end of both universities long before the end of the Middle Ages. It is true that university members enjoyed the legal privilege of immunity from civil jurisdiction granted to clerics (benefit of the clergy); but on this was superimposed a series of grants of royal protection that made it effective. The juxtaposition of spiritual and temporal was of the essence of Paris and Oxford, as of so many medieval universities. They were at once concerned with knowledge and faith; they had the interest of both papal and royal authority. Physically they were, like any other corporation, part of the city, without which they could not have survived; institutionally they were international, immune from urban control but subject to spiritual jurisdiction. They escaped their local ties for the intervention of both king and pope.

It is therefore unrealistic to treat Paris and Oxford as mere extensions of the church, any more than it would be tenable to think of them primarily in terms of their respective towns or even, in some ways, kingdoms. They contained elements of all these, but they were subordinate to their distinctive nature as self-regulating communities of masters and scholars.

It was their pursuit of learning that set the universities apart. It distinguished them as separate bodies enjoying, like all guilds and corporations, their own forms of organization. But it also made them more than mere corporations. As the guardians of knowledge they dealt in an international medium which, unlike wool fells or foodstuffs, could not simply be regulated as a local monopoly. On the contrary, to be a university (a *studium generale*) was to have attained to a universal eminence that attracted masters and scholars from all parts. The position of Paris and Oxford, Bologna and Padua, until the later fourteenth century, was the antithesis of local. Universities during the high Middle Ages were, in fact, nearer to constituting an independent order, as Alexander of Roes recognized when he said, in about 1281, "By these three, namely the priesthood, the empire and the university [*studio*], the holy Catholic church is spiritually sustained, increased and ruled as by three virtues. . . ." [1] The universities' role was at once professional and ideological. They had a monopoly of higher education—as opposed to learning, which continued independently in the monastic, cathedral, and religious schools as

[1] *De translatione imperii*, H. Grundmann, ed. (Leipzig, 1927), 27.

well as being individually pursued by men like Raymond Lull and Arnold of Villanova. Increasingly from the second half of the thirteenth century entry into the higher reaches of the church or medicine or the law was through having received a university training. There was little higher learning, wherever it might be practiced, that did not bear the stamp of the university; the university set the standards in a subject, prescribed the texts, the topics to be treated, the issues to be raised. It helped to mold the very form of intellectual expression—based on the syllogism—as practiced in the disputations of the schools (i.e., where the teaching in the universities was carried out). The universities in thus preparing men for a career not only professionalized teaching but also made learning vocational. It was directed to training men in the comprehension of a body of knowledge they could employ in the service of the church or in law or medicine or teaching. In a limited sense a medieval university was thus not so different in function from a modern university. The majority of its members were governed by the same demands of the syllabus and examinations; they were graduated into a comparable hierarchy in which status went with attainment, from mere student to bachelor and then master or doctor. These aspects dominated much of the life of a medieval university but they should not obscure the profound differences in conception from its modern counterparts. These sprang from divergent attitudes toward truth and knowledge.

The medieval university also gave institutional expression to the medieval belief in higher and lower degrees of knowledge. Only the understanding contained in God's word represented pure, absolute truth. It could only be seized supernaturally through some kind of illumination or direct revelation from God; what remained to man's own natural powers could never be more than incomplete. Its uncertainty varied in the degree to which it depended on the senses (the most uncertain source of all); the more the mind was able to turn away from the transitory flux and multiplicity of the external world to the unchanging ideas within the soul, the higher its knowledge. But full comprehension was reserved for the blessed in the next world.

Such an attitude had two very important consequences. The first was to put the search for truth in any full or absolute sense beyond the scope of all human enquiry. There was little notion of building up a body of knowledge that, even if it could never be complete, could lead to a growing comprehension of the nature of reality; little, that is to say, of the modern assumption that investigation of the natural and human world can lead to fundamental insights in nature and human nature. The medieval outlook on reality was a priori. The last word had been said by the Bible. At most, reason and natural experience could elucidate and amplify its truths, but they could never aspire to more than a secondary role, to explain and fill in the details.

This standpoint made for a tendency to disregard experiment and investigation of the natural world of the senses, and for a hierarchy of knowledge, with theology at the apex. It was enshrined in the division between the faculties of the university: at the base came arts, which, largely through the educational reforms of Charlemagne's empire in the later eighth and early ninth centuries, were, as we shall see in Chapter Three, regarded as providing a general grounding in the rudiments of knowledge. Above the arts faculty came the three higher faculties of theology, law, and medicine, which could normally only be entered after having first passed through the arts course. The notion of higher and lower kinds of knowledge dominated medieval intellectual activity, as we shall have plenty of occasion to see.

The second consequence of this attitude was that the search for truth was seen as the comprehension of texts. Virtually all study in all the faculties of a medieval university consisted in commenting and discussing a prescribed body of writings. Knowledge, however relative, as in, say, the works of Aristotle, was to be found in the expositions of the accepted authorities; the supreme authority was the Bible, in the light of which all others were to be judged. Commentary, disputation, and question were the means of elucidating their meaning and reconciling apparent contradictions, or, when this could not be done, of establishing logically the correctness of one interpretation over another. For that reason higher research as we know it today did not constitute a distinct activity in the medieval universities; the very act of learning was carried out as the investigation of the accepted sources of truth. The mode was the same for all—for a mere master and for a St. Thomas Aquinas. The difference was that

Thomas was able to attain to a deeper understanding and to formulate the accepted truths into a new system. He did so through the common media of commentaries, disputed and free questions, and *summae*, all the outcome of the techniques current in the university and the religious schools, and more particularly of his own teaching at Paris and in the *studia* of the Dominican order. Even the remarkable new scientific methodology of Robert Grosseteste, which we shall consider in Chapter Five, derived largely from his *Commentary* on Aristotle's *Posterior Analytics;* although it gave rise to a new experimental approach to scientific problems, speculation and calculation remained the dominant forms of medieval science.

The effect of this outlook on knowledge was to make medieval university education far more directly ideological and vocational than, until recent times at least, modern university education. On the one hand, all profane knowledge, as taught in the arts faculty, was regarded as subordinate to higher theological understanding; because the arts, as we shall see in Chapter Three, increasingly came to center on Aristotle's logical, philosophical, and scientific works, this meant, as we have said, an inherent tension between natural knowledge—largely pagan in origin—and the dictates of faith. Most of the great clashes over the relation between them occurred at Paris from the 1260's to the 1280's. On the other hand, since all education was considered as leading to some higher end, whether theological understanding and the priesthood or the more secular professions of law and medicine, the university was not principally a place of indefinite study for its own sake. The courses in the higher faculties, especially theology, were so long that the minority who continued in them to the final degree of doctor had spent upwards of twelve years in study.[2] Among these survivors only a small number remained as teachers after the obligatory period of one or two years that followed the mastership and doctorate. This was even more true of the arts faculty, which was almost invariably a stepping stone to a career elsewhere or study in a higher faculty; it was expressed in the saying that one should not grow old in the arts faculty (*non est consenescendum in artibus*). As a result, one of the distinctive aspects of the medieval universities

[2] For what follows see Chapter Three.

The Grand Pont of Paris.

north of the Alps was that the majority of the masters teaching
at any given time were merely temporary; the entire system was
based on a continuous succession of masters who taught for one
or two years before giving way—usually with relief—to those

newly graduated, on whom the obligation then fell. The permanent, full-time scholar-teacher of either the Italian universities or those of the post-Renaissance era was virtually unknown in northern Europe in the thirteenth and fourteenth centuries. Accordingly the role and nature of a medieval university cannot be directly compared with a modern university, even though they have many corporate features in common, above all their power of granting degrees.

One of the greatest institutional differences between medieval and modern universities was that, despite their monopoly of higher education, medieval universities were economically unprivileged until the later fourteenth century. They were corporations of masters and scholars with little more than the scholarly privileges that went with their corporate recognition; they had virtually no common property or wealth; their schools and lodgings were rented houses and rooms; their meeting places were churches or the premises of the religious orders. The very books they used were as often as not hired from stationers and booksellers overseen by, but not part of, the university. This lack of possessions paradoxically gave the universities their greatest power; for it meant their complete freedom of movement. They could at short notice quit one place for another at virtually no cost to themselves and a minimum of hardship. Those who suffered were the citizens of the town they were deserting; the livelihood of the towns-people was bound up with the presence of often thousands of alien scholars for whose needs of food, lodging, diversion, and so on they provided. The friction that arose from the close involvement between members of university and the local inhabitants was the most frequent cause of the many affrays and riots in the university towns of the Middle Ages; one of their accompaniments was the secession of universities from town to town. Thus Padua's university originated from the migration of scholars from Bologna in 1222; the university at Cambridge arose from the dispersion of Oxford university in 1209. The more established a university the more cataclysmic such an exodus could be, not least to the king and government who wanted order and stability. In the case of both Paris and Oxford the kings of France and England were particularly concerned to prevent the masters and scholars of either university from seceding, and both universities received lavish grants of privileges frequently renewed and extended throughout the thirteenth and fourteenth centuries. As the universities became increasingly well-endowed they became more vulnerable to external pressure, until by the later fifteenth and the sixteenth centuries the once invincible weapon of strike and dispersion had lost all effect. By then it was the universities—and more peculiarly the colleges—that had everything to lose by threats of closure.

The same progression to increasing privilege is apparent in the composition of the medieval universities. Although it would be an exaggeration to regard them as ever having been open to all talents they were certainly more open in the first two centuries of their existence than again at any period until comparatively recent times. It is virtually impossible to be exact either about student numbers or the social classes from which they were drawn. So far as the latter are concerned, all the indications are that there was no neatly defined sector from which they came. Negatively, it can be firmly stated that the universities were not primarily aristocratic preserves, as they were to become from the fifteenth century onwards. As we have said, universities in the thirteenth and fourteenth centuries were essentially places of vocational training; accordingly those who went to them were in the main concerned to qualify for a future career. The most lucrative, hence most popular, of the professions was law; and it was probably among its students that the wealthier elements of the university were to be found, as well, perhaps, as those with least bent for study. There is a good deal of evidence from the letter collections of medieval students—so skilfully put together by the late C. H. Haskins [3]—to suggest that many of the students were from comparatively modest backgrounds; they were supported at a university by their parents to learn a profession and were expected to apply themselves. There is not the remotest trace of the notion of a university as a finishing school. On the contrary, the main theme of these letters—which were used as models, often taken from real letters, for correct letter composition—was the student's need for more money; his letter, for the most part elaborately stereotyped, was designed to justify his re-

[3] C. H. Haskins, *Studies in Mediaeval Culture* (reprinted in New York, Ungar, 1958), Chapters 1–3.

quest by explaining the demands of a life of high thinking and hard living. Such collections of letters were widespread and are to be found for all the main universities, among them Bologna, Padua, Naples, Paris, Orleans, Oxford, Cambridge, Toulouse, and Montpellier.[4] The artificiality of most of the letters points the more clearly to the recurring topics of financial need and the need to succeed; there are sometimes undertones of sacrifice in supporting a son at a university, as in the case of one who was admonished to remember his sisters and told that he should be supporting his parents rather than taking money from them.[5]

Beyond these considerations, many clerks already in holy orders attended a university to better themselves or because the ecclesiastical authorities, from the pope down, sponsored them. They constituted a more mature element compared with the mass of the arts students—by far the most numerous—who were mostly adolescents and young men between fourteen and twenty years of age. Ecclesiastics selected on promise and members of the religious orders came closest to being the ones who received a university education on merit. This was particularly true of the friars, above all the Dominicans and the Franciscans, who undoubtedly attracted to themselves the most outstanding speculative minds of the thirteenth century. They represented a standing challenge to the secular masters, not only for intellectual eminence, which tended to draw most of the theological students away from the secular theologians to the schools of the friars, but also because, as we shall consider in Chapter One, they stood outside the corporate life and obligations of the university. They, like their secular counterparts, regarded a university education as a means to an end—as training for their subsequent responsibilities in the order. They had an even more rapid turnover of teachers than the secular masters and doctors; only a few, of whom St. Thomas was one, remained teachers throughout their careers. At both Paris and Oxford the role of the mendicant orders in the universities was central, as we shall have frequent occasion to see.

Finally, medieval universities were not simply seats of learning; they were centers of life. As concentrations of mostly young

[4] *Ibid.*, "The Life of Mediaeval Students as Illustrated by their Letters," especially pp. 10 ff.
[5] *Ibid.*, 14.

men, frequently turbulent, they accentuated the manners and behavior of society at large, in eating, drinking, and living as well as in learning and praying. They have been depicted in this aspect by C. H. Haskins [6]; no attempt will be made in this book to repeat what he did so inimitably. It is enough to remember that for every lecture attended or question disputed there were probably as many, or more, missed for sleeping or gaming or drinking or idling [7]; that then, as now, there was no single plane on which university life was conducted. If study was its badge, it was worn only by some. The universities were of this world; they were as close to the market place as to the cathedral. They taught men to serve themselves as well as God. This gave them their universality; it enabled them to uphold the canons of a theocentric society just because they accepted men in their worldly condition. The profanities of the Goliards,[8] the paganism of the Latin Averroists [9] were suppressed without killing the milieu from which they sprang. Not that the excesses and failings associated with the schools, above all at Paris, were condoned. They were denounced in sermons and satirized by moralists like John of Garland.[10] But there was no attempt to offer the universities up in sacrifice because of them. From the thirteenth century onward they became as indispensable to society as they have been for most of the succeeding ages.

The following chapters will try to describe the place of the universities at Paris and Oxford in the society of the high and later Middle Ages.

[6] *Ibid.*, especially Chapter Three, "Manuals for Students," pp. 72 ff.
[7] *Ibid.*, 57. Cf. the rhyme quoted there:
> *Vox in choro, mens in foro,*
> *Vel in mensa vel in thoro.*

[8] The Goliards were groups of vagrant students and clerks who had deserted their vocation for a life of freedom and song, by which they lived. The origin of their name is unknown but it came to mean troubadour or jongleur. They were rebels against authority and Christian values, praising the pleasures of this world and satirizing the church for failing to live by its own commandments. They came near to blasphemy and libertinism in their exaltation of man's natural impulses, echoes of which can be heard in the *Roman de la Rose*. For an excellent brief account see J. Le Goff, *Les Intellectuals au moyen age* (Paris, 1957), 30–40. See also Helen Waddell, *Wandering Scholars* (London, 1954).
[9] See Chapter Four, 122 ff.
[10] See pp. 222–238.

Part One

INSTITUTIONAL AND ACADEMIC

ONE

Paris University in the Thirteenth and Fourteenth Centuries

I ORIGINS [1]

Paris was the archetype of northern universities as Bologna was for those of Italy. It arose directly from the cathedral school of Notre Dame under a chancellor representing the bishop of Paris. In this it differed from Oxford; indeed the majority of universities were not the outcome of earlier cathedral schools. The difference was not merely formal, but had a direct bearing on the evolution of Paris as a university. Much of the early history of the university, to the third decade of the thirteenth century, centered on the masters' struggle for autonomy, particularly over examining students and granting degrees.

The difference in origin also made for direct episcopal intervention in matters both of doctrine and discipline; Oxford, on the other hand, was subject to the distant oversight of the bishop of Lincoln. Yet the distinctiveness of Paris did not lie exclusively—or indeed predominantly—in its ecclesiastical origins. Equally formative was the influence of the schools that had

[1] For the origins of Paris see H. Rashdall, *The Universities of Europe in the Middle Ages*, F. M. Powicke and A. B. Emden, eds., (Oxford, 1936) Vol. I, 271 ff.; H. Denifle, *Die Entstehung der Universitäten des Mittelalters bis 1400* (Berlin, 1885), 655 ff.

grown up on the left bank of the river about the church of St. Geneviève in the eleventh century. These, together with the school of the abbey of St. Victor, helped to create the city's pre-eminence in logic and theology. The left-bank schools owed their importance principally to Peter Abelard (d. 1142). His presence as a teacher there, as elsewhere, had drawn students from all parts to hear him demolish his opponents.

Among these opponents was William of Champeaux, who had withdrawn from the cathedral school to the abbey of St. Victor. During the twelfth century St. Victor was the home of specula-tive mysticism and a center of biblical exegesis.[2] Hugh (d. 1141), one of its greatest luminaries, was also an outstanding educationalist who stressed the importance of profane knowl-edge. St. Victor did not play any part in the formation of the university; but its presence in Paris contributed to the prestige of the city in these fields of study. This fame was one of the main factors in the rise of the university; it made Paris an intellectual center to which teachers and students came from everywhere. Neither Abelard nor the cathedral school alone could have achieved this; the one was too transitory, the other too local. Neither Abelard's gifts as a teacher nor his personal magnetism sufficed to keep in being the external schools of St. Geneviève after his departure; by 1143 the majority had vanished.[3] A more permanent institutional form was needed to give such groupings stability. The cathedral school of Notre Dame provided it. But in the process of becoming a university it was superseded as a ca-thedral school.

Nothing could be more misguided than to see one as the log-ical outcome of the other. The university at Paris was, as we have mentioned, almost unique in its episcopal origins. The majority of cathedral schools—Chartres, Laon, Rheims, Tours, Lincoln, York, to mention only a few—remained such despite a standing comparable to that of Paris. Paris was the exception. To explain why entails explaining the nature of a university. Let us begin with terminology. The word *universitas* had, during the thirteenth and fourteenth centuries, no specific application to a university; it connoted any corporate body or group with an in-

---

[2] For the latter see B. Smalley, *The Study of the Bible in the Middle Ages* (Oxford, Blackwell, 1952), 83 ff.
[3] Rashdall, I, 271 ff.

dependent juridical status.[4] It could be constituted from three or more persons in a profession who could form their own association (*collegium*) to protect their rights. Provided they were recognized either in common law or by some higher authority, they could elect their own officers, make statutes, and be represented as a legal person through a proctor or delegate.[5] The very flexibility of these notions in the thirteenth century is exemplified in the free use of terms like *universitas, collegium, consortium, procurator, syndicus,* to describe the university at Paris in whole or in part.[6] Their significance lies not in any exclusive application to the university, but rather in its recognition as a corporation. This was established by 1215 [7] at the latest, as we shall consider later. For the present it represents the first and in many ways the fundamental element in a university. Corporate identity—however widely or narrowly interpreted—was the condition of its independent existence. That ultimately such a body concerned with higher education should come to be called a university is entirely incidental.

The actual designation given to a university at this time was *studium generale* or frequently *studium.*[8] Here again we must beware of pressing terminology too hard. The presence or absence of *generale* cannot be taken as the difference between a university and a nonuniversity. During the thirteenth century indeed *studium* (a place of study) was the usual expression for a university. It recurs in references to Bologna, Paris, and Naples (the first foundation by a prince—the emperor Frederick II in 1224).[9] In none of their numerous letters and decrees concerning universities did Popes Honorius III and Gregory IX go beyond *studium. Studium* was likewise used by Philip II of France in his charter to privileges to Paris university in 1200.[10] The word *generale* appears from about the end of the fourth decade

[4] Denifle, *op. cit.,* 30, who gives Hugolinus' definition: *universitas est plurium corporum collectio inter se distantium uno nomine specialiter eis deputato.*

[5] Post, "The Paris Masters as a Corporation," *Speculum,* 9 (1934), 422–3.

[6] *Ibid.,* 423 ff.

[7] *Ibid.,* 428.

[8] Denifle, *op. cit.,* 5 ff.

[9] *Ibid.*

[10] *Ibid.,* 7; *Chartularium Universitatis Parisiensis (Chart.),* H. Denifle and E. Chatelain, eds. (Paris, 1889–97), Vol. I, No. 1.

of the thirteenth century, when it is to be found in a reference to Naples; a little later in 1245 it was applied by Pope Innocent IV to his new school of studies at Rome.[11] Its use, however, remained perfunctory until the fourteenth century. By then it had become a technical term for those *studia* that had the right to confer a general license to teach *(ius ubique docendi)*.[12] In theory this carried universal recognition, the possessor of a degree from a *studium generale* being accepted at any other university without further examination. This was the aim of Gregory IX's statutes for his new foundation at Toulouse; its members were to enjoy the same privileges as those at Paris, and those who satisfied the examiners there were to be exempt from further examination elsewhere.[13] Although in practice degrees from one *studium generale* were rarely accepted automatically by another— even Paris and Oxford imposed mutual examination [14]—the *ius ubique docendi* became the juridical hallmark of a university by the end of the thirteenth century. As so often happens this occurred after the main event, when the most important universities had been established. It was designed to control the founding of new ones. The power to do so had by then become associated with either papal or imperial recognition; at first this conferred the general privileges of a *studium generale,* but by the end of the thirteenth century it meant primarily the *ius ubique docendi.*[15] Henceforth whether an institution of higher learning was a general or merely particular place of studies depended upon whether its degree was valid elsewhere, which for new universities turned on possession of the *ius ubique docendi.* By the fourteenth century its grant was usually included in the foundation charter.

There was, however, a third source of university status that antedated any formal act of recognition by popes or emperors or, in the case of Spain, kings. This was custom. It concerned the older universities, especially Bologna, Paris, Padua, and Oxford. Of these the first two had effectively become *studia generalia* by

---

[11] Denifle, *Entstehung,* 14.
[12] *Ibid.,* 20 ff; Rashdall, I, 9 ff.
[13] *Chart.,* I, No. 99; Denifle, *Entstehung,* 20.
[14] Rashdall, I, 14.
[15] Rashdall, I, 9.

the end of the twelfth century without any specific charter of foundation. Far from being anomalies they set the standard for those that came after them, Bologna becoming the model for the majority of Italian universities and Paris for those north of the Alps. Here in the beginning had been the deed; the word came much later for Bologna and Paris—which received in 1291–2 the privilege of the *ius ubique docendi* from Nicholas IV [16]—and even later for Padua; but for Oxford never at all.[17] With characteristic orderliness fourteenth-century jurists classified the ancient foundations as customary *studia*.[18]

The discrepancy reflects the difference between theory and practice. From the standpoint of strict terminology, Bologna, Paris, and Padua were universities after Naples and Palencia, while Oxford, in perhaps its heyday of the first half of the fourteenth century, was not on a par with the emperor Charles IV's newly constituted university at Prague in 1348. In practice this meant little. *Post hoc, ergo propter hoc,* in the case of universities as in so many others, makes bad counsel. Both Paris and Oxford—our main concerns here—became what they were by the power of their appeal and the strength of their support. Excellence in one or more of the higher subjects—law, theology, and medicine—the existence of which marked off a place of higher studies from a mere local school in arts or grammar, drew masters and students to Bologna, Paris, and later Oxford and Montpellier from far and wide. It was this fact that above all made them general as opposed to local *(particularia) studia*.

The universities formed an artificial and predominantly alien body, numbering thousands of individuals, which could not be assimilated to the normal life or institutions of a city. Neither the urban commune of Bologna nor the cathedral school at Paris sufficed in themselves for such concentrations. In each city, as also at Oxford, the authorities had to come to terms with their distinctive demands; in each these went beyond merely local considerations, to involve emperors, popes, and kings. The outcome was some form of independent recognition. It did not, however, come easily or quickly. These early universities evolved

---

[16] *Ibid.,* 10; *Chart.,* II, No. 578.
[17] Rashdall, *loc. cit.;* Padua eventually received a bull in 1346.
[18] *Ibid.*

through struggle; they survived only because of outside support from emperor, pope, or king. Hence much of their history, especially for the formative phase, is bound up with their relation to external authority.

So far as Paris was concerned this centered on the masters' attempts to gain academic independence of the chancellor. It is a commonplace that Paris was the archetype of the masters' university, whereas Bologna was the model of the students' university. Each university became what it was largely because of this difference. In Paris the role of the masters was central to the emergence of the university. It began within the framework of the cathedral school presided over by a chancellor.[19] In the eleventh century the master appointed to preside over the cathedral school became a member of the cathedral chapter. Called variously chancellor (as in Paris), *scholasticus,* or *magister scholarium,* he supervised the cathedral school and sometimes all the other schools in the diocese. He accordingly stood outside or at least above the school, subject only to the bishop and the chapter. He was not directly concerned in the teaching; that was the responsibility of masters in the school. But because he licensed them to teach they owed their livelihood to him. It was this position that seems early to have led to simony on the chancellor's part, either in his demanding a share of the masters' fees or his selling them the license to teach. The latter practice was forbidden at the Council of London in 1138.[20] Under Alexander III, pope from 1159 to 1180, there was a sustained effort to put an end to such abuses. The pope's aim was the provision of free teaching: to allow all clerks in the diocese and city to instruct "freely and without hindrance," as he put it in his first extant letter on the question to the dean and chapter at Chalons-sur-Marne in 1166–7.[21] In the decretal *Quanto Gallicana ecclesia,* 1170–2, he recognized the right of the chancellor or master of the school to grant the license to teach (*licentia docendi*) and to

[19] For an account of the early relations between the chancellor and Paris masters see G. Post, "Alexander III, the *Licentia docendi,* and the Rise of the Universities" in *C.H. Haskins Anniversary Essays in Mediaeval History* (Boston, Houghton Mifflin, New York, 1929), 255–77.

[20] *Ibid.,* 258; J. D. Mansi, *Sacrorum conciliorum nova et amplissima collectio* (*Concilia*), XXI, 17, 514.

[21] G. Post, "Alexander III"; *Chart.,* I, Introduction, No. 12.

judge the fitness of the candidate.[22] At the Third Lateran Council in 1179 Alexander renewed the ban on selling the *licentia docendi*, which should be conferred on any learned men seeking it.[23] The penalty for violating it was, as in *Quanto Gallicana ecclesia*, the deprivation of the benefices of the chancellor and masters concerned.[24]

These measures were directed principally at the ordinary cathedral and diocesan schools rather than at Paris, where they do not seem to have been strictly applied. Alexander seems to have allowed the chancellor to take payment for licensing a master (*precium*).[25] As late as 1212 the chancellor was refusing to grant the license to a candidate who did not pay, even when supported by masters' testimony to his learning.[26] In that year Innocent III prohibited the chancellor from taking fees.[27]

The financial aspect, however, is secondary to the main one that Alexander III's legislation had confirmed the chancellor in the all-important function of appointing masters. Although theoretically he was circumscribed by the obligation to license without fee any learned man who presented himself, in practice judgement lay with him. If Alexander III set the precedent of regulating the chancellor's activities he also helped him to entrench himself so firmly that it took the support of another and even greater pope, Innocent III, to enable the masters, in the first decades of the thirteenth century, to wrest control from him. The chancellor's prerogatives, however, were not confined to conferring the license; he could also withdraw it; in addition, he was a spiritual judge with power of excommunication and his own prison.[28] Thus he possessed extensive disciplinary authority that he was not slow to use in times of stress.

It was essentially a local authority. At first it probably did not extend to more than a handful of masters, all of whom came within the purview of the bishop and chapter. The chancellor was merely their representative, and the school an extension of

[22] *Chart.*, I, Introduction, No. 4; G. Post, *loc. cit.*, 261–2.
[23] G. Post, "Alexander III," 262; *Chart.*, I, Introduction, No. 12.
[24] Post, "Alexander III"; Mansi, *Concilia*, XXII, 18, 227–8.
[25] Post, "Alexander III," 272 ff.
[26] *Ibid.*, 270; *Chart.*, I.
[27] Post, "Alexander III"; *Chart.*, I, Nos. 14 and 16.
[28] Rashdall, I, 304 f.; Denifle *Entstehung* 688.

their activities. It is the paradox of the Paris university that it evolved not by becoming independent of the control of the church but by substituting the pope's oversight for control by the bishop and chancellor. The ecclesiastical framework was expanded, not broken. Consequently Paris to a unique degree came directly under papal supervision, with the result that the curia was involved in most of the important events there until the fourteenth century.

The major factor in the change from a local to an ecumenical overseer was the growth of numbers at Paris. A chancellor sufficed for a cathedral school, even for other schools in the diocese; but not when one cathedral school had multiplied into several schools filled with masters and students seeking to practice their professions or learn new ones. The existing structure could not contain them. At most the chancellor could attempt to regulate the teaching and authorize the teachers. But by the last third of the twelfth century this was no longer a matter of dealing with individuals. By then the chancellor was being confronted with the growth of an organized body of masters constituted into their own association or guild. It was during the ensuing forty years that the cathedral school passed into a *studium generale* (though not yet called such). The transition was anything but painless. It entailed breaking the integument of the cathedral school, the masters displacing the chancellor and chapter as the governing body and the license becoming a professional qualification subject to their acceptance. From this there emerged a self-regulating body of teachers and scholars, subject to over-all ecclesiastical jurisdiction but enjoying extensive corporate privileges and governed by its own elaborate procedure. Control of day-to-day scholastic affairs passed from the hands of the chancellor into those of the masters. This was part of the universal growth of monopoly in the crafts and professions by guilds or associations of their members. It constituted a revolution that involved the transfer of power and therefore invariably some form of struggle.

At Paris, as in most such cases, there is no single date for the creation of a masters' guild. The formative years were probably from the 1140's until the 1180's. Although the first specific mention of a separate body of masters is not until 1208, there are many earlier references to their presence as a distinctive element.[29] As early as 1169 Thomas Becket suggested their mediation in his dispute with Henry II of England; [30] his one-time secretary, John of Salisbury, has much to say about the number of masters both around the cathedral and on the left bank.[31] John, like Stephen of Tournai a quarter of a century later,[32] commented on the great increase in numbers, especially of younger masters.[33] From Stephen of Tournai (c. 1192) we also learn of clashes between the scholars and monks of the abbey of St. Germain-des-Prés, one of the recurrent features of university life in the thirteenth century.[34] The majority were engaged in logic and dialectic, but law and theology were also well-established studies,[35] for the teaching of which, as we have already seen from Alexander III's decrees, payment was taken.[36] The pope himself sought a benefice for one master Theobald to enable him to study theology there.[37] The spread of the schools is indicated as early as 1127 when lodgment in the cathedral cloister was reserved for its members.[38] When John of Salisbury studied at Paris in the 1160's one of his masters, Adam de Parvo Ponto, was already established, as his name tells us, on one of the Seine bridges—which became a center of logic and philosophy.[39]

How early the masters gained a distinct authority cannot be said. They may have sent representatives to the pope in their dispute with the abbey of St. Germain in 1192.[40] In 1180 Alexander III had affirmed the jurisdiction of the masters at St. Germain and at Rheims over their own students, free from all out-

[29] E.g. *Chart.*, I, *Introduction*, Nos. 2, 3, 5, 6, 8, 9, 10, 13, 15, 16.

[30] *Ibid.*, No. 21, p. 23.

[31] *Ibid.*, Nos. 19 and 20; Rashdall, I, 289.

[32] *Chart.*, I, No. 48.

[33] Rashdall, I, 289, note 2, referring to *Metalogicon* (C. C. J. Webb, ed.), I, 24, 25.

[34] *Chart.*, I, Introduction, No. 47.

[35] Cf. the letter of Guy of Bazoches, *Chart.*, I, Introduction, No. 54. Also *ibid.*, Nos. 26, 27, 35, 48, 51, 52.

[36] For independent evidence see also *Chart.*, I, Introduction, No. 24.

[37] *Ibid.*, No. 13.

[38] Rashdall, I, 288.

[39] *Ibid.*; *Chart.*, I, Introduction, No. 55.

[40] *Chart.*, I, No. 47. This is suggested by Post, "Paris Masters," 434.

side interference; [41] but this represented less any special legal authority than the customary power of teachers over pupils.[42] Even had it meant more, it would have been superseded by Celestine III's bull of 1194, putting all secular causes that involved clerics at Paris under the ecclesiastical courts; it thereby merely confirmed that masters and students alike, in enjoying benefit of the clergy, were subject to canon law.[43] It is with Innocent III that the masters' tacit and customary privileges become explicit and increasingly defined. Most of this occurred in the last eight years of his pontificate (1208–16), when the earlier developments reached a climax. But at its very beginning in 1198 there is mention of the masters' collective advice (*de communi consilio magistrorum*) being given to the bishop on a matter of discipline.[44] In 1207 Innocent intervened directly in their affairs when he ordered the bishop of Paris to limit the number of masters in theology to eight,[45] a provision that was not kept. Then in 1208–9 he recognized the right of the masters to act as a body.[46] There can be little doubt that here the pope was putting into words what already existed in fact. The letter, addressed to all the masters in theology, canon law, and arts, was in reply to a letter from the masters asking permission to reinstate one of their number whom they had expelled for not observing three of their statutes, concerning dress, the correct order of lectures and disputations, and attendance at the funerals of dead masters. As Rashdall observed, they show a close analogy with the statutes of the ordinary guilds.[47] But whether he was correct in concluding that they represented the earliest statutes is at least open to question and at most subordinate to the fact that Innocent confirmed their validity; hence the masters' right to act as a legal corporation.[48] He accepted their election of eight sworn officers to enforce their rules, failure to swear obedience to which had caused the expulsion of Master G. before he

---

[41] *Chart.*, I, Introduction, No. 5.
[42] Rashdall, I, 290, note 1.
[43] *Chart.*, I, Introduction, No. 15; Rashdall, *loc. cit.*
[44] *Chart.*, I, No. 16.
[45] *Ibid.*, No. 5.
[46] *Ibid.*, No. 7.
[47] Rashdall, I, 300.
[48] This aspect is the one stressed by Post, "Paris Masters," 423.

thought better of it and sought readmission. Equally significant, Innocent employed the terms *universitas* and *consortium* to describe the masters' association, and he gave judgment in favor of taking back masters on grounds of both canon law and custom.[49] In the inchoate state of corporation theory at that time his action was to treat the masters as a corporation *de facto* if not yet *de iure*. Even this distinction is artificial, especially as within six years Innocent's initial recognition was embodied in the statutes granted to the university by his legate Robert de Courçon. They had been preceded in 1212–13 by the masters' appointment of three representatives to a joint meeting with three from the chancellor before judges delegated by the pope.[50] Robert de Courçon's statutes in effect embodied statutorily the decisions reached there. These had regularized the chancellor's jurisdiction over licensing and imprisonment, complaints against his abuse of both having caused Innocent III to intervene.[51] After hearing the evidence the pope's arbitrators decided against the chancellor on both counts. Henceforth he was to grant licenses in theology, canon law, and medicine to any candidate considered worthy by the majority of the masters in those subjects. For arts degrees the chancellor was to act together with six of the masters in arts. The chancellor in turn could continue to bestow the license (at his discretion) in any subject independently of the masters. But in no circumstance was he permitted to exact an oath of obedience or payment for doing so; nor was he to imprison any clerk—that is, master or scholar—unjustly or demand money when injuries had been inflicted. All doubtful cases were to be decided by the pope's official.

These provisions were tantamount to incorporating the masters as a separate body. They at once gave the masters an independent standing in relation to the chancellor and curtailed the chancellor's power toward them. They did more: as resulting

---

[49] . . . *et tam iuris canonici quam nostri moris existat* . . . (*Chart.*, I, No. 7).

[50] *Ibid.*, No. 16. Post, "Paris Masters," 429. Innocent also authorized the masters to appoint proctors in a bull issued between 1210 and 1213. *Chart.*, I, No. 24; Post, "Paris Masters," 434, who makes it clear that it referred to the masters as opposed to scholars.

[51] *Chart.*, I, No. 14.

from papal intervention, they effectively substituted papal for episcopal control of the schools. The chancellor might be still the officer of the chapter, but it was the pope to whom he was now answerable. The pope's role was thus central to the independent standing of the masters and thereby of the university.

The juxtaposition of papal and magisterial power was given lasting expression in the statutes of 1215.[52] For the first time the masters' position was comprehensively set out. They were to be of at least twenty-one years of age in arts and thirty-five in theology; there was to be a compulsory period of two years lecturing in arts on texts that were prescribed; conduct, dress, attendance at funerals were all specified; the license was to be granted free of all conditions and payments; and, perhaps most important of all,

". . . the masters and scholars can make, both between themselves and with other persons, obligations and constitutions supported by faith or penalty or oath in these cases: namely, the murder or mutilation of a scholar, or atrocious injury done a scholar, if justice should not be forthcoming, arranging the prices of lodgings, costume or burial, lectures and disputations, so, however, that the university be not thereby dissolved or destroyed."

This was to grant the masters the right of acting as a *collegium,* with the power of framing its own statutes and of binding its members to observe them, and, by implication, of expelling those who broke them. There can be little doubt that with this step the masters were now a corporation, a *universitas magistrorum et scolarium* both in its own internal structure and in relations with the outside world. It had already sent three representatives to parley with the chancellor in 1211–13; it was now authorized to act over a whole range of matters concerning the interests of its members. That these included fixing the cost of lodgings shows how far the university had come to form a distinctive community. The words "that the university be not thereby dissolved or destroyed" are convincing evidence that it was something separate from the cathedral school physically as well as juridically.

[52] *Ibid.,* No. 20. Translated in L. Thorndike, *University Records and Life in the Middle Ages* (New York, Columbia University Press, 1949) No. 15.

The 1215 statutes resumed forty years of corporate development. In no sense were they a foundation charter. They took the university as it had come to be and sought to regularize its practices. Nor should these be seen exclusively in the light of the struggle between masters and chancellor. The license was merely the outcome of a complex series of scholastic exercises, just as the chancellor was only at the apex of an increasingly elaborate network of authority. In that sense the confirmation of the masters' power at the expense of the chancellor's was merely a recognition of the facts. Moreover, however much of this was formally due to the pope, in actuality it depended on royal support. Ultimately the university owed its existence to the concentration of schools in Paris; it could only survive by coming to terms with the city. That it chose more than once to secede from the city is not to deny that it could have flourished elsewhere; it rather affirms the importance of Paris in its history. Much the same can be said for the university's internal life, which revolved increasingly around the faculties, nations, and their different officers as well as the new and disturbing presence of the mendicant orders.

The history of the university therefore presents us with a threefold perspective, in its relations with both spiritual and temporal authority and with the city, and in its development as an institution. Frequently they are inseparable, as in the disputes between the university and citizens or friars, leading invariably to the intervention of one or both powers of king and pope. Since it was largely through having to overcome such conflicts that the university evolved, we shall first consider the external context during the thirteenth and fourteenth centuries, and then the university's internal evolution.

II THE ATTAINMENT OF INDEPENDENCE

The 1215 statutes were not the first document to be addressed to the university, even if they may be said to constitute its first formal recognition as a corporate entity. Before the papacy, under Innocent III, came consistently to be concerned in its affairs Philip II, the king of France, had already taken it under his protection. Whether he was the first king to have done so is uncertain; [53] but his charter of 1200 is the first extant grant of privileges.[54] Unlike Innocent III's letters of a few years later it makes no mention of a university. Issued in response to an appeal by the masters for protection, following the death of several students in a tavern brawl, it conferred important immunities on the Paris scholars. All citizens were to swear to report and help to bring to justice anyone seen maltreating a scholar. The offender was to be dealt with by the king's provost; the present provost having been arrested for his part in the riot, future officers were to promise on appointment, before the assembled scholars, to uphold their privileges. These included freedom from arrest and sequestration [55] by the lay authorities, thereby reaffirming the clerical immunity that Celestine III had pronounced a few years previously. The canons of the cathedral were excluded from these new concessions—an additional sign that they were directed to scholars and masters in general rather than a defined body. They certainly had no bearing on the university as a corporation.

The charter of 1200 did not remove the causes of friction between townsmen and scholars any more than the statutes of Robert de Courçon in 1215 solved the conflict between masters and chancellor. It was followed in 1210 by a further royal decree defining the crimes for which a scholar could be arraigned: homicide, adultery, rape, and the infliction of injury.[56] These initial interventions by king and pope were the beginning of a close and continuous involvement in the university over the next two centuries. Only rarely did they conflict; for the most part they had different ends. Whereas the pope sought to oversee the

[53] Rashdall, I, 291, mentions a reference to Louis VII as having authorized the masters to suspend their lectures. See also P. Kibre, *Scholarly Privileges in the Middle Ages* (Cambridge, Mass., Mediaeval Academy of America, 1961) 85.
[54] *Chart.*, I, No. 1.
[55] Following Rashdall's interpretation of *capitale Parisiensium scholarium* (I, 297–7), which, he argues cogently, means chattels, whereas previous authors had understood *capitale* as rector or master.
[56] *Ibid.*, No. 13.

university from the point of view of the ecclesiastical hierarchy, increasingly acting instead of the bishop, the king regulated its place within the city and, on occasion, the kingdom. Although the king's authority was local and less spectacular, it often occasioned the more ecumenical actions of the papacy. Indeed the major events in the university's history during the thirteenth century—the great secession of 1229–30 and the conflict between the seculars and mendicants 1254–61—grew directly out of local happenings. Each led to the convergence of both royal and ecclesiastical jurisdiction, leaving a lasting impression on the structure of the university.

So far as relations with the church were concerned, the decade or so after 1215 saw the climax of the university's struggle for independence from the cathedral. This was now no longer simply over the chancellor's abuse of his prerogatives, but bore directly on the masters' rights of governing themselves that Robert de Courçon had acknowledged. Moreover, it now involved the bishop of Paris, who sometime before 1219 had excommunicated the entire university for conspiracy in attempting to make its own statutes.[57] In that year Pope Honorius III intervened on the university's behalf, commanding the ban to be lifted and prohibiting the chancellor's power of imprisonment.[58] Once again the pope had come to the rescue of the university; once again the masters had invoked his aid, sending proctors to him.[59] The need for papal support shows the precarious position of the university at this time; far from evolving naturally from the cathedral school it needed fostering from outside to keep it in existence. Not that it was a sickly child or that the wrongs were all on the side of the chapter. The scholars and masters—in arts especially, where many were no older than present-day undergraduates—were a potentially explosive force that only too frequently became actual. Riots and turbulence were never far away, whether in their dealings with the local populace or with ecclesiastical authorities. One of the reasons given by the bishop of Paris for excommunicating the university in 1219 was the

[57] *Ibid.*, Nos. 30, 31.
[58] *Ibid.*
[59] *Ibid.*, No. 31.

need to put down the armed bands of scholars who were threatening the peace of the city.[60]

Two years later the bishop was again appealing to the pope to intercede.[61] His allegations against the members of the university included the making of illegal constitutions by the masters and scholars, which they were sealing in their name with their own newly made seal; [62] the imposition of severe penalties on those not acceding to their illegal decrees; and the fixing of rents in defiance of the authority of both king and chapter. The pope commissioned Stephen Langton and two other bishops to investigate these complaints, meanwhile suspending the use of the university's seal, which he commanded should be broken. The masters, however, still continued to use a seal until 1225, when the papal legate, in response to the protests of the canons, broke it. Nor, despite the fury of masters armed with sticks and swords, did they gain another seal until 1246.[63] On the other main issues, however, the pope once again came down firmly on the side of the university. Although there is no record of his final judgment, his interim measures reaffirmed the masters' rights.[64] The chancellor was to grant the license freely, without demanding an oath of obedience or other conditions, to any candidate supported by the masters' testimony; neither bishop, chancellor nor any other member of the chapter could excommunicate members of the university, and the chancellor's gaol was to be demolished. Any settlement, however, that may have been reached as a result of the pope's arbitration was no more enduring than previous ones. In 1228 the pope, now Gregory IX, was again acting—this time through the archbishop of Rouen and other French prelates—to resolve substantially the same differ-

---

[60] *Ibid.*, No. 30; Kibre, *op. cit.*, 90–1.

[61] *Chart.*, I, No. 41.

[62] Kibre, *op. cit.*, 91, says that the seal belonged to the cathedral chapter but the words *"Abutiontur etiam quodam sigillo nomine universitatis magistrorum et scolarium nuper facto"* (*Chart.*, I, No. 41) explicitly state that this was a recent creation of their own.

[63] *Chart.*, I, No. 45, Note 3; Rashdall, I, 317; Kibre, *loc. cit.*; Post, "Paris Masters," 438 ff.

[64] *Chart.*, I, No. 45. It is likely that a settlement was reached, from mention of an agreement in 1228; *Ibid.*, No. 58.

ences.[65] It took the physical departure of the university finally to establish its corporate independence; and this was only achieved through the joint efforts of pope and king.

The trouble leading to the great dispersion of 1229–30 arose from another series of riots that broke out in a tavern during the carnival of 1228–9.[66] According to Matthew Paris they finally led the queen regent, Blanche of Castille, to call out the provost and his soldiers,[67] who killed and wounded some of the students. The masters suspended lectures in protest; when no redress was made they met on Easter Monday and resolved to leave the city in a month for six years if none was by then forthcoming.[68] It was not; so they went, some to other schools in France, some to Oxford in England, where Henry III welcomed them.[69]

The new king Louis IX and the pope Gregory IX were not long in going to the university's rescue.[70] In August 1229 Louis reaffirmed the privileges granted by his grandfather, Philip II; in November Gregory wrote strong letters to William of Auvergne, bishop of Paris, reproving him for his inactivity, and to the king and his mother enjoining them to act against the culprits. How quickly, and in what ways, the king and his mother responded is not known. The university, however, did not return to the city for nearly two years, probably until the beginning of 1231. In April of that year a stream of papal letters was directed to securing the university's privileges vis-a-vis both the cathedral and city. The centerpiece was the celebrated bull *Parens scientia-*

---

[65] *Ibid.*, No. 68. In addition to the questions of the license and the making of statutes, the masters' power to expel erring members was also included.
[66] See Rashdall, I, 334 ff. for an account.
[67] H. R. Luard, ed., *Historia majora,* III (Rolls Series, London, 1872–83), 166 ff.; Rashdall, I, 335.
[68] In Rashdall's view this was because of hostile ecclesiastical influence at the court (*loc. cit.*).
[69] *Chart.*, I, No. 64.
[70] *Ibid.*, Nos. 66, 67, 69, 70, 71; Rashdall, I, 337, says that Gregory peremptorily required the king and queen mother to punish the offenders, implying that the pope was the first to act; but Louis IX had already reaffirmed the university's privileges of 1200 in August 1229 (*Chart.*, I, No. 66) three months before Gregory's letter to him and his mother on November 29 (*Chart.*, I, No. 71).

rum,[71] which, if still lacking definitiveness, finally established the masters' supremacy over the chancellor. The chancellor had now to swear publicly before the bishop or the chapter and two representatives of the university to bestow the license on any candidate adjudged worthy by the masters in the faculty concerned; also to uphold the liberties of the masters in "making due constitutions or ordinances" on teaching, dress, funerals, price of lodgings, and power to enforce them by expulsion. Most significant was the recognition of the masters' right to suspend lectures in case of death or injury or extortionate rents. In return the bishop of Paris had to punish any delinquents among the university and, if they were guilty, to imprison them in his own prison; the chancellor's prison was "utterly forbidden." But no scholar could be arrested for debt, nor was any payment to be made for the license (which was to be granted unconditionally) or for release from excommunication. Scholars were not to carry arms, and there was to be no protection for disturbers of the peace or the idle. For the rest, these privileges were to be maintained by the king and observed by everyone else. For a document so precise in certain respects—prescribing, among other things, the length of the long vacation, the reading of Priscian and the procedure for disposing of the goods of a scholar who died intestate—it still left considerable room for dispute over the license. The chancellor, for all his obligation to consult the masters and respect their confidences, could nevertheless "give or deny according to his conscience the license asked for." But if this was to remain an endemic cause of contention, it was never again the central issue.

Parens scientiarum did not end the disputes between university and city and chapter, but it meant the passing of the chancellor's control. He still remained nominal head of the university for another century, and occasional conflict could still flare up around him; but as a force in the life of the university his day was done. *Parens scientiarum* robbed him of most of his judicial powers; it gave to the university a set of inviolable privileges that made it virtually immune from the local ecclesiastical authorities. Paradoxically, the pope's support of the masters and scholars against the cathedral threw the university increasingly

[71] *Chart.,* I, No. 79; Thorndike, *op. cit.,* No. 19.

upon the support of the king and his officers as a counterweight to the hostility of the church locally. The years following Gregory IX's charter of liberties saw a further development of the tendency—already apparent in the years preceding it—for the bishop to displace the chancellor as the university's main opponent. In 1237 the masters accused the bishop of granting licenses in canon law in the absence of a chancellor and of excommunicating those who sought to tell the pope.[72] Gregory IX in reply [73] once again confirmed his earlier statutes on the license and bound the bishop to obey them. Soon after *Parens scientiarum* he had renewed for a further seven years the masters' immunity from excommunication without papal consent. He did so again in 1237.[74] The pope's zeal for the university's liberties had led him to extend the same privileges granted at Paris to his new foundation at Toulouse in 1231; [75] it was also the masters and scholars at Paris to whom he presented his book of decretals in 1234.[76] Gregory's solicitude for the university continued through the pontificates of his immediate successors, except for Alexander IV (1254–61). But even by 1261, after nearly seven years of struggle, and the suspension of the university's privileges for a time in 1256,[77] the masters and scholars enjoyed extensive rights and immunities.[78] These included exemption from summons outside Paris; [79] their own seal; [80] the right to tax their members for university purposes; [81] independent conservators of the apostolic privileges awarded by the papacy; [82] and freedom, periodically renewed, from the ban of excommunication without papal consent.[83] Together with the

---

[72] *Ibid.*, No. 115.
[73] *Ibid.*, No. 117.
[74] *Ibid.*, Nos. 95, 113.
[75] *Ibid.*, No. 99. He had then gone on to assure them at Paris that this in no way derogated from their statutes (*ibid.*, No. 101).
[76] *Ibid.*, No. 104.
[77] Ibid., No. 407.
[78] For a comprehensive treatment of the question see Kibre, *op. cit.*, 99 ff.
[79] *Chart.*, I, No. 142.
[80] *Ibid.*, No. 165; granted by Innocent IV in October 1246.
[81] *Ibid.*, Nos. 352, 376; Kibre, *op. cit.*, 117–18.
[82] *Chart.*, I, No. 377 (1262); Kibre, *op. cit.*, 119.
[83] *Chart.*, I, Nos. 161, 383, 405, 406.

rights granted, and successively upheld, in *Parens scientiarum,* the university's independence of both city and chapter was never again seriously challenged after Gregory IX's pontificate.

III THE STRUGGLE WITH THE FRIARS

The danger that now arose was of another kind. It had previously come from underprivilege; now it was from privilege. That this was based on continuing papal support made it the greater, for it caused the university to bite the hand that so faithfully fed it. This was the implication of the struggle between the secular masters and the mendicant orders, which broke out in 1253 and lasted for more than a decade. What began as another assertion of university privilege, accompanied by the usual suspension of lectures and threats to disperse, became a trial of strength between Pope Alexander IV and the university. If it ended with the pope successfully asserting his will this was not at real cost to the university. Its pride certainly suffered, but its powers remained unimpaired and the tendency to abuse them at the expense of both the Paris chapter and citizens undiminished. Indeed, the conflict enhanced the importance of the university, which became the arena of an ecumenical dispute over the role and justification of the mendicant orders. The local issues of privilege merged into those affecting fundamental Christian principles. The pope in arbitrating over the one was also involved in the other. In that sense more than the interests of the university were at stake; and Alexander IV for all his clumsy incomprehension of university sensibilities was acting as much in terms of the church as in terms of events at Paris. This is equally true of the Paris masters; on the one hand they showed all the jealousy of any local association concerned for its rights; on the other, the struggle took on a correspondingly wider import—with mendicancy and perfection the main issues. We shall consider these theoretical questions in the second part of the book.

The cause of the conflict was another clash between scholars and townsmen, this time in 1253. Attempts to regulate them had been made two years previously, after the widespread outbreaks of disorders, caused by the sect of Pastoreaux,[84] in Paris and

[84] Kibre, *op. cit.,* 101 ff.

other cities. The university now suspended lectures in protest against "a recent and monstrous outrage against innocent scholars." [85] The offenders were duly punished. The friars, however, had refused to join with the rest of the university in ceasing lectures; and the masters now turned their attention to them. This was not the first time the mendicants had dissociated themselves from the rest of the university; they had remained aloof during the great dispersion of 1229–30, continuing to teach at Paris.[86] The masters had not forgotten this. They were fearful and resentful of the mendicants' privileges, which for over twenty years had enabled them to have their own independent schools and organization, free from the demands of the university, and yet enjoy chairs in and membership of the theological faculty. They taught the full range of subjects in arts, philosophy, and theology—medicine and law were excluded from their curriculum—in their own provincial *studia*.[87] Within the Dominican order, especially, *studia* developed at every level from the individual priory to the provincial schools, serving all the houses of a province and the general schools to which members were sent from throughout the order. Theology was the universal subject; but gradually special *studia artium* and *studia naturalium* were established for the study of metaphysics and natural science as found in Aristotle; later in the fourteenth century this was extended to special schools for the Bible, Arabic, Greek, and Hebrew—in the last three cases to further missionary work. The two main mendicant orders thus constituted self-contained systems of learning and study—a decentralized university with its base in the priory schools and its apex in the general schools [88] —in no way inferior to the universities or dependent on their license. Inevitably this led to a one-way traffic. The friars established their *studia generalia* in most of the same cities as their

[85] *Ibid.*, following *Chart.*, I, No. 219.
[86] This is contained in the masters' *Apologia* of 1253, *Chart.*, I, No. 230, which recounts the history of their relations with the friars.
[87] Rashdall, I, 371 ff.; and especially the excellent account by W. A. Hinnebusch, "Foreign Dominican Students and Professors at the Oxford Blackfriars," in *Oxford Studies Presented to Daniel Callus* [Oxford, Oxford Historical Society (OHS), 1963], 101–34.
[88] Hinnebusch, *op. cit.*, 101.

secular counterparts: Bologna, Paris, and Oxford; [89] their conventual schools provided them with the equivalent of a university education; the study of arts was wholly confined to them but further qualification in theology at a university was optional. Accordingly friars entering the university went directly to the theological faculty, having already been through their own arts course; nor did they need a license from the university in order to teach in their own conventual schools; recognition from their superior was sufficient. The trouble between the mendicants and the secular masters at Paris was part of an almost universal conflict over the role of the friars in relation to the secular church. It extended to the hearing of confessions, to burials, preaching, pastoral, and sacramental duties, and was exacerbated by the mendicants' claims for the spiritual superiority of mendicant poverty and by the support they received from the papacy. At Paris, as in other spheres, it raised the question of their *raison d'être;* but with less cause, as it would appear at first sight. Why, it may be asked, should the friars with their own schools have sought entry into the university? The answer is partly that they went there, as elsewhere, to save souls—and this entailed preaching and learning among the masters and scholars. But it was also partly through other circumstances. When the Dominicans (in 1217) and the Franciscans (in 1219) first arrived at Paris [90] they did not immediately seek entry into the university; they established their own schools for their own members. Not unnaturally the fame of Paris in theology led them also to send students to study for degrees in the theological faculty. In 1229 Roland of Cremona, who was to be the first Dominican professor

[89] They could only obtain degrees (in theology) from Paris, Oxford, and Cambridge until the mid-fourteenth century. At Bologna and other Italian universities the friars'—especially the Dominicans'—schools formed the theological faculty until the middle and later fourteenth century (*ibid.*, 102, 118).

[90] Both were strongly supported by Honorius III (*Chart.*, I, Nos. 35–40, 42, 43, 44). The Dominican house was the convent of St. Jacques on the left bank (hence the name Jacobites). Previously the site of the hospital of St. Jacques, it was given to them by the dean of St. Quentin, John de Barastre, appointed by Honorius III their teacher in theology (*Chart.*, I, No. 43). The university also made over certain rights (*ibid.*, Nos. 42, 43). The Franciscans, after living at first near St. Denis, settled in 1230 on land owned by the abbey of St. Denis and presented to them in 1234 by Louis IX, who bought it from the abbey (Rashdall, I, 348, note 1; *Chart.*, I, Nos. 37, 76).

A Dominican lecturing.

in theology at Paris, received the license from Bishop William of Auvergne. But it was only with the dispersion of the rest of the university that the friars, who remained at Paris, became directly involved in teaching. They opened their schools to secular students in theology, first under Roland of Cremona and then under his successor, Hugh of St. Cher. The teaching of theology thus continued uninterrupted with the approval of the chapter. The Dominicans, whether by design or accidentally, thus gained their first chair in the theological faculty. They retained it on the return of the seculars to Paris in 1231; and shortly afterwards added to it when Roland of Cremona's master, John of St. Giles, assumed the Dominican habit without relinquishing his chair. He was followed shortly afterwards by Alexander of Hales, one of the most eminent theologians of his day, who went over to the Franciscans. Of twelve chairs in theology the mendicants occupied three by 1231. Other religious orders began to do the same—Cistercians, Premonstratensians, and later Augustinian and Carmelite friars. These events of 1230–1 seem to have been the beginning of secular resentment against the mendicants, if the masters' letter of February 1254, written in the heat of the moment, can be taken as a reliable guide to events of twenty years before. According to it, both the Dominican chairs had come through duplicity: the first behind the university's back "with the connivance of the bishop and chancellor of Paris"; the second "against the will of the then chancellor." They also deplored the multiplication of "successive doctors for themselves" that resulted from having two chairs.[90a]

The role of the mendicants in the theological faculty in the years after 1231 is uncertain, but undoubtedly their growth in numbers and privileges was a major element in the tensions between them and the secular masters. It is again expressed in the same letter of the masters. Only three of fifteen chairs in the theological faculty remained to the seculars by 1254; the cathedral canons had another three and the mendicants the remainder: in addition to the three that had originally gone to the Dominicans and Franciscans, new religious orders had established schools and had swallowed up, it would seem, another six. Moreover, by 1254 some of the foremost theologians were mendicants, including St. Thomas Aquinas and St. Bonaventure, who were shortly to hold a Dominican and a Franciscan chair respectively. The secular masters were feeling the effect of their competition:

"They considered furthermore that the state of the city and the reputation of the theological faculty . . . could hardly support twelve chairs because of the scarcity of the scholars studying with us, since now in cities and other large-sized places generally the said subject is taught by the same friars and others not without great peril. Therefore they perceived more clearly than light that, after nine of those twelve chairs were occupied, as they were about to be irrevocably by the said colleges, which because of the continued succession of friar teachers would never thenceforth revert to secular masters, two or three at the

[90a] *Chart.*, I, No. 230.

most would be reserved for secular persons who flock from every region under the sun to the university of Paris." [90b]

For the ordinary masters, then, the prospect was one of extinction by the mendicants and religious; their encroachment here, as in other spheres, was depriving the seculars of their *raison d'être* and their livelihood. The masters' letter clearly shows that they were losing their students to the friars. The friars taught them in their own schools, where, in addition to the holders of the two Dominican and one Franciscan chair—whose occupants were continually changing—they had their own lectors. Until 1250 members of the two orders seem to have shown no inclination to apply for the license in theology from the university, probably because they received their own, and the chancellor of the day was in turn not giving it to those who did not apply. On May 30, 1250, Innocent IV wrote commanding the chancellor to grant it to whomever he considered suitable, especially religious, regardless of whether he was asked.[91]

This presaged the first real trouble. It opened the loophole that had always existed in the masters' control. If exploited it would give the friars entry to the theological faculty independently of the seculars. The mendicants had certainly taken part in faculty meetings; [92] but until now their challenge had been from without, as more popular teachers, rather than from within. To prevent this new danger from materializing the masters in the theological faculty passed a statute in February 1252—the first recorded by any faculty—to control the admission of the mendicants.[93] Its restricted applicants to those who had studied at one of the recognized Paris colleges and who had been examined and approved and had lectured in one of the recognized schools of the university; in future each religious order was to have only one college and one master in theology. The act was expressly designed to end the proliferation of masters in theology "beyond

[90b] *Ibid.*

[91] *Ibid.*, No. 191; Rashdall, I, 376, whose assumption that this applied only to the mendicants has been corrected by his editors; but this does not affect the main issue that it would have directly favored the mendicants and bypassed the masters.

[92] *Chart.*, I, Nos. 108, 178; Rashdall, I, 375.

[93] *Chart.*, I, No. 200; Rashdall, I, 377–8.

necessity." It would make all masters in theology subject to faculty approval and prevent the inundation by the mendicants. Failure to comply would mean expulsion from the society of masters. Thus, a generation after winning formal independence from the bishop and chancellor, the masters were now confronted with a new threat to their monopoly. For a time their attempt to enforce it succeeded because they had papal backing; but they met with failure when Innocent IV was succeeded by Alexander IV. A generation later they were to reassert their authority. But in 1254 they were taking on the mendicants and the papacy, then at the flood tide of success, and had temporarily to bow to their force.

They did not do so easily. The failure of the mendicants in 1253 to come to the support of the university, for a second time, released the university's pent-up hostility against them, the more powerful for being compounded of a righteous sense of betrayal as well as resentment.[94] This time the masters of the whole university joined in the action against the three mendicants, solemnly expelling and excommunicating them for disobedience to the university and for violating papal privileges. In addition it was decreed that in future no one would be admitted as a master unless he had first sworn before three other masters to observe the university's statutes, papal privileges, and secrets, to comply with any future cessation of lectures, and to bind the bachelors whom they taught and examined by the same oath. Failure by any master, bachelor, or scholar to observe a cessation would lead to eternal exclusion from the university.[95] Events now moved quickly. The friars, long buttressed by papal support, appealed to Innocent IV. On July 1, 1253 the pope wrote lifting the friars' excommunication and urging their readmission to the masters' consortium,[96] injunctions he repeated during July and August.[97] The masters replied with their open letter, already referred to.[98] It was a sustained *apologia* for their long suffering at the hands of the mendicants; it recounted the gradual encroachment on the masters' rights leading up to recent

---

[94] Cf. their letter of February 1254, *Chart.*, I, No. 230.
[95] *Ibid.*, No. 219.
[96] *Ibid.*, Nos. 222, 223.
[97] *Ibid.*, Nos., 224, 225, 226.
[98] *Ibid.*, No. 230.

events. After stressing the need to limit the number of mendicant masters and schools, which had led to the faculty of theology's statute in 1252, it described in detail the present struggle. The Dominicans emerge as the main villains. They were accused by the masters of attempting to make support for the cessation conditional on receiving their two chairs in perpetuity; when this was refused they had held aloof. By this action they had delayed redress of the university's wrongs for seven weeks. It was to prevent a recurrence that the masters had introduced their measures. Even so, they had sought to mitigate the Dominicans' position by allowing their oath to the university's statutes to be subject to the observance of their own rule. But the friars had still insisted on their chairs being made perpetual. They were then excommunicated for "rebellion and contumacy," to which the Dominicans replied with false slanders to the regent of France and the apostolic see. This led to their having falsely obtained papal letters to lift the ban on them which one of their traditional enemies, a canon of the Paris chapter, had used to suspend the whole university of masters and scholars alike. The masters nevertheless had stood firm. On the resumption of the academic year in October their beadles had been sent round the classrooms to announce the ban on the friars to new scholars; this had led to an affray in one of the friars' classes, which it had taken the rector to quell.

Nor did the masters stop at words; in order to present their case at the papal court they levied a tax on members of the faculties to meet the expenses involved.[99] Innocent IV's response was favorable. In a series of letters in July and August 1254 he effectively confirmed the master's position; he first reaffirmed the inviolability of their statutes [100] and then endorsed the right of the university to raise money to support William of St. Amour, its proctor in Rome, by a *pro rata* tax on all masters and scholars.[101] Three months later, on November 21, he imposed extensive restrictions on the mendicants' rights of preaching, hearing confessions, celebrating mass, and officiating at burials.[102] It

[99] *Ibid.*, No. 231.
[100] *Ibid.*, No. 237.
[101] *Ibid.*, Nos. 238, 239.
[102] *Ibid.*, No. 240. These last bulls betray a growing alienation from some, at least, of the friars, whom he called blasphemers, killers of souls, and

seemed that the Dominicans and Franciscans, especially, were about to have to withdraw along the whole of their front with the secular church. Then Innocent IV died, to be succeeded by Alexander IV, and the situation completely changed.

One does not have to be partisan for the Paris masters to feel that they were hardly treated by the new pope and that he was lacking in an understanding of the issues involved. The masters were defending rights that had been won in half a century's alliance with the papacy. Yet here was a pope undermining them. He began in December 1254 by removing Innocent's recent restrictions on the mendicants' rights of preaching, hearing confessions, burying the dead and other sacramental functions.[103] The following April he issued the celebrated bull *Quasi lignum vitae,* a root-and-branch vindication of the mendicants.[104] After reciting at inordinate length the history of the conflict, the pope lifted the ban of excommunication and ordered the restoration of the expelled friars. In future, cessations were to be valid only if voted by a two-thirds majority of each of the faculties—a measure that gave the mendicants, more than a third of the theological faculty, a power of veto. At the same time the pope affirmed the chancellor's power to grant the license to whom he thought fit, thereby putting the admission of religious to the faculty of theology in his hands.[105] The pope reiterated to the masters in theology his command for the friars to be readmitted within fifteen days, entrusting the task to the bishops of Orleans and Auxerre.[106] The masters, however, remained adamant. Turning the title of the pope's bull to mean the cross of death (*quasi lignum mortis*),[107] they declared the pope's command would mean the end of the university; neither the canons nor the mendicants

usurpers of the functions of the church. C. Thouzellier, in "La Place du *De periculis* de Guillaume de Saint-Amour dans les polémiques universitaires du XIII⁰ siècle," *Revue historique,* **156** (1927), 69–83, has pointed to the resemblance in tone with William of St. Amour's attacks on the mendicants. See pp. 259 ff.

[103] *Ibid.,* No. 244.

[104] *Ibid.,* No. 247.

[105] Rashdall, I, 383, says this implicitly conceded the second Dominican chair; but the gravamen of the charge over the second chair was that it had been obtained without the chancellor's assent.

[106] *Chart.,* I, Nos. 248, 249.

[107] *Ibid.,* No. 256, dated October 2, 1255.

in the theological faculty would vote with the secular masters; and without them a two-thirds majority would be impossible. Thus their right of cessation—their sole means of defense—would be lost. Rather than be faced with that or renew their association with the mendicants, they preferred to renounce all their privileges and dissolve the university. They were a society bound together by ties of friendship, not force, and nothing could compel them to keep it in being if they should decide otherwise. It was a plea not unlike that to be made fifty years later by the Franciscan Spirituals: to be left alone to observe their rule undefiled by those who had betrayed it. Even if there was a touch of histrionics in their declaration that "we do not prohibit them from having as many schools or scholars, secular or regular, as they want and can get," the sincerity of their wish to be allowed to live their own life, "in one part of the city peacefully and quietly," cannot be doubted. Already the dispute was being overlaid by doctrinal issues; a third of the masters' letter was devoted to a defense of William of St. Amour's work (almost certainly *De periculis*), which the friars were attacking; the questions of poverty and perfection were now coming to the fore. These theoretical attacks, which we shall consider in Part Two, had their practical counterpart in the lives of the friars, for whom Paris during the winter of 1255–6 was a far from congenial place. According to the reports of the Dominican general Humbert, the masters had imposed a boycott on members of the order; [108] they were attacked in the streets, abused, pelted from the houses, and treated as traitors. Whatever their support in the battle of words, the friars were intensely vulnerable on the streets.

Even at the ecumenical level, however, the struggle was moving away from resounding declarations. Alexander's response to the masters' reply to *Quasi lignum vitae* was not a further counter-reply, but a series of more practical measures designed to restore the friars. In November and December of 1255 a succession of bulls was sent to the ecclesiastical authorities in France instructing them to act against those masters who refused to accept the friars.[109] They were to be suspended and deprived of their benefices. He also ordered the chancellors of Notre

[108] *Chart.*, I, No. 273; also Nos. 250, 272, 275.
[109] See Kibre, *op. cit.*, 108 ff.; *Chart.*, I, Nos. 261, 262.

Dame and St. Geneviève to withhold the license from anyone who would not uphold the provisions of *Quasi lignum vitae*.[110] In the new year he began to intervene directly in the affairs of the university: at the end of January and in February he absolved any member from having to contribute to the university's finances and from any sentence of excommunication that might be imposed for having refused.[111] Even more noteworthy, Alexander authorized two cardinals to examine a Cistercian, whom he then licensed to teach theology at Paris, enjoying all the privileges and immunities of the university; the masters were ordered to admit him. Nothing seems to have come of it,[112] but the pope continued to enjoin the punishment of recalcitrant masters and to encourage the licensing of friars, among them at this time Thomas Aquinas.[113] He also actively took the mendicants' part in their persecution at the hands of the seculars, which by mid-1256 seemed to be abating.[114]

The pope was coming to single out certain of the ringleaders, foremost among them William of St. Amour who had been the masters' proctor at Rome. In April 1256 he warned them against being led into evil ways by William and a few others.[115] The struggle now centered increasingly on William of St. Amour. As so often, the principles—though not forgotten—became overlaid by personalities. Not that in William's case they could be dissociated; his *De periculis novissimorum temporum* expressed the widespread hostility of seculars everywhere to the incursions and pretensions of the mendicants; it had received a greater impetus from the recent affair of the *Evangelium eternum,* which had led to the condemnation of a young Franciscan, Gerard of Borgo San Donnino, at Paris and implicated important members of the order.[116] William's depiction of the friars as the "false prophets of the last times" formed a rallying point in the struggle between the two sides. These went beyond the two parties at the univer-

---

[110] *Ibid.,* Nos. 259, 260. For the chancellor of St. Geneviève see ref. 155.
[111] *Ibid.,* Nos. 263, 264, 267.
[112] *Ibid.,* Nos. 265, 266; Kibre, *op. cit.,* 109.
[113] *Chart.,* I, Nos. 269, 270.
[114] *Ibid.,* Nos. 272, 275.
[115] *Ibid.,* No. 271.
[116] See pp. 256 ff.

sity. In June Alexander made a frontal attack on William and three of his confrères, Odo of Douai, Nicholas of Bar-sur-Aube, and Christian of Beauvais.[117] First, he ordered them to be deprived of their benefices, expelled from the body of masters, and excommunicated; then, ten days later, he asked the king of France to imprison William and Christian and to expel the others. The reasons at this juncture were the now standard ones that they were refusing to comply with papal decrees to admit the friars. A month later William and others were summoned to an ecclesiastical council of the provinces of Sens and Rheims to answer charges of defaming the mendicants.[118] The seculars and mendicants there were split over whether to call a council to decide. Eventually the king sent William's *De periculis* to Rome; [119] in October Alexander condemned it following its examination by a commission.[120] Although he did not damn it as heretical, he found it "perverse and reprehensible against the power of the pope and the curia," to say nothing of the mendicants. He therefore banned it eternally with every copy to be burned within eight days; anyone found in possession of one after that, or espousing its doctrines, would be excommunicated.

Gradually, resistance to the pope's decrees on the mendicants melted away; only William remained as a standing obstacle to the pope's will. By October 1256 Odo of Douai and Christian of Beauvais submitted at Anagni to the provisions of *Quasi lignum vitae* and accepted the entry of both Thomas, a Dominican, and Bonaventure, a Franciscan, as masters in the theological faculty; they also professed assent to William of St. Amour's condemnation.[121] For all the pope's combination of cajolery and threats toward the Paris masters and William of St. Amour [122] the masters remained loyal to him: they renewed appeals as regularly as the pope rejected them.[123] They were no more successful in gaining the French king's intercession, although Louis IX

[117] *Chart.*, I, Nos. 280, 282.
[118] *Ibid.*, No. 287.
[119] *Ibid.*, No. 289.
[120] *Ibid.*, No. 288, 291.
[121] *Ibid.*, No. 293; see also No. 294.
[122] *Ibid.*, Nos. 296, 297, 301, 303, 304, 305, 306, 307, 308.
[123] *Ibid.*, Nos. 309, 332, 343.

did himself make one unavailing attempt.[124] The pope's obduracy also for a time led him into a *volte face* over the granting of the license in the arts faculty; he insisted that its new statutes demanding an oath of obedience to the faculty did not absolve a candidate from swearing to uphold the pope's decrees. The chancellor was to license no one who would not do so. Once again dealings with William of St. Amour were prohibited.[125]

To the end, however, and well beyond it, William eluded the pope. In 1270–1 he was living in Franche Comté and in correspondence with Nicholas of Lisieux, despite Alexander's repeated demands for his expulsion.[126] He died in 1272. The pope's obsession with William of St. Amour apart, he gradually mellowed toward the university in his later years. In August 1259 he sought to undo his earlier disregard of the arts faculty's privileges by instructing the chancellor of St. Geneviève to license no one who had not been examined and passed by four masters in arts. The chancellor of St. Geneviève had clearly been taking advantage of the pope's former indulgence.[127] The pope also reaffirmed a number of the university's judicial immunities from outside arrest or interference; [128] and perhaps most noteworthy of all, he now sanctioned the taxation of masters and scholars for university needs.[129] At the end of 1260 the pope came nearer to conciliating the university over its repeated pleas for the restoration of William of St. Amour when he authorized the bishop of Paris to absolve those who had been excommunicated for possessing copies of *De periculis*.[130] Thus the smoke of the greatest explosion of the university's history gradually lifted, leaving most of the older landmarks standing. The university—

[124] *Ibid.*, Nos. 353, 355, 356, 357.
[125] *Ibid.*, Nos. 333, 337, 338.
[126] Kibre, *op. cit.*, 116; *Chart.*, I, Nos. 439, 440.
[127] *Chart.*, I, No. 346.
[128] *Chart.*, I, Nos. 149, 351.
[129] *Ibid.*, No. 352.
[130] *Ibid.*, No. 367. After the pope's rejection of its appeals for Willliam in June and July the university renewed them in September; this time the pope did not reply (*Chart.*, I, Nos. 353, 354, 355). It is of interest that the bishop of Paris had on this occasion taken up the university's call, an indication of how the opposition to the mendicants had spread to the secular church, overlaying the older animosities between university and the Paris chapter.

contrary to Rashdall—had never dissolved, though it had threatened to do so; the pope, for all his fulminations, had never gone beyond tinkering with its privileges. The basic structure had remained unimpaired; the issue had been its widening to admit the mendicants. In retrospect Alexander IV's actions can only appear a disturbing and pointless exercise in papal prerogative which, had they been maintained, could have done both the friars and the university nothing but harm. The significance of the struggle lay in the tenacity with which the university had resisted and in the deep-rooted hostility felt toward the friars. It emerged a more cohesive force, not least in its financial organization.

IV RELATIONS WITH AUTHORITY FROM THE LATE THIRTEENTH CENTURY

After Alexander IV the university never again had to suffer such sustained intervention from any quarter until Louis XII in 1499; nor was its existence ever again in doubt. Alexander's pontificate was an aberration. His successor Urban IV (1261–4) resumed the policy of earlier popes, confirming most of the existing privileges,[131] and providing support once more against the cathedral chapter.[132]

It would be tedious to recount all the incidents of his and successive pontificates. The heroic period was over. Although friction and conflict—frequently violent—continued throughout the later Middle Ages, these were mainly of a local nature.[133] The wider issues involving the university were doctrinal and intellectual, not institutional. There were renewed outbreaks between the masters and the chancellor in 1271 and 1282, the masters again suspending lectures on both occasions. But the university now had the whip hand over the chancellor, and the issues revolved round his failure to answer to the masters, whose effective head by then was, as we shall discuss later, the rector. An-

---

[131] *Ibid.*, Nos. 376–384.
[132] *Ibid.*, No. 385.
[133] A detailed account until the end of the fifteenth century is to be found in Kibre, *op. cit.*, 120–226.

other and prolonged dispute of the same nature lasted from 1290–6, until it was finally settled by Boniface VIII; in the course of it pope Nicholas IV in 1292 formally accorded the university the right of granting the *ius ubique docendi* to those receiving its license.[134a]

By the end of the thirteenth century the kings of France were increasingly becoming the guardians of the university's privileges.[134b] This was an inevitable accompaniment of the growth of royal power and a corresponding decline in papal authority, especially in the struggle between Boniface VIII and Philip the Fair. It was then that the university had to choose for the first time between king and pope. With a king as determined as Philip was to assert his authority—and not merely to vindicate himself—the choice could hardly have gone to the pope. Not that the university's support for the king was entirely the result of royal pressure; from early in his reign Philip followed the almost invariable pattern of confirming—and indeed extending —the university's privileges, especially over the provost's oath of protection and exemption from imposts.[135] He sought also to safeguard foreign students passing through the kingdom to and from Paris, in 1297 specifically forbidding the molestation of Flemish students during the war with Flanders.[136] When the trouble between Philip and Boniface reached its height in 1302 each side took the unprecedented step of summoning assemblies of French prelates and doctors of theology and canon law to condemn the other. Philip came out on top, prohibiting any prelate or master from leaving his kingdom and gaining the assent of the university to his own council's decision to call a general council to try Boniface for his "enormous, horrible and detestable crimes." [137] Boniface replied in August by suspending the university's power to license masters in theology and law; but any effect it might have had was only transitory because

[134a] *Chart.*, II, No. 578.
[134b] E.g., *Chart.*, I, Nos. 466, 467; II, 531; also documents cited in Kibre, *op. cit.*, 129 f.
[135] *Chart.*, II, 531, 589, 597, 603, 606, 609, 612, 614, 624, 644, 631, 657, 660, 688, 700, 707.
[136] *Ibid.*, No. 602; also 638, 646, 648.
[137] *Ibid.*, No. 621 and 634: earlier in 1297 some of the masters in theology had agreed that Boniface VIII was a usurper (*ibid.*, pp. 604, 604a).

Boniface died the following year and his successor, Benedict XI, lost little time in restoring the right to the university.[138]

The epoch of Boniface VIII and Philip IV marked a watershed in the history of the university no less than in Christendom as a whole; or, more exactly, the changes in society as a whole also affected the university. The king rather than the pope now became the main power regulating its relations with the outside world; the chancellor and the bishop were no longer the force they had been in the past, nor were the mendicants a challenge to the secular masters' rights. The papacy still involved itself keenly in the university's affairs, but this involvement was now almost exclusively doctrinal and ecclesiastical, concerned above all with providing the seculars with benefices. As universalism waned the university became increasingly French. The object of the king's solicitude was to preserve it from the jealousies of his officers and subjects; his high court of parlement became the main adjudicator in the university's suits. Only occasionally was appeal made to the pope, and then on matters of form rather than content as in the dispute between the rival jurisdictions of the courts of papal conservator and bishop in 1346–7.[139] There was one final dénouement between the university and the chancellor John Blanchart in 1385–6, which ended in his resignation and replacement by Pierre d'Ailly, who had led the attack on him.[140] Although the case had been taken to the papal court at Avignon, d'Ailly's eighty-three charges against Blanchart and his deputy, involving numerous witnesses, raised no wider issues than the chancellor's abuse of his office and self-enrichment by illegally taking fees for the license. That it originally arose through a dispute over seating at an inception banquet testifies to its trivial nature compared with earlier disputes.

By then, however, the university's ecumenical standing—juridically and, up to a point, intellectually—had been undermined by the twin effects of the Hundred Years' War and the Great Schism. We shall consider their intellectual and doctrinal implications in Part Two. Institutionally they meant that the univer-

[138] *Ibid.*, Nos. 636, 637, 639, 640, 643, 645.
[139] *Ibid.*, Nos. 1129, 1137.
[140] *Chart.*, III, Nos. 1491, 1512, 1513, 1515, 1517, 1518, 1522, 1527. For a full account, see Kibre, *op. cit.*, 169 ff.

sity was no longer the intellectual center of Christendom; the devastation and unrest caused by the war—leading in 1356 to Etienne Marcel's insurrection at Paris [141]—made France less attractive to foreign students, especially those from England, France's adversary. At the same time the second half of the fourteenth century saw a wave of new universities founded in the German empire: Prague, Heidelberg, and Vienna, to name only three. These all drew scholars who in a previous age would have gone to Paris. The Schism, beginning in 1378 and lasting for forty years, completed the gallicizing of the university at Paris as it similarly affected the French church. Although the university advocated renunciation by each of the rival popes (the *via cessionis*), the division within the papacy was perpetuated by division among the kingdoms of Europe. Whereas France supported the pope at Avignon, the Empire and England supported his opponent at Rome; far from being overcome at the General Councils of Constance and Basel these rivalries were enshrined in the system of voting and deliberating by nations.

It is not surprising, therefore, that the history of the university during the fourteenth century is in its external facets principally a record of its relations with the kings of France, their officers, and the Paris populace. In the ceaseless succession of incidents and injuries to persons and privileges—some serious, many trivial, and most tedious—there were two main strands. One was the unwavering protection of the university by king after king, no matter what the external circumstances; even during King John's imprisonment in England after his defeat at the battle of Poitiers in 1356 the dauphin maintained the policy his father had followed and resumed after his return in 1360.[142] It lasted throughout the fourteenth century and well into the fifteenth, and was only finally reversed by Charles VIII in 1488 and then Louis XII in 1498 when he wholly abolished scholarly exemption from civil jurisdiction.[143] The papacy had already withdrawn the right of cessation in 1462. This was not only the logical outcome of the university's long dependence on royal authority; it was also the historical effect of the unceasing conflicts to which resentment at

[141] There is a break of fourteen months in the records from February 25, 1346 to April 23, 1347 (*Chart.*, III, pp. 42–3, note 3).
[142] Kibre, *op. cit.*, 11 ff.
[143] *Ibid.*, 220 ff.

the university's possession and abuse of its privileges had led. If the university had largely been nurtured by the papacy it had been kept in being and indulged by the French monarchy; like any corporation it had come to see its rights as overriding all others. The genuine struggles to survive that had marked the great disputes of the thirteenth century became in the fourteenth century mainly jealous and often fractious assertions of privilege. They built up a legacy of hostility from the local populace and others whom not all the kings' ordinances could curb from breaking into violence. This was the other element in the later history of the university: regular royal declarations of university privilege were as regularly matched by their infraction. By the end of the fourteenth century, for all its intellectual luster, which was still to be seen in men like Gerson and to a certain degree d'Ailly, the university was living on past capital; its rights and immunities were a source of discord that sooner or later had to be ended.

V INTERNAL DEVELOPMENT

If university's relation to authority altered little after 1300, institutionally it continued to develop throughout the fourteenth century. This lay mainly in the growing autonomy of its constituent groups, above all the faculties, nations, colleges, and their officers, on the one hand; and in the increasing definition of its organs and channels with the outside world, on the other, especially the royal and ecclesiastical courts whose jurisdictions were crystallized largely as the result of the constant affrays between members of the university and the Paris populace. They were all closely interrelated and often inseparable; but for the purposes of discussion we shall consider them under separate headings, beginning with the nations and the rector.

The Nations and the Rector. The system of nations and their relation to the rector was *par excellence* the distinctive feature of Paris university's internal organization. When they first emerged is not known. Unlike the corresponding institutions at Bologna, they were an outcrop of the basic structure, grafted on to the masters' association and concerning only the arts faculty. As such they included all the masters, local and foreign, and were governed by them, not the scholars as at Bologna. But far from their having only a local authority—as but part of a part of the university—the nations came to be a major factor in its affairs. The reason for this was twofold. In the first place, the arts faculty was by far the most numerous section of the university, containing two-thirds of its total members; as also the youngest and the most volatile it was in the forefront of its actions. Moreover, the bachelors in the higher faculties were—excepting the mendicants—usually already masters in the arts faculty from which they had graduated before going on to the study of theology, law, or medicine. Until they became masters or doctors (the terms were interchangeable) in one of these higher subjects they continued to be members of the arts faculty and belong to a nation there.[144] In the second place, and here lay the anomaly, from the arts faculty came the rector. He was chosen by the nations, but by the second half of the thirteenth century he was *de facto* head of the university. The role of the nations therefore extended—if only indirectly—beyond their own faculty.

The nations at Paris, as at the other early universities, were not formally established; they first appear in the second decade of the thirteenth century, mentioned by Honorius III in 1222,[145] although the term was employed in a literal, nontechnical sense by Philip de Hervengt some time before 1181.[146] Honorius referred expressly to "scholars according to their nations" avenging their injuries. There is no further mention of them until 1245 when Innocent IV granted the same immunities to faculty officials, elected by all the nations, as faculty members enjoyed.[147] But it is only in 1249 that the division into four nations and their election of the rector are made clear, the pope laying down the procedure.[148] Among other provisions, the nations were to seal their agreement with their own seals. The Paris masters, in their celebrated letter of October 1255,[149] spoke of the antiquity of

---

[144] See authorative study by P. Kibre, *The Nations in the Mediaeval Universities* (Cambridge, Mass., Mediaeval Academy of America, 1948), 15.
[145] *Chart.*, I, No. 45.
[146] *Ibid.*, Introduction, No. 51.
[147] *Ibid.*, No. 141.
[148] *Ibid.*, No 187.
[149] *Ibid.*, No. 256; see 42–3 above.

their four nations whose seals they were using in the absence of a common seal.

The Paris nations, unlike those at Bologna, were large, heterogeneous groupings; the lack of clear-cut geographical divisions led to frequent conflict.[150] There was the French nation, which included masters from the Île de France and Paris, southern France, Italy, Spain, and the East. The Norman nation comprised the masters from Rouen and Brittany and later, by 1275, the six episcopates of the province of Rouen. The Picard nation was composed of those from the Low Countries and northern France, in the fifteenth century dividing into two regions of the Picards and Flemings. Lastly, the English nation, perhaps the most diverse of the four, brought together masters from the British Isles, Normandy, Holland, part of Flanders, Germany, Scandinavia, Finland, Hungary, and the Slavic lands. In the thirteenth century the English were separated from the other regions; this was superseded in the fifteenth by a division into three provinces of High and Low German and the Scots, the English element by then having become infinitesimal as a result of the 100 Years' War.

In many ways the nations were the heart of the university. Besides constituting, as we have said, the majority and the most vital element, they were the basic units of university life for members of the arts faculty. Honorius III's admonition of 1222 was to the nations to refrain from violence; the masters in their letter of 1255 used the seals of the nations to express their corporate identity. It is not surprising in so diverse a society that men naturally gravitated to their own kind; and the records of the university abound in clashes between the different groups. The fiercest ones often involved the mediation of the pope or king, directly or through their representatives, as for example in 1266, 1278, 1281, 1328, 1356.[151] The outbreak of the Great Schism in 1378 led to clashes between the partisans of the rival popes. The French and Norman nations, as well as the three higher faculties, supported Clement VII, while the English-German nation and the Picards were in favor of Urban VI. In September 1381 Urban's backers suggested secession to Prague, a threat that materialized in the

---

[150] P. Kibre, *The Nations*, 18 ff.
[151] *Ibid.*, 22 ff.

departure of a number of masters to the new universities of Vienna, Heidelberg, Erfurt, and Cologne after the university officially declared for Clement in February 1381.[152] As the university gradually lost its international character in the fifteenth century, so the importance of the nations diminished, although they were not finally abolished until after the Revolution in 1793.

During the thirteenth and fourteenth centuries, however, they were indispensable to the university's functioning. At their height they were responsible for the corporate life of their members; and each nation was run as an independent organization.[153] To begin with, the nation guaranteed the individual scholar's legal privileges and immunities, its members coming almost too easily to the defense of one of their number. It also had its own schools, which, being solely concerned with arts subjects, were located on the left bank of the river, most of them in the Street of Straw (Rue du Fouarre, Vicus Straminis), so called because the students sat on straw to hear the lectures. Many of the schools were to be found there, belonging to all the nations and including the celebrated school of the Seven Arts of the English-German nation. Each nation supervised its constituent schools. Those attending paid the fees to the proctor of the nation concerned. The students could also attend the schools of other nations, and masters were forbidden to take scholars for themselves or to prevent scholars from going outside their own nation's schools.[154]

The nation was also responsible for the examinations leading to the license. We shall consider their nature in Chapter Three; here it will be enough to enumerate them. Before the license could be granted candidates had, by the middle of the thirteenth century, to pass through a number of preliminary stages. The first was responsions: a test conducted by the master before the pupil could begin to determine—that is, engage in a series of disputations over the first half of Lent on prescribed texts. The qualifications as laid down in the English-German nation's statutes of 1252 [155] included a minimum age for determining of

[152] *Ibid.*, 26–7.

[153] This account is mainly based on Kibre, *The Nations,* 90 ff.

[154] E.g. *Chart.*, II, No. 570, cited by Kibre, *The Nations,* 95.

[155] *Chart.*, I, No. 228, translated by Thorndike, *op cit.*, No. 26; for this, as

twenty years, a declaration by the student that he had attended a recognized master's school and followed his disputations for two years, had heard lectures on prescribed texts and performed the requisite exercises, had spent five or at least four years continuously at Paris or another *studium generale,* and would continue to study in one of its schools for another year. For a worthy candidate these provisions could be waived. The examiners—who were to collect the money from the bachelors—consisted of a committee of three variously appointed: by the proctor of the English-German nation in the January or February before the examination or by the whole nation, in the case of the Normans.[156] Whatever the method, they were responsible to the whole faculty, to which they had to take an oath. Only by their unanimous agreement could a candidate be approved and recommended for the license.[157] By the middle of the thirteenth century no English-German scholar could gain a degree without having first determined; and this requirement applied to the whole arts faculty by 1279.[158] The determiners usually took their degree under a master of their own nation. Those who did not pass beyond the grade of bachelor received letters of testimony from their masters, signed with the nation's seal after having been sanctioned by a full congregation of the masters.[159] In the examination for the license each nation supplied one examiner, chosen by the abbot or chancellor of St. Geneviève; the examiners, too, had to swear to the faculty of arts that they would act fairly.

From these provisions it is apparent how largely teaching was in the hands of the nations. The masters' recommendation of a candidate for the license was—as we remarked earlier—only the culmination of an elaborate scholastic process by the second part of the thirteenth century. In the arts faculty this was centered on the nations. Thus the French nation by 1328 had established a

for much else known about the regulation of the nations, see G. C. Boyce, *The English-German Nation in the University of Paris in the Middle Ages* (Bruges, 1927) 73 ff.

[156] *Chart.,* II, No. 1008; Kibre, *The Nations,* 100.

[157] Boyce, *op. cit.,* 81 ff.; *Chart.,* I, No. 227; *Chart.,* II, No. 673, note 2.

[158] Boyce, *op. cit.,* 87; *Chart.,* I, Nos. 201, 485.

[159] Boyce, *op. cit.,* 95–6.

regular system of overseeing its schools: [160] each year five masters were appointed to visit each of them to fix the stipend of those teaching; for example in 1320 it was to be thirteen and fourpence for each determiner. Particular stress was put on establishing which masters were genuinely teaching (regent masters). The money to be paid by their pupils had in turn to go to the proctors before the assembled nation.[161] In the later fourteenth and fifteenth centuries the French nation spent considerable sums on buying schools in the Street of Straw, besides maintaining those elsewhere in the area. It sought to stop their proliferation in 1328,[162] however, because too many had been opened by the masters who received payment for their upkeep. Each year all teaching posts were re-allocated; every master wishing to teach had to apply or re-apply. Those accepted undertook to lecture continuously from the beginning of October to some time in Lent (the Grand Ordinary). The nations also jointly decided the organization and content of the courses within the arts faculty as a whole; but they deliberated separately and voted on their decisions individually, each nation having a single vote. Agreement was often not gained without friction; the French nation in particular, because of its greater numbers, in 1266 claimed that it should provide three of the four examiners for the license, but the papal legate (Simon de Brion, the future Martin IV) rejected it.[163] In 1338 the number of candidates for the license was fixed at sixteen, six from the French nation, two from the English-German and four each from the Normans and Picards.[164]

Amidst all the legalism that inevitably forms such a large element of the documents of any institution, we should not forget that the nations were above all educational associations. Teaching and the passing of examinations were their main function. Moreover, they were masters' organizations; their perspective was that of the masters' interests and activities. Financially it is reflected in the fact that fees were the nation's principal

[160] *Chart.*, II, No. 807; Thorndike, *op. cit.*, No. 69.
[161] *Chart.*, II, No. 793; Kibre, *The Nations*, 94 ff.
[162] Kibre, *The Nations*.
[163] *Ibid.*, 101.
[164] *Ibid.*

source of income. There were fixed scales of payment, as we have seen, by candidates who were preparing for the license, and for taking the different examinations. The money was collected by the masters who taught them; there was also an entrance fee, in common with all guilds and professional associations, for those becoming masters (incepting). This varied according to the entrant's means and the state of the nation's finances, which, being limited, were liable to fluctuate. Expenditure on schools or other property or a recent feast could rapidly bring them to a low ebb.[165] In 1336 the French nation demanded twenty *solidi;* in 1319 the Normans asked 16 *solidi.* The money in both cases was to be paid to the respective proctor. Poor scholars were frequently dispensed from payment at the time. Other sources of revenue were from fines on newly elected officers, for example, ten *solidi* from proctors in the French nation in 1336; but these, like the entry fees, were probably quickly spent in celebration at the nearest tavern.[166]

Periodically measures were taken to restrict this more conspicuous consumption;[167] all the nations made expenditure a matter for a general congregation of its members. It was the function of the proctor and the other officers of the nation to oversee its finances. They had control of the *archae,* or coffers, containing its funds, documents, and other valuables. Originally the proctor was principally concerned with collecting money. He was the nation's chief officer, as his title *procurator* shows, acting on behalf of the rest of its members. Proctors were first mentioned in connection with the nations in 1249, where, as we have seen, they represented the four nations in electing the rector.[168] Qualifications for the proctor's office varied from nation to nation, but in all of them a proctor had to be at least twenty-one years old and a regent master (i.e. one officially teaching in the faculty). Election was indirect, made through electors appointed by each

---

[165] *Ibid.,* 83; and especially Boyce, *op. cit.,* 164 ff.

[166] Kibre, *The Nations,* 84.

[167] E.g., The Picards in 1373 (Kibre, *The Nations,* 85; and *Chart.,* III, No. 1384) and the English-German nation in 1391 (Kibre, *The Nations,* 86; *Chart.,* III, No. 1592).

[168] *Chart.,* I, No. 187. For what follows see Kibre, *The Nations,* 66 ff. and Boyce, *op. cit.,* 39 ff.

nation; this was usually done by its different subgroupings, for example the five provinces of Paris, Sens, Rheims, Tours, and Bourges in the French nation.[169] Although the post of proctor was, until the fifteenth century, held only for a month, except during the long vacation, and, in the English-German nations at least, was an obligation that could not be evaded, later records suggest that passions sometimes ran high; charges of election-eering and its usual accompaniments of fraud, bribery, and cor-ruption are to be found among the documents of all the nations in the later fourteenth and the fifteenth centuries.[170]

At Paris, as at Bologna but unlike Oxford, the proctor's finan-cial duties gradually passed to a special officer, the receptor, elected each year by each nation separately. The proctor's duty became the government of the nation: he had one of the three keys to its *archae;* and on appointment he had to uphold the statutes and promise to punish transgressors as well as to relin-quish his office without delay at the end of his term. During it he kept the nation's book of statutes and its seal. His was the right to summon congregations of the nation and preside over them. He was also the nation's link with the faculty and the uni-versity, reporting to the rector matters of common concern. The nation was in turn bound to obey the rector by the oath its members took as bachelors and on becoming masters (incep-tion).[171] The proctors had judicial authority over both the scholars and masters; they could deprive scholars of the privilege of the schools for living in houses banned by the university; each proctor acted as a court of first instance, and the four constituted a tribunal of the faculty, together with the rector's court.[172] The proctors were subject to the nation's assembly in all matters of policy; but as its representative in the university congregations they were subject to university decisions, and could subsequently be disowned by the regent masters of the nation.

---

[169] Kibre, *The Nations;* the Normans had a peculiar system known as "finding the black bean" by which the electors were appointed by the master who drew the black bean from a cap in which all the other beans were white.

[170] *Ibid.,* 68–70.

[171] *Ibid.,* 71.

[172] *Ibid.,* 72; *Chart.,* I, No. 137.

The meetings of a nation, over which the proctor presided, were usually held weekly—normally on Sunday mornings—at the Mathurins (the house of the Trinitarians, an order of mendicant friars, next to the chapel of St. Mathurins, from which it took its name) or the church of St. Julien-le-Pauvre. These, together with the Dominican and Cistercian convents, were established assembly places for the faculties, which, like the university, had no premises of their own. Although summoning these meetings was the exclusive right of the proctor, he was assisted by the beadles, who were also elected at such congregations. The beadles were the noncommissioned officers of the university,[173] to be found at all levels. There were two in each of the nations; they accompanied the proctor in most of his duties, forming a permanent cadre on which the administration was based. The head beadle was the proctor's chief agent, visiting the schools with him, proclaiming congregations, statutes, and vacations, and being present at all inceptions.[174] In the thirteenth century the office was annual, but during the fourteenth and fifteenth centuries it was a life appointment, as the subbeadle's was, made through the nation's assembly. The beadle carried a mace as the insignia of his office on ceremonial occasions. He kept a register of all graduates and masters of arts. Failure in any of his duties or revealing the secrets of the nation or university was punishable by fines of part or all of his stipend.

Finally, in addition to the receptor or finance officer, elected in the nation's assembly annually, there were messengers (*nuntii*). Chosen by the proctor, they acted as intermediaries with the rest of the university and the outside world, not least with families and relatives of scholars. They enjoyed the same privileges as the scholars. Their numbers seem to have been considerable, leading to protests against them by the German nation in 1470.[175]

Beyond their formal attributes the nations were places of reli-

---

[173] Boyce's phrase, *op. cit.*, 60.

[174] *Ibid.*, 61 f.; Kibre, *The Nations,* 75 ff.; *Chart.*, I, No. 418, translated by Thorndike, *op. cit.*, No. 33.

[175] Kibre, *The Nations,* 80, who also quotes figures from A. Budinszky, *Die Universität Paris,* which give 162 *nuntii* from the French nation and 60 for the Germans; it is not clear at what date or for how long these were supposed to be.

gion and living as well as learning. Attendance at masses and
other religious services formed an important part of the masters'
functions; and elaborate provisions were made to fine defaulters.
Each nation also had its own patron saint in addition to those of
the university—the Virgin, St. Nicholas, and St. Catherine—
whose day was duly kept. Celebrations of any kind were one of
the features of medieval university life; and many of celebrations of the nation were directly financed by successful candidates on passing an examination. Although festivities were not
confined to the masters, it must always be remembered that the
nation was a masters' institution run by and for those who
taught. As such it reflected the concerns of magisterial life—
teaching, payment, representation, and exercise of authority,
academic, religious, and moral.

The rise of the rector to be head of the university is not the
least of the anomalies in its earlier history; nor are the stages by
which it occurred especially clear. The problem of how the chief
of the arts faculty—the lowest of the four faculties—came to
preside over all of them is made harder by the frequent and in-
exact use of the word rector.[176] Early mention of him in 1237
and 1244 does not differentiate him from the proctors; [177] that
first occurs in 1245,[178] and again in 1249 when provision is
made for his election by representatives ("intrants") of the four
nations.[179] Although it was not until 1274,[180] that he was expressly called head of the arts faculty, the earlier references,
from 1249 onward, leave little doubt that he had enjoyed that
position for twenty-five years previously.[181] He was expressly
recognized as head by Simon de Brion, the papal legate, later
Pope Martin IV, who in 1275 called for obedience by the nations to the rector, the proctors, and the beadles.[182] This, however, was not the same as headship of the university; the frequent use of the term *universitas* in conjunction with the rector's

---

[176] See especially Denifle, *Entstehung,* 106 ff.
[177] *Ibid.,* 113–14; *Chart.,* I, Nos. 95, 113.
[178] *Chart.,* I, No. 137; also No. 136.
[179] *Ibid.,* No. 187.
[180] *Ibid.,* No. 447; also No. 485.
[181] *Ibid.,* Nos. 231, 246, 328, 330.
[182] *Ibid.,* No. 460.

name in the years before 1260 can almost invariably be read to mean the arts faculty.[183] The one exception is perhaps the most instructive: it occurs in the celebrated masters' letter of 1254, previously discussed, which speaks of the beadles returning for the help of the "rector of our university" in their attempt to read out the edict of separation to a classroom of the friars. Since this letter was from the secular masters as a whole it cannot be made to refer exclusively to the faculty of arts.[184] On the contrary, it seems to be the direct outcome of a united front among the seculars in defense of their rights against the mendicants. This appears to have been a catalyst in the development of the rector's power, just as the earlier struggle against the chancellor led to the autonomy of the masters. Moreover, the one almost certainly fostered the other. The effective rejection of the chancellor's headship—for that is what the masters' assertion of their independence in effect entailed—meant the need for a substitute in time of crisis. The mendicants occasioned the crisis; the rector provided the substitute. For the moment at least—if we are to believe the letter of 1254—the rector in asserting his authority spoke for the whole university, and not, at this time, just for the faculty of arts. Six years later, in the immediate aftermath of the struggle for survival, the university again seems to have let the rector act for it: in the presence of the proctors and in response to the appeals of the three higher faculties he petitioned for the revocation of acts made by him and the proctors.[185] There was no question, however, of the rector enjoying a formal constitutional position within the university as a whole; his pre-eminence at this time was purely *ad hoc*. Nevertheless he had been its spokesman, and over the next twenty years he consolidated his hegemony until by the 1280's it had been effectively accepted by the faculties of law and medicine. It was not done by legal

[183] Denifle, *Entstehung*, 110 ff.; and *Chart.*, I, XXIII–V.
[184] I agree with Rashdall, I, 330–1, note, in opposing Denifle's view that the rector was not head of the arts faculty before 1274, and of the university before the middle of the fourteenth century. Denifle's grounds were that the name of the rector was not before then mentioned in the appropriate statutes. Denifle's approach here is too formal; it leads arbitrarily to dismissing the written evidence as well as failing to give due weight to its context.
[185] *Chart.*, I, No. 373.

means; unlike the masters wresting control from the chancellor, the arts faculty had no grounds for imposing its own head on the superior faculties. It was rather the survival of the fittest. The overwhelming numbers of the artists compared with the other faculties—fivefold in the rolls sent to the papal curia in 1348 and 1363 [186]—as well as their youth—put members of the arts faculty in the forefront of the struggle against the chancellor and mendicants. Just as the university's independence was forged in conflict, so was the rector's authority. It was achieved by usurping the power that could only be effectively wielded by the arts faculty. There was, however, another element in favor of the rector. Many of the members of the higher faculties would have belonged to the arts faculty, where they had to take an oath to observe its statutes. Rashdall has pointed out that the formula of the oath changed significantly in the course of the thirteenth century. Originally it bound the bachelor in the arts only so long as he should profess the faculty of arts. By about 1280 this clause had become "to whatever state you shall come." [187] As the rector was head of the arts faculty by then, the obligation to obey him continued after passing on to one of the higher faculties; in due course it led to an explicit oath of obedience to him.[188]

Above all, recognition by the other faculties of the rector's headship should not be seen as the surrender of independence; it was rather the acceptance of his presidency in matters of common concern. As we shall discuss shortly, his main function was to preside over the general assembly and take the consensus of opinion that was reached separately by each of the faculties. The latter preserved their own internal organization and statutes. Accordingly, acknowledgment of the rector was more a matter of form than of substance, in which dignity rather than self-interest was involved. Perhaps for that reason recognition was longest coming from the faculty of theology, the one closest to the chancellor and the chapter. Both of the other faculties, medicine and law, seem to have gained corporate seals considerably

[186] Denifle, *Entstehung*, 123.
[187] Rashdall, I, 328–9; *Chart.*, I, Nos. 231, 501; Rashdall puts the change "sometime after 1256" on no apparent grounds.
[188] *Chart.*, II, No. 1675.

later, in about 1270 [189]—against which the chancellor characteristically was the one to complain. Although in 1279 the deans of
the two faculties were disputing the form of summons to an assembly by the rector, they had in 1276, jointly with the rector
and proctors, given their assent to a deed; only the eight masters
of theology appended their names individually.[190] Even the protests of the theological faculty in 1283–4 concerned the form of
summons, which it held should be through its dean and "by sup-
plication and request," thereby by implication conceding the rector's right to convene a general assembly of the university.[191] It
persisted in this attitude until finally in 1341 the arts faculty
agreed to notify the dean personally.[192] To treat this as the
point, however, as Denifle does,[193] at which the rector became
acknowledged head of the university is not even to take the
shadow for the substance, since the theological faculty continued
to dispute the rector's precedence; nor was it alone in doing
so.[194] This did not alter the relationship between the rector and
the faculties any more than the pope's letter addressed to the
"rector and masters of the University" in 1358 did. These were
matters of form and terminology that were the continual cause
of friction.

More telling is the way in which the rector was able to assert
his claims of precedence in the 1280's and 1290's, with papal
backing. They were the years, as we have remarked earlier, of
the last and real disputes with the chancellor, except for 1386,
which was in another category. In 1281 the chancellor Philip de
Thori was accused of bypassing the masters in granting the license; he riposted with the equally time-honored charges that
the masters had been making illegal statutes. But he also asserted that he—the head of the university—had been summoned
by a beadle to appear at university congregations. The arts fac-

---

[189] *Ibid.*, I, Nos. 446, 451; Rashdall, I, 326.

[190] *Chart.*, I, Nos. 490, 493; also 416.

[191] *Ibid.*, No. 515; Rashdall, I, 327.

[192] *Chart.*, II, 1051; Rashdall, I, 402 ff.

[193] Denifle, *Entstehung*, 110 ff.; *Chart.*, I, XXIII–V; he is followed in this by
Kibre, *The Nations*, 103.

[194] *E.g.*, in 1347, 1353, and 1386; Rashdall, I, 403.

ulty's reply, made through their proctor at Rome in 1283 or 1284, is doubly revealing.[195] First, it unequivocally rejected the chancellor's claim to be head of the university; to concede it would be to give the university two heads and so make it a monstrosity. On the contrary, it acknowledged no head beyond the rector save the pope. Second, it was explained that the chancellor had been cited to appear before the university not as chancellor but as one of the regent masters.[196] Now this could only have been as a member of the theological faculty of which the chancellor —as we shall discuss later—was *ex officio* member. Hence it shows that the rector was by this time presiding over meetings of the whole university as a matter of course—a supposition further confirmed by the pope's reply, which made no mention of this fact, but merely declared that thenceforth the chancellor could not be compelled to attend university meetings, although he could be respectfully invited.[197] This injunction was repeated again in 1286 as the result of further trouble between the university and the deceased Philip de Thori's successor.[198] That it involved more than the arts faculty is clear from an agreement made in July 1281 that questions of privilege concerning one faculty were a matter for them all.[199]

Thus, despite the lack of any precise constitutional formulation, the rector's position as *de facto* head of the university was established and implicitly acknowledged by both the higher faculties and the papacy by the 1280's. It was not, however, comparable with the chancellor's position, and there was no question of one superseding the other. The chancellor had in the days of the cathedral school been in charge of it, appointed by the bishop or chapter and enjoying indefinite tenure; his powers were at once spiritual, judicial, and educational; hence the prolonged struggle that was needed finally to dislodge him. By 1281 only his education prerogative of granting the license remained, but even here his scope was restricted as we have recounted; and after the grant of the *ius ubique docendi* in 1292 he con-

[195] *Chart.*, I, No. 515; Rashdall, I, 330.
[196] *Chart.*, I, p. 618.
[197] *Ibid.*, No. 516.
[198] *Ibid.*, No. 528.
[199] *Ibid.*, No. 505, cited by Kibre, *Scholarly Privileges*, 124.

ferred it in the name of the pope. The case of the rector was
different. To begin with he was elected by the representatives of
the nations; he was thus drawn from the masters and was one of
them, unlike the chancellor, who qua chancellor—as opposed to
being a member of the theological faculty—stood over and
above the university. In the second place the rector's tenure was
very limited—a month or six weeks—until Simon de Brion's reforms of 1266, after which it became three months.[200] It was
therefore a rotating office, subject to the closest scrutiny as well
as an elaborate voting procedure, which, in contrast to the chancellor's office, made its holder more like a tribune or at least an
elected president. It carried none of the personal or judicial prerogatives of the chancellor's position. Like the election of a pope,
on which it was modeled, it demanded a majority agreement, or
failing that, acceptance of the decision by an approved adjudicator, normally the retiring rector. Friction was inevitable and frequent, but in this case it was over the exercise of rights, not the
struggle to attain them.

The main functions of the rector were twofold. At the university level he convened and presided over congregations of the
university.[201] He did not take part in its debates but had the
chairman's prerogatives of deciding what could be discussed and
when it should be voted on. Within the arts faculty after 1275 he
acted for the faculty between meetings. Together with the four
proctors he constituted a court of the first instance for questions
of discipline from which appeal could be made to the assembly
of the university. The rector also controlled part of the funds of
the faculty of arts for common expenses; he also authorized the
sale of parchment.

He had no authority over the government of the other faculties. The medieval university was a federation of its faculties. In
itself it possessed no buildings, organization, or income. Accordingly, the decisions affecting the university as a whole were
taken by the faculties, which retired to their own accustomed
places to consider the question at issue. Voting at a general con-

---

[200] *Chart.*, I, No. 492; it was confirmed in 1313 (*ibid.*, II, No. 699). For
what follows see Kibre, *The Nations*, 107.
[201] Kibre, *The Nations*, 108; *Chart.*, II, No. 1032, for an account of a
congregation of the university.

gregation of the university, which met usually at the church of Julien-le-Pauvre or the chapter house of the Mathurins, was by faculties. Each nation and each of the three higher faculties had one vote; a majority of the seven votes carried a decision, although dissentients could obstruct it by refusing to affix their seals. The rector had no casting vote; he could only sum up in his conclusion.[202] His position therefore expressed the state of the university, which existed in the faculties.

We have already considered the nations of the arts faculty. They were not synonymous with the faculty, which was governed by their representatives under the rector. Like the higher faculties, the faculty of arts had its own statutes for teaching, examining, payment of fees, discipline, and so on. Nevertheless, it was largely dominated by the need to reconcile the interests of the different nations, each of which, as we saw earlier, had its own seal. The three higher faculties of law, medicine, and theology were likewise each a distinct corporation within the university. The word "faculty" as meaning a distinct discipline or branch of learning seems to have been first applied to Paris in a bull of Honorius III in 1219, although it had been used in the same sense by Boethius in the fifth century.[203] The existence at Paris of the four main studies of arts, law, medicine, and theology, dates from the later twelfth century at least.[204] It is not until 1252, however, that we find the first recorded statute by one of the higher faculties, that passed by the masters in theology against the mendicants.[205] Deans do not appear in documents before 1264, and the faculties of law and medicine do not seem to have had seals until the 1270's.[206] Of the higher faculties, that of theology was in the most singular position because it was closest to the original cathedral school. As a consequence,

---

[202] Rashdall, I, 329 speaks of the "almost superstitious importance attached to his rectorial conclusion," but on what grounds he does not say; his view that "the oath of obedience to the rector was the keystone of the academic constitution" (*ibid.,* 329–30) seems exaggerated.

[203] *Chart.,* I, No. 29; also No. 48 (1224); Rashdall, I, 324, quoting Denifle, *Entstehung,* 70.

[204] Rashdall, *ibid.,* 22; and especially C. H. Haskins, *Studies in the History of Mediaeval Science* (reprinted New York, Ungar, 1960), 126 ff., 356–76.

[205] *Chart.,* I, No. 200, dated February.

[206] Rashdall, I, 326; *Chart.,* I, Nos. 399, 416, 446, 451.

both the chancellor and the canons of Notre Dame belonged to it and had the right to teach without the authorization of the other masters. It was thus far more under the aegis of the chancellor and canons. As late as 1264 the chancellor claimed to be *ex officio* dean in the face of strong opposition from the masters.[207] The canons, as we saw, not only could teach independently but were a threat to the corporate identity of the faculty; they also repeatedly refused to pay the taxes levied by the university—which was another source of discord.[208] For these reasons the masters of the theological faculty were in the forefront of the struggle against the chancellor and the mendicants, even if, unlike those in the arts faculty, they were not so involved in the brawls and physical skirmishes.

Benefices and Fees. Both Paris and Oxford were ecclesiastical universities. Although they came increasingly under temporal jurisdiction in the fourteenth and fifteenth centuries, they owed much of their privileges and benefits to papal intervention and all their members enjoyed ecclesiastical status. From early on popes had sought to send promising ecclesiastics to Paris to study. To provide for them they looked to the local churches to give such priests benefices, the fruits of which they could enjoy while studying. Alexander III is the first example of a pope to do so;[209] he was followed by Innocent III, who in one case had to resort to threats of excommunication, and was in general not particularly successful.[210] Honorius III went further with his bull *Super speculum* of 1219,[211] in which he asked prelates and chapters to provide promising young priests with benefices so that they could study theology. As a counter to the attraction of the "lucrative sciences"—law—those engaged in the study of theology were to receive the income from their benefices for five years. This policy was not intended to provide for a class of professional theologians, nor did it succeed in doing so in the thirteenth century. Masters who received benefices—and in France

---

[207] *Chart.*, I, No. 399.
[208] Kibre, *Scholarly Privileges,* 126, 146 ff. As we observed earlier, Philip Augustus's charter of 1200 exempted the canons from its privileges.
[209] *Chart.*, I, Introduction, No. 13.
[210] *Ibid.*, Nos. 15 and 16.
[211] *Ibid.*, No. 32.

they were few—did so because they were ecclesiastics, not teachers.[212] Even Louis IX, devout son of the church, was adamant when it came to control of benefices.[213] Only when the papacy settled at Avignon did the situation change; with John XXII regular rolls of nominees for benefices (*rotuli nominandorum*) were carried from the university to the papal curia. John XXII, alarmed at the decline in numbers at the university, appealed in 1316 to all prelates of the church to provide the masters and scholars with benefices.[214] Whether he was the first pope to initiate the practice of *rotuli* is not certain—the first extant rolls date from Clement VI's pontificate [215]—but he provided the impetus, directly disposing of benefices in his characteristically masterful way that brooked no opposition. The succeeding Avignon popes, particularly Clement VI, were distinguished by their patronage of scholars, so that by the time of the Great Schism papal benefices had become one of the university's most vested interests. Its desire to preserve them led to a series of sharp conflicts with Charles VI, King of France, in the first decades of the fifteenth century.[216]

They must not, however, be regarded as a substitute for income through fees. Benefices came only late into the life of the university. How widespread their effects were is not known; nor is there any evidence that they affected the scales of payments that we have mentioned in the case of the nations, which date mainly from the fourteenth century. The officers of the nation, including the rector, had as one of their main duties the collection of money.

Robert de Sorbon openly stated that the scholars paid their masters,[217] and we have the testimony of the masters themselves to their dependence on taking pupils, in their celebrated

[212] See Post, "Masters' Salaries and Student Fees in the Mediaeval Universities," *Speculum*, 7 (1932), 181–98, at 184.

[213] Kibre, *Scholarly Privileges*, 227 ff.

[214] *Chart.*, II, No. 729; see also Nos. 730, 738; and Kibre, *Scholarly Privileges*, 229 ff.

[215] *Chart.*, II, No. 1062, dated July 1342; Rashdall, I, 555.

[216] Kibre, *Scholarly Privileges*, 232 ff.

[217] Quoted by C. H. Haskins, *Mediaeval Culture*, 55; and cited by Post, "Masters' Salaries," 197.

letter of 1254. Above all, the proctors' vindication of the faculty of arts from Philip de Thori's charges in 1283–4 contains a sustained defense of the taking of fees: "Our masters teach for their own benefit and for that of the scholars . . . but they cannot have food without money. If the chancellor wishes them to teach for nothing, he must then provide them with food since without it no man can work or do any good." [218] In common with the masters of the other universities, those at Paris earned their living professionally by their teaching.

Colleges. From early on, however, provision was sought for poorer scholars. It took the form of colleges, which in the beginning were little more than hospices providing board and lodging. As time went on they came to take the place of the nations as the units of student life. But until the fifteenth century they concerned only a minority of the scholars. They arose because the university as a physical entity did not exist independently of its constituent parts. From the beginning their endowment was the concern of individuals or bodies like the nations seeking to provide for a particular group of scholars. They were ancillary to the nations and faculties, playing no role in the teaching or intellectual life of the university at this time. Their importance—or that of certain celebrated ones among them—belonged to the future. They should not therefore be seen as a distinct element; nor should their importance be exaggerated. They were created for a limited practical object. Moreover, except for the most illustrious of them—like the Sorbonne, founded about 1257 by the king's chaplain, Robert de Sorbon,[219] or the College of Navarre, founded in 1304 by Joanna of Navarre, queen of Philip IV—they could not compete with the colleges of the religious orders, the attraction of whose teachers we have earlier mentioned. The majority of students probably lived in houses supervised by masters of the university; they enjoyed almost unlimited freedom, beyond having to pay the rent authorized by the university. It was not until 1289 that students were required to have their names and an inventory of their goods included in the list (*matricula*)

---

[218] *Chart.*, I, No. 515, p. 608.
[219] For its earlier statutes see *Chart.*, I, No. 448, translated in Thorndike, *op. cit.*, No. 42.

of a master in order to be eligible for the university's privileges.[220] For the rest it was for the master of their house to decide the discipline to be imposed on them.

Although Paris has been called "the true home of the collegiate system," [221] it did not come into its own until the sixteenth century, when the Sorbonne stood for the whole university and its hall and schools held the public disputations of the theological faculty. During the thirteenth and fourteenth centuries, however, life and teaching still centered on the schools of the nations and faculties. The corporate identity of the nations made for the main differences between the colleges at Paris and those at Oxford and Cambridge. The colleges at Paris had less autonomy and were, until the founding of the College of Harcourt in 1311, most exclusively for scholars. That is to say, whereas the Oxford colleges from the first were more like self-governing corporations, well endowed and largely independent, those of Paris were overshadowed by the faculties and nations that possessed those very traits.

University Rights and Privileges. In one sense the history of the university in its external relations is the history of the evolution of its rights and privileges.[222] These were of the following kinds: ecclesiastical status *(privilegium fori)* rendering its holders immune from secular jurisdiction, which all members of the university as clerks enjoyed at least from the time of Celestine III; exemptions and immunities granted by the kings of France, beginning with Philip Augustus's charter of 1200 and maintained and extended until the fifteenth century; and the papal privileges, such as the right to strike and, later, enjoyment of benefices *in absentia.* In addition the university had supervisory rights over both its properties and a substantial class of university dependents, such as booksellers and stationers. For these

[220] *Chart.*, II, No. 561; Rashdall, I, 521.
[221] Rashdall, I, 498; see also A. L. Gabriel, *Student Life in Ave Maria College* (South Bend, Ind., Notre Dame University Press, 1955). Twenty colleges were founded at Paris between 1300 and 1336 (*ibid.*, 243).
[222] In addition to Kibre, *Scholarly Privileges,* see, for a resumé of the main features, S. Stelling-Michaud, "Les Universités au moyen age et à la renaissance" in *XI Congrès International des Sciences Historiques, Rapports,* I (Stockholm, 1960) 110 ff. Also M. M. Davy, "La Situation juridique des étudiants de l'Université de Paris au XIII ͤ siècle," *Revue d'histoire de l'église de France,* 17 (1931), 297–311.

different categories there grew up courts or procedures that we shall examine briefly.

Legally the university had to do with four different courts. There was the bishop's court to which all ordinary criminal or ecclesiastical cases concerning scholars were brought, as well as certain civil cases in which they might be involved. There was the Chatelet, the provost's court; as "conservator of the royal privileges of the university" it dealt with civil actions outside ecclesiastical jurisdiction (i.e. those over property). This was the result of royal protection of the university, but for which these cases would have been tried in an ordinary secular court. Third, there was the papal representative's court, the court of the apostolic conservator, which maintained papal privileges awarded to the university.

Finally, during the fourteenth century, as the university looked increasingly to the king for protection, we have seen that it made more and more use of the high court of parlement, and there were sometimes clashes between the bishop's court and the court of the apostolic conservator. In the main, however, the distinction between these different kinds of jurisdiction corresponded to the different areas of authority from which the university derived its privileges. Their extraordinary nature scarcely needs stressing. They were partly the outcome of the university's successful struggle to emancipate itself from the chancellor's often arbitrary jurisdiction, which he had effectively lost by the time of *Parens scientiarum* in 1231, and partly inherent in the distinctive and precarious nature of the university; its survival depended on a double support against the incursions of both the chapter and the city. The pope provided one, the king the other. The university's success in establishing its privileges was due largely to this artificial position. Certainly in its earlier phase, until the later thirteenth century, it had little to lose—and everything to gain—by threatening to disperse. It possessed few buildings and little property;[223] its members lived and met in hired rooms and convents. It was the religious, including the mendicant orders, who had the colleges and enjoyed stability, and they did not participate in the cessations or dispersions.

---

[223] The first record of the transfer of university property is to the Dominicans, *Chart.*, I, No. 42.

A scribe at work.

Thus, paradoxically, the university achieved its corporate privileges largely because it lacked any material foundations. Its strength lay in being bound neither to place nor possessions. As it came to depend on them it became more vulnerable, until finally it lost its weapon of cessation, which had long lost its edge in an increasingly aristocratic milieu.

An aspect of the growth of these material interests was the control the university was able to exercise over its immediate clients, especially those involved in producing and supplying books: the *stationarii* or *librarii,* who combined the functions of printer, publisher, and bookseller.[224] The main concern of the university was the copying and hiring out of the standard text (*exemplar*) of an authorized work. The exemplar was first copied into a series of separate sections or pieces (*pecia*), usually of eight pages (four folios); they were then examined by four masters and, if correctly transcribed, passed for general

[224] For an account see Kibre, *Scholarly Privileges,* 251 ff. (with bibliography); and Rashdall, I, 421 ff.

hire. The title of the work then went on to the official list of titles which the *stationarius* could hire out, each at an authorized price and with the number of *peciae* stated.[225] Masters and scholars could also borrow individual *peciae,* which they could in turn copy for their own use, the price again being fixed by the appointed masters. Thus at one time a number of people could be copying parts of the same standard text. As well as having been a way of satisfying contemporary demand it has provided posterity with an indication of the relative popularity of different works, to say nothing of the perplexing textual problems of their different recensions. The university also vetted the qualifications of the *stationarius,* who together with the various scribes, binders, and illuminators whom he employed, had to take an oath of obedience to it. Those doing so often received university privileges in return.[226] In 1323 the *stationarii* recognized by the university numbered twenty-eight or twenty-nine, the first statutes drawn up for them dating from 1275.[227] These statutes, like subsequent ones, contain indications that they were not always observed, especially in regard to the circulation of faulty exemplars and fraudulence; such breaches caused the university in 1342 to summon the *stationarii* to a general congregation, when it was decided thenceforth to make them take the oath of obedience every year instead of every two years.[228] Further measures followed in 1370, 1376, 1382, and into the fifteenth century. The university also exercised strict control over parchment; before it was sold to the university it had first to be brought to St. Mathurins for inspection by the rector or his representative, who then fixed its selling price.[229] Enforcement of this control also led to difficulties lasting well into the fifteenth century.

Other areas of regulation included the faculty of medicine's continuous war against unlicensed medical practitioners; [230] its exclusive right to practice medicine in the Paris area probably

[225] See *Chart.,* I, No. 530, translated in Thorndike, *op. cit.,* No. 49, for such a list.

[226] *Chart.,* I, Nos. 462, 661; II, Nos. 661, 733, 825; cited in Kibre, *Scholarly Privileges,* 252.

[227] *Chart.,* I, No. 462.

[228] *Ibid.,* II, No. 1064; Kibre, *Scholarly Privileges,* 254.

[229] *Chart.,* II, No. 574 (dated 1292); cited by Kibre, *Scholarly Privileges,* 255.

[230] For this see Kibre, *Scholarly Privileges,* 261 ff.

dated from 1220, and it was in 1271 that it drew up a series of statutes designed to exclude "shameless and brazen" usurpers.[231] In the fourteenth century the faculty, in an effort to stamp out the usurpers, turned to both the pope and the king for help; John XXII, Clement VI, Charles VI, and his successor all passed decrees against the offenders apparently without lasting success.

As the university evolved, then, it not only became more privileged, but its privileges came to consist more in its rights over persons and property; in seeking to preserve them it was now asserting its authority rather than seeking protection from others. This is apparent from the cases we have been considering; it is also to be seen in the university's acquisition of control over its own benefices. Among these were the chapels of St. Martin des Orgres and St. Catherine du Val des Écoliers, which it gained as a result of prolonged internecine war with the abbey of St. Germain, going back to 1192. It centered on the so-called field of scholars—Pré aux Clercs [232]—and reached a climax in an especially bloody encounter during May 1278; [233] to expiate their wrongs the abbot and monks had *inter alia* perpetually to endow two chapels, to which the abbey later added a further two in 1335. The university received more from other sources in much the same way, so that by the fifteenth century it had the patronage of a considerable number of benefices. These, together with papally provided benefices and other endowments, helped to transform it from rags to riches by the fifteenth century. Its increasing assimilation to the higher reaches of society made the final loss of its judicial privileges in 1499 a formality. By then it was entering a new aristocratic phase that rendered otiose the old forms of protection. The center of gravity was shifting from the university to the endowed colleges, membership of which became a mark of honor rather than a recognition of need. The original association of masters and scholars, owning little but the license to teach, was now long since a privileged corporation.

[231] *Chart.*, I, No. 434, translated in Thorndike, *op. cit.*, No. 40.
[232] For an account see Kibre, *Scholarly Privileges*, 241 ff. and bibliography given there.
[233] *Chart.*, I, No. 480.

TWO

Oxford University in the Thirteenth and Fourteenth Centuries

Oxford's university has a close affinity to Paris in its academic and intellectual life. There were, however, important differences in their institutions and history that were a direct outcome of their different milieux. Paris in the thirteenth century and the first third of the fourteenth was the international focus of speculative and theological thought; most of the great doctrinal systems and conflicts were, as we shall see, associated with it. The price of such luster was a prolonged struggle for autonomy first against the chancellor and cathedral chapter and then against the mendicants; even then the university's importance made it the constant object of papal observation as in the great condemnations of 1277. Oxford—in the eyes of Christendom at least—was never so important, and enjoyed a much freer history in consequence. It was not part of a capital, never had a cathedral school, and was in a more distant kingdom where the papal writ did not run so freely. The resulting differences were substantial, especially as they affected the institutional and juridical structure of the university. Institutionally they are to be seen in the different role of the chancellor, both within the university and especially toward the city; in a much greater integration of the faculties; in the nonexistence of nations as separate organizations; and in a correspondingly greater importance and autonomy of the colleges from their outset. Historically, there was no struggle for independence, either against the chancellor or the mendicants, and little intervention—after the initial grant of privileges—by the papacy. Whereas at Paris the motive force of development was the university's relations with ecclesiastical authority, at Oxford it lay in relations with town and monarchy. From almost first to last it owed its position to the king; it was a position of independence from all outside authority, ecclesiastical as well as temporal, and of hegemony over Oxford and its burgesses. Accordingly its main struggles were local ones; none had the international repercussions of those at Paris. But if Oxford's history was in the main confined to Oxford—principally because of the exclusive protection exercised by the kings of England— its intellectual life was part of Christendom's, as we shall consider in Chapter Five. For that reason the more local scale of its evolution is of no less relevance than the wider canvas of Paris's history.

I ORIGINS

At first sight a university of international standing in Oxford, rather than in London or one of the great cathedral cities, appears to be an anomaly.[1] There is no evidence for Oxford's existence before the tenth century and none for the university's connection with the monastery of St. Frideswide's there. Indeed the striking thing about the emergence of the university is that it was from the first untramelled by any monastic or cathedral leading strings. Its schools grew up around the parish church of St. Mary.[2] The city developed from a walled town by the Thames created by the Anglo-Saxons to prevent the Danes from crossing the river. Its artificial foundation is strongly suggested by the regular gridiron form of the streets, which meet at right angles with Carfax as their center.[3] Its growth in impor-

---

[1] For a resumé of the question see H. E. Salter, *Medieval Oxford* (Oxford, OHS, 1936), 6 ff.

[2] Rashdall, III, 10. This led him to conclude that Oxford originated from a migration of scholars from Paris about 1167, 11 ff., a theory generally rejected; *ibid.*, Introduction, XVI ff., Appendix I.

[3] Salter, *op. cit.*, 7–8.

tance was partly geographical, as the meeting of the routes to Bristol, Southampton, London, Buckingham, Bedford, Cambridge, Brackley, Northampton, Worcester, and Warwick, as well as to southern Ireland. In about the year 1100 Henry I built a royal palace at Woodstock a few miles away; in 1121 came St. Frideswide's Monastery, to be followed in 1129 by Osney Abbey. These additions, combined with Oxford's advantageous position, must have brought Oxford into direct regular contact with both king and religious life. When the university came into being is not known. It was certainly there by 1200. As early as about 1117 Theobald Stampensis, a .eacher of European fame, taught there for four years and had at least fifty pupils.[4] According to the Osney chronicler, the scholar Robert Pullen lectured there in 1133, and the celebrated Italian civil jurist Vacarius in 1149;[5] among known English scholars there were Robert Crickslade (c. 1149–1174) and Walter, archdeacon of Oxford, provost of the Church of St. George's-in-the-Castle (transferred to Osney Abbey in 1142), and patron of Geoffrey of Monmouth. The presence of such names points to the existence from about 1120 of schools at Oxford whose numbers must have increased in 1167, when Henry II prohibited English scholars from studying abroad.[6] Throughout Christendom at this time such schools were of indigenous growth, the result of the new demand for education in an expanding society. It would therefore be otiose to look for a sudden date or a deliberate act of foundation any more than in the case of Paris or any other *studium*. The later twelfth century was probably the period when an organized body of masters emerged from the Oxford schools. Giraldus Cambrensis in 1184 spoke of having entertained "the doctors from the different faculties"; since the bishopric of Lincoln was vacant from 1166 to 1186 they must have been largely, if not entirely, autonomous.[7] Daniel of Morley (between 1175 and 1200), John of

[4] *Ibid.*, 29 f.

[5] Rashdall, III, 11 ff., in accordance with his view of the university's origin in 1167, sought to place Vacarius's sojourn twenty years later (19 ff. and 21, editor's note).

[6] Salter, *op. cit.*, 92; Rashdall, III, 13; *Chart.*, I, Introduction, No. 20.

[7] Salter, *loc. cit.*; also Rashdall, III, 25, who translates the passage from Giraldus *Opera*, J. S. Brewer, ed., I Roll Series (London, 1861) 72, 73.

Constantine (a scholar between 1186 and 1190), and Alexander Neckham (master at Paris who was resident at Oxford in 1191 or 1192) all provide further testimony to the existence of a *studium generale* by the end of the twelfth century; its importance for contemporaries is to be seen from an estimate of its numbers as 3000.[8] In 1201 comes the name of its first master of the schools: Master J. Grim.[9]

If early Oxford lacks the landmarks of Paris in the twelfth century—with Abelard and the schools of Notre Dame and St. Geneviève—its recorded history as a university begins at almost the same time and in comparable circumstances, if not with the same subsequent vicissitudes. In 1209, following a scholar's manslaughter of a woman, the mayor and burgesses led an attack on his hostel; a number of scholars was arrested and several were executed. A cessation of lectures was ordered in protest, masters and scholars migrating to Reading, Paris, and Cambridge, from which the latter's foundation dates.[10] England at the time was under papal interdict; its lifting in 1214, on King John's submission to Innocent III, enabled the pope to intercede for the university. Through the papal legate he published what came to be a charter of liberties, comparable to Philip II's at Paris in 1200.[11] In recompense for their wrongs the burgesses were to swear to take only half the rent on hospices and lodgings for ten years; and for another ten years not to charge more than the rate current before the dispersion, to be enforced by a joint commission of two masters and two burgesses. The burgesses were also to pay fifty-two shillings annually for poor scholars and to provide them with an annual feast on St. Nicholas' Day, and they were not to overcharge masters and scholars for food and necessities. Finally, the burgesses were to swear to uphold the clerical immunities of members of the university from lay arrest, and to report any violation to the bishop of Lincoln or his representatives. The masters and scholars for their part were to be allowed

[8] Rashdall, III, 33.

[9] *Snappe's Formulary,* H. E. Salter, ed., (Oxford, OHS, 1924) 318, quoted in Salter, *Medieval Oxford,* 93.

[10] Rashdall, III, 34.

[11] H. E. Salter, ed., *Mediaeval Archives of the University of Oxford,* 2 vols. (Oxford, OHS, 1920–21), I, 2–4.

to return to their studies, excepting those who had not obeyed the cessation, who were suspended for three years.

The charter is significant in two respects. It defines explicitly the ecclesiastical status of members of the university, exempting them from civil jurisdiction, and it contains the first reference to a chancellor of the university in the phrase "bishop of Lincoln, or the archdeacon of the place [Oxford], or his official, or the chancellor or whom else the bishop of Lincoln shall depute to this office"; it recurs in a slightly different form. In each case it seems to imply the lack of any fixed officer as head of the university at that time. This could either have been because of a vacancy that the archdeacon or his deputy was filling, or because the office of chancellor did not yet exist. But this should not obscure the fact that a master of schools had, as we have seen, already been mentioned in 1201. It seems indisputable therefore that before 1214 there was an officer who presided over the schools; even if we do not know the nature or extent of his authority, analogy with other schools under the aegis of the church suggests that he would almost certainly have been acting for the bishop or the chapter, and this would have included granting the license to teach.[12]

The year 1214 marked the inauguration of the chancellorship, but not immediately of a new régime; indeed we learn from Oliver Sutton, bishop of Lincoln from 1280 to 1299, that Robert Grosseteste was the first chancellor of the university but was not permitted by the then bishop of Lincoln—his immediate predecessor—to use that title; he had to continue to call himself "master of the schools." [13] The position of chancellor was therefore in direct succession to that of master of the schools; the office must have come into being after 1214, after the return of the masters and scholars to Oxford, because the papal letter was addressed to the prior of Osney, the dean of Oxford, and Master

[12] This agrees with Rashdall, I, 38 ff.; but not when he goes on to conjecture that, because of the prolonged vacancy at Lincoln in the later twelfth century, the license may not have been granted and that the masters conducted their own inceptions and elected their own head. Against this view of what he calls "scholastic anarchy" is the absence of any reaction by the masters to the imposition of a chancellor after 1214.

[13] Salter, *Snappe's Formulary*, 52, 319; Rashdall, III, 41.

Adelard, "rector of the schools." [14] The significance of this development lies less in the precise point at which the chancellor superseded the master of the schools than in the fact that his office originated in the course of the evolution of the university; it had not pre-existed as part of the cathedral chapter. In consequence the position of chancellor at Oxford was radically different from that at Paris; it was far more that of intermediary between bishop and university than at Paris where, although a member of the theological faculty, the chancellor stood outside the society of masters. The chancellor, at Paris the symbol of alien rule, became at Oxford the symbol of self-rule.

The main reason must be sought in the absence of a cathedral school and the bishop's distance from Oxford. The lack of immediate control by him, or subjection to the authority of the chapter, inevitably gave the masters a much greater scope. The nearest episcopal representative was the archdeacon of Oxford.[15] He probably never had any jurisdiction over the clerks of the university; it was transferred by the bishop to the chancellor after the latter's office had been instituted in about 1214. In 1281 the bishop agreed that any penalties for those who had been found wanting were to be imposed by the chancellor. In 1346 the archdeacon renounced all rights over members and servants of the university other than the proving of wills.

Only once, in 1290, did a chancellor appear in person before the bishop to receive his office.[16] The procedure was for a deputation from the university of regent masters (whose number varied from five earlier to two later, one of whom was a proctor), to go to the bishop for him to confirm their election of a chancellor. Each party sought to maintain that it had the power of appointment; in order to reconcile their claims it became customary for the bishop to accept the absent candidate chosen by the university with the saving clause that it was he who had nominated him. In that way he reserved his right *de iure* to make the appointment, even though *de facto* the election had been made by the university; such an arrangement shows clearly

[14] Salter, *Mediaeval Archives*, I, 4, 6.
[15] On the archdeacon's relation to the university see H. E. Salter, ed., *Registrum cancellarii Oxoniensis* (Oxford, OHS, 1932), I, XV–XVI.
[16] Salter, *Snappe's Formulary*, 43.

that—in opposition to Rashdall [17]—the chancellor was far from being principally the bishop's officer, who only later became part of the university. Had such a change occurred it would have filled the annals of the university as the struggle at Paris did. Moreover, evidence that the masters did not consider the chancellor in that light is seen in the distinction they later made between his spiritual jurisdiction and his temporal power (*regiam potestatem*).[18]

As it crystallized the chancellor's authority at Oxford was in inverse proportion to that of his Paris namesake; even if they had more than their title in common they diverged widely in their roles. Whereas after 1231 the chancellor at Paris had little of his original powers beyond conferring the license, at Oxford he combined these original powers with those of the Paris rector and the chief magistrate of a city. Only the latter caused friction—and then not within the university. As the bishop's representative (technically his "nominee"), through his court he exercised spiritual control over the scholars as clerks; he had general supervision of the schools; and he could excommunicate or deprive offenders of the license and other privileges. His spiritual powers gained their main force from his right to arrest and imprison, which had to be in the king's prison as the bishop's prison at Lincoln was too far away. This and extensive other powers were provided by a succession of royal grants beginning with Henry III in 1227 and subsequently confirmed and extended in his reign and by his successors. These gave the chancellor jurisdiction over any legal action involving a clerk of Oxford (both master and scholar); it made his court unique in combining ecclesiastical and lay powers, and contrasts directly with the tripartite division between the bishop's, provost's, and papal conservator's courts at Paris.

The chancellor, however, attained—if he did not receive—his office through election by the masters as we shall consider later. He was chosen by the masters not imposed on them as at Paris. The difference was reflected in the different course of events at the two universities. At Oxford the ecclesiastical au-

[17] Rashdall, III, 40 ff.
[18] Salter, *Snappe's Formulary*, 61; in their dispute with Bishop Walter Wetheringsete of Lincoln (Rashdall, III, 43, editor's note 3).

thorities and the papacy were scarcely involved; there were no appeals from the masters to the pope against the chancellor; and even when dispute broke out between the mendicants and the university it was the king, not the pope, who interceded. Since the main conflicts centered almost wholly on the university's privileges over the city, they lacked both the ecumenical and constitutional impact of those at Paris. The university's institutional evolution took place with little reference to outside agencies. Although educationally and intellectually it had, as we shall see in Part Two, close affinities with Paris, it was more genuinely autonomous. There was less interaction between its external events and internal development, as we must now consider.

II RELATIONS WITH TOWN AND AUTHORITY

After 1214 the university's external history was dominated by its relations with the town and, through these, with the monarchy. There was an almost regular sequence of appeal from town or university to the king, leading to confirmation and often extension of the university's rights in the city. It began with Henry III who in 1227 formally guaranteed the university's existing privileges.[19] Henry also showed his solicitude—which never waned—when two years later he invited the dispersing scholars from Paris to study in England.[20] His first direct intervention in the disputes between town and university came in 1231, in response to the latter's complaints about high rents. Besides calling on the traditional four-man commission to fix just rents, he extolled the virtues of the university, which he declared brought honor to the whole kingdom in drawing students from all parts of it and from overseas.[21] He repeated his decree on rents in 1244, 1248, 1256, and 1268.[22] The king also sought to put down the common abuse of bogus scholars, in 1231 ordering the sheriff

[19] Kibre, *Scholarly Privileges*, 270; her account traces relations down to the end of the fifteenth century as they concern the university's privileges.
[20] *Chart.*, I, No. 64; and Salter, *Mediaeval Archives*, 17–18.
[21] Kibre, *Scholarly Privileges, Calendar of Close Rolls, Henry III* (1227–31) (London 1902) 587.
[22] Kibre, *loc. cit.;* Salter, *Mediaeval Archives*, I, 18, 21, 28.

to expel those at Oxford and Cambridge who were not under the direction of a master; the sheriff was also to arrest and imprison in the king's gaol any scholar—true or false—indicted by the chancellor or masters.[23] Thus from an early stage the chancellor's jurisdiction was buttressed by temporal support. It was considerably reinforced in 1244 after forty-five scholars had been imprisoned for·attacking the Jews. The king now extended the chancellor's authority to include all cases of debt, rents, and prices of food and movables which involved scholars; the Jews were also limited to taking an interest rate of twopence on the pound per week.[24] These decrees were confirmed in 1286 by Edward I. By then there had been numerous other royal interventions. In 1248 the murder of a scholar led to a further charter from Henry III making the town corporately responsible for the murder or injury of scholars and repeating the earlier provisions for the taking of interest.[25] In addition the chancellor and proctors were now to be present at the assizes of bread and ale, which could not proceed without them unless they purposely failed to attend. A new element of discord was thereby introduced into town and gown relations that was to grow more intense in the fourteenth century. This was followed in 1255 by a charter for the appointment of four aldermen and eight burgesses to help the mayor and civic authorities in keeping the peace; it also regulated the buying and selling of food and the assizes of bread and ale. But most important it added criminal offenses by laymen to the chancellor's jurisdiction; henceforth a layman doing a clerk injury was to be imprisoned in the castle or the town gaol, according to the gravity of the offense, and only to be released with the agreement of the clerk or—if he proved unreasonable in his demands for satisfaction—of the chancellor.[26] Thus the chancellor now had powers that extended beyond that of any ordinary ecclesiastical court. It did not prevent a conflagration in 1263, which caused the university for a time to

---

[23] Kibre, *Scholarly Privileges,* 271; Rashdall, III 83–4; *Close Rolls* (1227–31), 586.
[24] Kibre, *Scholarly Privileges,* 272–3; Rashdall, III, 85; *Calendar of Patent Rolls, Henry III,* (1232–47), 424.
[25] Salter, *Mediaeval Archives,* I, 18–19.
[26] Rashdall, III, 86; Salter, *Mediaeval Archives,* I, 19–21.

secede to Northampton. They did so on the king's orders, probably because of the disturbances connected with the civil war; the return to Oxford, following the capture of Northampton in 1264 by royalist forces, was likewise made at the king's command. It again resulted in confirmation of the university's privileges; all houses and properties were restored and the chancellor was empowered to settle outstanding disputes with the townsmen. The king also pardoned members of the university for their transgressions during the recent hostilities.[27] This was more than a formality because many of the scholars seem to have fought against the king at Northampton.[28] The university in the king's eyes seemed able to do no lasting wrong. In 1265 he granted its members immunity from service on all assizes and juries,[29] to be followed in 1268 and 1269 by a final reaffirmation of their rights and liberties.[30]

These were, as we have seen, by now extensive; and Edward I pursued much the same policy towards securing them as his father, if with a firmer hand. He had early to display his authority when dissensions within the university during 1273 erupted into open conflict between the Northern and Southern students in January 1274.[31] Peace was not finally made until the end of March, but not before fifty scholars had been taken to London and charged with murder; in consequence students were in future banned from carrying arms. This was one of the few occasions when the ecclesiastical authorities came on the scene, the archbishop of Canterbury decreeing that the chancellor's sentences of excommunication were to be acted on within the whole of his province.[32] In the main the university's privileges con-

---

[27] Salter, *Mediaeval Archives,* Nos. 16 and 17, 24–6; Rashdall, III, 86 ff.; Kibre, *Scholarly Privileges,* 276.

[28] Rashdall, *loc. cit.,* Kibre, *loc. cit.*

[29] Salter, *Mediaeval Archives,* I, No. 18.

[30] *Ibid.,* Nos. 20, 22.

[31] *Ibid.,* No. 28, and Appendix I, Nos. 1 and 2.

[32] I am at a loss to understand why Rashdall, III, 91, should have called Edward's letters patent of 1275 "a new era" in Oxford privileges. They gave the chancellor jurisdiction over all personal actions when a scholar was involved, which Rashdall interpreted as for the first time extending to the scholar as plaintiff. His own words "it is not clear" to describe the earlier position are sufficient to make one hesitate before drawing firm conclusions.

tinued to be a matter for the king alone. If their substance did not greatly change under Edward I they received greater clarification, as one would expect from that king. At the same time a new element appeared. After a succession of confirmations or judgments in the university's favor in 1283, 1287 and 1288, the long-suffering burgesses turned. In 1290 they appealed directly to parliament against the chancellor's oppression; [33] they accused him of freeing the mayor's prisoners, imposing crushing fines on citizens, and taking for himself food declared unfit for human consumption. The king made this the occasion for a comprehensive charter of university liberties. All the main issues raised by the burgesses were decided in the university's favor. To call it the university's *magna carta* would be inappropriate because it had long enjoyed what was now confirmed; unlike *Parens scientiarum,* the 1290 charter was not a defense against oppression but a license of authority, or rather its continuance, over the mayor and burgesses. The chancellor was to have cognizance over all crimes, except murder and maiming (mayhem), to which a scholar was party; his recently won control over the royal bailiffs was confirmed, with the latter having the right of appeal to the king's court; confiscated food was to go to the hospital of St. John as alms. For the first time we find the university's officers and servants, parchment dealers, illuminators, and so on, included in its privileges as well, but in ordinary merchandising they were to be taxed like any other traders.

The comprehensive nature of these privileges constituted an unbreakable hegemony of the university over the city. Repeated attempts by the burgesses to seek redress from king or parliament against abuse by the university led only to reaffirmation of the privileges, as in 1297–8 when in recompense for the death of a clerk, those responsible were excommunicated and the city had to, pay the university £200 indemnity. Here, in addition to royal support, the bishop of Lincoln had also intervened,[34] in marked contrast to such happenings at Paris. It is hard to dis-

[33] Salter, *Mediaeval Archives,* I, No. 50; Rashdall, III, 93 ff.; Kibre, *Scholarly Privileges,* 279–80.
[34] Kibre, *Scholarly Privileges,* 280; and Salter, *Mediaeval Archives,* I, Nos. 32–41 (especially the editor's introductory remarks) and Appendix I, No. 3.

believe the burgesses in their complaint that Oxford had become a hotbed of criminals who were able to masquerade as clerks and so able be delivered from prison when arrested by the bailiffs. As they put it,

". . . if a clerk wound or beat or does violence to a layman, for which he is imprisoned by the bailiff, he will at once be delivered by the chancellor without writing [written security], and if a layman ill-treats a clerk he will be imprisoned by the chancellor, and will be there a month or forty days, and will not be delivered without grievous ransom both to their common chest and the injured party, so that it grievously seems to the commonality that there is not one law for the clerks and the laymen." [35]

This was benefit of the clergy with a vengeance. It could only mean dissension and unrest between town and university, which marked much of Oxford's history in the fourteenth century. On this occasion the burgesses had to suffer their now accustomed humiliation of having to renew their oath to the university's liberties and privileges; they had also to restore any prisoners committed by the chancellor but subsequently released by the bailiffs; altogether fourteen bailiffs were punished or banished; and a further 600 marks had to be paid to the university as a result of the royal commission's findings.

Not surprisingly, the burgesses sought to avenge their ignominies; one of the most persistent ways of doing so was to cheat the university.[36] The resulting friction is most apparent in the disputes over the assizes of bread and ale. We have earlier seen that the university was first admitted to them in 1248 by royal award; this enabled it to ensure that prices had been arrived at fairly. The fixing of prices took place twice yearly, and it became customary for Henry III and his successors periodically to confirm the burgesses' obligation to adhere to their prices—especially in selling to the university. Edward I went further in extending it to the quality of these and other victuals: in 1290 over the question of putrid meat that was to go to St. John's hospital; in 1293 and 1305 over unclean water in the beer and bad wine in the taverns. Edward II, for all his other preoccupations, also concerned himself with these matters and instituted various measures to punish offenders; these now involved the correct assaying of weights and measures, another source of friction. The members of the university claimed that they received short measure in wine sold to them. Both monarchs also sought to control thirty "regrators" (retailers),[37] mainly women, who bought goods from the market and sold them in their shops at a higher price. There had long been regulations controlling their activities, which were licensed: they were not allowed to sell meat; they were only to purchase food on two market days and after 9 A.M.; in 1305 their number was fixed at thirty-two and their conditions were reaffirmed, and again in 1310. Failure to adhere to these regulations led the king in the following year to allow anyone to sell food freely, but strangers could not act as regrators. The problem recurred later in Edward II's reign and in that of his son, Edward III, at some time affecting virtually every kind of consumer goods. Petitions from the scholars to the king complaining of extortionate prices were as regularly answered by ordinances for regulating them.[38] It is a familiar cycle, and medieval governments, for all their authoritarian methods—or rather tone—were no more able to break it than later ones.

There were also periodic appeals still to be heard in the reign of Richard II for royal intervention against the burgesses' more unhygienic practices, such as depositing their refuse in the streets, which accumulated in the holes they would not repair, as well as melting tallow and slaughtering animals in the public thoroughfares and at Carfax.[39] Such frictions were endemic in any medieval city; examples of similar complaints abounded among the students in the schools of the left bank at Paris, and were just as unsatisfied. The difference was that at Oxford they were heeded—if not remedied—and the protests of the bur-

---

[37] *Munimenta civitatis Oxonie,* H. E. Salter, ed. (Oxford, OHS, 1917). Introduction xxii–iv and Nos. 9, 11, 17, 20.
[38] *Ibid.,* 84–5; Salter, *Mediaeval Archives,* I, Appendix II, No. 1; Salter et. al., *Oxford Formularies,* I, 71, 72–3, 77–8.
[39] Kibre, *Scholarly Privileges,* 287 ff.

gesses against the clerks of the university invariably recoiled on them in some new grant or confirmation of existing privileges to the university. This pattern continued throughout the reign of the three Edwards and beyond; in 1305 Edward I even banned tournaments and jousts from the environs of the city in order that the scholars should not be disturbed by noise; [40] in 1311, in response to more than one university request, he ordered the mayor and bailiffs to house imprisoned scholars separately or build another jail.[41] In 1309 Edward II reaffirmed the chancellor's power to compel burgesses and other laymen to appear in his court; [42] he upheld the chancellor against the Dominicans in 1314, refusing to let them appeal to papal privilege, as we shall discuss later; he supported the chancellor against the mayor and burgesses on the occasions when they clashed, as in 1314 and 1315, confirming in the latter year and again in 1327 the university's previous liberties.[43]

Edward III took a similar course of interceding for the university on issues with which its rights and privileges had come to be associated, notably custody of the assizes of bread and ale and weights and measures in 1327, 1328, 1330, 1332, and 1336.[44] He also sought to enforce the keeping of the peace in 1329 by prohibiting the carrying of arms. But these had little effect on what seems to have been a worsening atmosphere by the 1340's. By then a hundred years of royal favor had given the university authorities a stranglehold on the life of the city, juridically, economically, and psychologically. What had originated as benign protection under Henry III had become, no doubt unwittingly, active oppression under his successors. There was not a case and hardly a clause in the succession of appeals to the king and government that went in favor of the town.

From the 1290's the tempo of government intervention on the side of the university seems to have increased, coming, after Edward I's charter of 1290, to center increasingly on the assizes

[40] *Ibid.*, 286; Salter, *Munimenta*, 5–6.

[41] Kibre, *Scholarly Privileges*, 287; Salter, *Munimenta*, 20–1.

[42] Salter, *Mediaeval Archives*, I, No. 45.

[43] *Kibre, Scholarly Privileges*, 191–2; Salter; *Munimenta*, 25–26; *Mediaeval Archives*, I, Nos. 51, 52, 55.

[44] Kibre, *Scholarly Privileges*, 297 ff.

of bread and ale and the regulation of foodstuffs. The chancellor's encroachment into these spheres of merchant life, backed by his judicial powers to summon burgesses who crossed him, was the last straw. The burgesses, having repeatedly failed to gain redress by lawful means, seemed to have turned increasingly to violence, never long absent at Oxford any more than at Paris. As early as 1329 the king appointed a commission to inquire into reports of widespread homicide, assault, and robbery.[45] Then in 1334 the university decided to secede to Stamford at the invitation of the Earl of Warenne. The masters and scholars complained at the unrest and lack of order at Oxford, not a new occurrence. On this occasion it seems to have been prompted by a recent outbreak between the Northerners and Southerners. The king, however, refused to permit the move, and instructed the sheriff of Lincoln to tell the masters and scholars to return to Oxford.[46] He followed this with an enquiry into the university's grievances and an order to the sheriff to protect the chancellor, masters, scholars, and their liberties as well as to prohibit the possession of arms in Oxford.[47] In 1336 he went further in making the chancellor's court free from royal interference and the chancellor immune from charges of false imprisonment so long as he was acting to keep the peace.[48] To this was added authority to take oaths of fealty to the king from the mayor and burgesses.[49]

Thus, once again, the chancellor, and by implication the university, had emerged stronger and more firmly entrenched than ever; but at the cost of still further feeding the burgesses' resentment. One of the main plaints in their appeals to king and parliament in the first half of the fourteenth century was the sheriff's

---

[45] Salter, *Mediaeval Archives,* No. 71.

[46] Salter et al., *Oxford Formularies,* I, 105–6, 107–8; Kibre, *Scholarly Privileges,* 300; Rashdall, III, 89. There are strong indications that the move was mainly by Northerners; seventeen northern masters remained at Stamford in spite of the king's prohibition (Rashdall, *ibid.,* 90, editor's note).

[47] Kibre, *Scholarly Privileges;* Salter, *Mediaeval Archives,* I, Nos. 81, 82, 84.

[48] Salter, *Mediaeval Archives,* I, No. 87. This followed (on April 12, 1336) a grant of April 8 by the king, extending the chancellor's jurisdiction over all clerks in the suburbs as well as the city of Oxford (*ibid.,* No. 86).

[49] Kibre, *Scholarly Privileges,* 301.

obligation, repeated annually on oath, to arrest trespassers at the chancellor's behest; the burgesses claimed this violated the city's charter of 1199 which excluded the sheriff from the town. Edward III, however, reaffirmed the provision in 1340, besides ordering the mayor and bailiffs in 1341 to do likewise in arresting disturbers of the peace and handing them over to the chancellor.[50] Another petition by the burgesses in 1346, reminding the king that they were his liegemen, not the chancellor's, met with no greater success than previous ones. It shows clearly their sense of frustration at being legally defenseless against the chancellor's powers; he was making statutes that were disinheriting them; they were being summoned to appear in his court, and they had no legal representative to support them there.[51]

There were signs that the burgesses were taking the law into their own hands. In 1346 the university complained that they were being kept from the assizes of weights and measures by force of arms; and two years later the archbishop of Canterbury and bishop of Chichester had to arbitrate in a dispute that had begun on the same issue but had widened into one of privileges.[52] It did not bring the dissension to an end. Further charge and countercharge followed until there came an explosion on February 10, 1355, in riots on St. Scholastica's day.[53] The wonder is that it had not occurred earlier. Even so, its long-term importance should not be exaggerated. Heads were broken, and so were halls; parts of the city were set on fire; shops and houses were looted; there were several deaths, how many is not known. But the pattern did not change. The king came to the defense of the university, which had, of course, suspended lectures.[54] He

[50] *Ibid.;* Salter et al., *Oxford Formularies,* I, 104–5; Salter, *Mediaeval Archives,* I, Nos. 91, 92, 100.

[51] Kibre, *Scholarly Privileges,* 302.

[52] Salter, *Mediaeval Archives,* I, No. 94.

[53] Kibre, *Scholarly Privileges,* 304; Salter, *Munimenta,* 126–8; Rashdall's account (III, 95 ff.) suffers from a false perspective, which magnified the outbreak into an event of unique importance leading to unprecedented privileges; in fact many privileges, such as those of the assizes, already existed.

[54] For what follows, see Salter, *Mediaeval Archives,* Nos. 97–102; Kibre, *Scholarly Privileges,* 303 ff.; Rashdall, III, 95 ff., who needs supplementing by the references given in the editor's notes.

began by taking the masters and scholars under his protection on March 5, 1355; in May he restored to them their privileges and absolved those who had been charged with offenses during the disturbance, the city having been put under interdict. In June he asked them to resume lectures and promised to act further to protect the university's peace and honor, which he did in a charter of privileges given on June 27. In this, after extolling its worth to the kingdom, he restored to the university and its servants all former liberties—which, together with those of the town had earlier been surrendered to him for his arbitration.

The concessions that the university received as a result went beyond anything that it had had before. The chancellor was now given sole jurisdiction over the assizes of bread, ale, weights and measures, forestalling, and regrating, with authority to punish transgressors. For the burgesses it was the obverse: many, including the mayor and bailiffs, were arrested; the sheriff was removed from office and the burgesses had to pay £250 damages and return the goods and chattels belonging to members of the university. Moreover, for the lifting of the interdict imposed by the bishop of Lincoln, the mayor, bailiffs, and sixty burgesses were to do annual penance on St. Scholastica's day at a special mass in St. Mary's Church, when they would also give tribute of a hundred marks to be paid in perpetuity. As well as submitting to the chancellor in all cases of felony, robbery, arson, or any other transgressions in which clerks were involved, they had to keep the roads and pavements in good repair and cleanliness. These concessions together with loss of the town's rights over the assizes gave the university everything that it had sought over the past fifty years. For the town it was unconditional surrender, its humiliation re-enacted in the annual ceremonies in St. Mary's. But it was also achieved second-hand; the university had to live with privileges received from others and only maintained from outside. In such circumstances lasting peace was not possible. Nothing was settled in 1355 that had not been settled before; in one sense it made the chancellor, with his increased responsibilities, more vulnerable, especially over the assizes. He accused the mayor and bailiffs of obstruction, and the burgesses in turn blamed him for the scarcity of bread.[55]

[55] Kibre, *Scholarly Privileges*, 308 ff.

In the main, however, the conflict between town and university seems to have abated in the later part of the century. The king periodically confirmed the university's privileges; he also had to intervene in 1362, and again in 1367 and 1369, to repeat an earlier ban on appeals from the chancellor's court to the pope.[56] But the mutual recriminations of chancellor and burgesses were not carried so frequently to the central government. The troubles of Richard II's reign doubtless had their effect in distracting royal attention from Oxford. Nevertheless in 1378 and 1380 the government followed previous policy of confirming the university's privileges. It also instructed the sheriff to arrest malefactors on the warning of the chancellor and urged the university to be vigilant in preserving the peace. The chancellor and the mayor were commissioned jointly to enforce the provisions of the assizes. The inhabitants were to keep the roads before their houses in good repair and the streets clean and free from rubbish.[57] The chancellor, besides having his earlier jurisdiction reaffirmed, was also to be free from interference by the courts of the Common Bench and other royal judges.[58] Beyond these grants the university was additionally exempted in 1380 and 1381 from paying the parliamentary subsidy levied in 1377.[59] On the other hand, the growth of the Wyclifite heresy brought ecclesiastical intervention, as we shall mention shortly. Henry IV's reign saw something like a return to the dialectic between royal support and civic hostility. The king almost at once confirmed the privileges of the university and went on to enlarge its boundaries, as well as to pardon those among its members who had committed offenses against the crown.[60] In 1406 came his institution of the new office of steward to try members of the university accused of felony.[61] Like his predecessors, the king turned a deaf ear to protests among the burgesses. The old animosities seem to have revived once again; for the following years

[56] *Ibid.*, 309; Salter, *Mediaeval Archives*, I, Nos. 114, 115, and Appendix II, No. 5; *Munimenta civitatis Oxonie*, 144.
[57] Salter, *Mediaeval Archives*, I, Nos. 119, 122, 123, 125, 126, 127, 128.
[58] Kibre, *Scholarly Privileges*, 312.
[59] Salter, *Mediaeval Archives*, I, Nos. 124, 129.
[60] *Ibid.*, Nos. 140, 141, 142.
[61] Kibre, *Scholarly Privileges*, 314–15 who calls it "stewart"; Salter, *Mediaeval Archives*, I, No. 143.

were marked by a renewal of unrest. They were, however, increasingly merged with the discontents and disorders in the kingdom at large, mainly as the cumulative effects of nearly a hundred years of war and the political and social strains they helped to engender. By the first decade of the fifteenth century the university's privileges were as complete as they were to be in the Middle Ages.

The striking fact in their achievement was the central role of the king, and equally striking was the virtual absence of any active part by the pope or church. Compared with Paris the influence of pope and church upon events at Oxford was nonexistent. Indeed, except for the initial charter of liberties of 1214 and their confirmation by Innocent IV in 1254, what official contact there was with the pope came mainly through the initiative of the kings. This is particularly true of the reigns of the three Edwards when resistance to papal intervention in their realm hardened into official policy. Under Henry III this had not yet occurred. In May 1246 Innocent IV empowered Robert Grosseteste, then bishop of Lincoln after his illustrious association with Oxford, to permit no one to teach in any faculty unless, following the custom of Paris, he had been examined and approved by the bishop or his deputies.[62] Rashdall saw in this evidence for the survival of the older régime such as must have prevailed up to 1214.[63] That may be; but it seems even more indicative of a papal attitude that regarded Oxford in terms of Paris. The fact was that Oxford had no comparable problem of relationship between the university and the chapter. The bishop at Lincoln, residing at least twenty miles away at Finghurst and usually many more, was, as we have seen, not continuously involved in the affairs of the university; only occasionally did he intervene, as in the riots of 1298 and 1355, and then on the side of the university; equally rarely did he attempt to assert his authority directly in the appointment of chancellor: one of the few times was in 1289, when bishop Oliver Sutton for a time insisted on the chancellor elect appearing in person to receive his office, a demand in which he did not persist.[64] The same bishop, however, had

[62] Salter, *Snappe's Formulary*, 299–300.
[63] Rashdall, III, 40.
[64] *Ibid.*, 40 ff.; Rashdall, III, 123.

supported the university against the burgesses in 1298; and in 1281 he had waived his earlier claim of visitation over the university in favor of the chancellor. Although he gave as his reasons his special affection for the university and his desire not to disturb the scholars in their study, he seems also to have to come to his decision under pressure from the archbishop of Canterbury and other prelates meeting at London; for in 1289 he excommunicated members of the university infringing his privileges.[65] Despite these disputes and further ones over the boundaries between the jurisdictions of the chancellor and the archdeacon of Oxford, finally settled in 1345, diocesan issues had no formative influence on the university's history.

The pope had scarcely more influence. Innocent IV's grant of liberties in 1254 may have been in response to the hostility of the new bishop of Lincoln, Henry of Lexington, who had succeeded Grosseteste in 1253; for the pope, in addition, appointed the bishops of London and Salisbury as apostolic conservators of the "rights, liberties and immunities of the university" to see that the scholars were not molested.[66] These duties carried none of the authority of their Paris counterparts, the chancellor's court, as we have seen, exercising all the powers of the papal conservator's court in the French capital. However serious these early disputes with bishop Lexington might have been, the university's independence was preserved by the king, not the pope. Even more noteworthy, it was the king who asked the pope for privileges on behalf of the university first in 1303–4 and again in 1317. On both occasions the appeal was for the *ius ubique docendi,* which had been granted to Paris in 1292. Edward I invoked "the testimony of venerable writings," showing that the French university had indubitably sprung from the English, to claim the same privileges for the latter.[67] He met with no response, probably because of the unsettled state of the papacy following Benedict XI's short pontificate and the peregrinations of his successor,

---

[65] Kibre, *Scholarly Privileges,* 278. For an account of the university's relations with the church during this period see Rashdall, III, 114 ff.

[66] Rashdall, III, 115; Kibre, *Scholarly Privileges,* 274; *Calendar of Papal Letters Relating to Great Britain and Ireland,* Vol. I, W. H. Bliss, ed. (London, 1893), 306.

[67] Salter, et al., *Oxford Formularies,* I, 6–7.

Clement V. Edward II renewed his father's petition in 1317, despite his other many preoccupations, and again in 1320 and 1321,[68] complaining that Oxford, the older foundation—an opinion, it seems, widespread at Oxford—did not enjoy the privileges of Paris. John XXII was not a pope to be pushed off his course, and Oxford had not responded to his defense of the friars in 1317.[69] This dispute, which dragged on until 1320, was the nearest that the pope came to arbitrating in the affairs of the university.

On the whole, however, the most influential ecclesiastical power was that of the archbishop of Canterbury. Three of the most momentous occasions concerned the intervention of Kilwardby in 1277, Pecham in 1284, and Courtenay in 1381, to condemn doctrinal errors associated with Aristotle, Aquinas, and Wyclif: we shall consider them in Chapter Five. But for the most part the archbishops were content to act as mediators, as in 1281 in the dispute with bishop Sutton and in the conflict with the friars in 1318, or more frequently as upholders of the chancellor's authority as in 1298 and again in 1303 at the beginning of the quarrel with the friars. The one outstanding exception was the clash between the university and archbishop Arundel in 1411. The cause of the trouble dated back to 1395 when the university—probably remembering the humiliation its chancellor, Richard Rigg, had suffered in 1382 at the hands of Courtenay—received from Boniface IX a bull exempting it from the jurisdiction of all archbishops, as well as bishops and ordinaries, even the pope's legate.[70] This was to give the chancellor power over normally exempt groups such as the mendicants and monks; they and all others seeking special privileges would no longer be able to enjoy them. It was also to go against a century of English policy towards the pope, given statutory expression in the statutes of Provisors and Praemunire of Edward III's reign. That king

---

[68] *Chart.*, II, No. 756; Kibre, *Scholarly Privileges*, 290.

[69] Salter et al., *Oxford Formularies*, I, 19–28.

[70] Bliss, *Papal Letters*, Vol. VI, 304; Rashdall, III, 128 ff. The sources for the episode are edited by Salter in *Snappe's Formularies*, 90–193. What follows is based in the main on my account in *Heresy in the Later Middle Ages*, II (Manchester, Manchester University Press, 1967), Chapter 8. See also Kibre, *Scholarly Privileges*, 310 ff.

had gone so far as to abrogate all papal bulls issued in response to the university's ban on the friars, even while himself lifting it.[71] It was thus not long before Boniface IX's grant ran into opposition. It was first denounced by representatives of the university's law faculties at the Canterbury convocation of February 1397. When this failed to move the university, Arundel, at the time both archbishop of Canterbury and papal legate, sought the king's help. Richard II ordered the university to renounce the new privileges on pain of losing all its others and reaffirmed Arundel's right of visitation. Before Arundel could put his powers to the test he was impeached and Richard was deposed.

It was not until 1411 that the matter was resumed. Arundel had been restored as archbishop by Henry IV and his position greatly enhanced. His renewed clash with the university arose over his measures to put down Lollardy. To this end he had in 1407 drawn up thirteen constitutions, all concerned with prohibiting the propagation of Lollard doctrines in one form or another and the translation of the Bible into English. The eleventh constitution bore directly on the university; it provided for a monthly enquiry by the heads of colleges and other houses into the opinions of their inmates. But it was only in 1411, after Wyclif's writings had been condemned in March of that year in 267 articles by a commission of twelve, that Arundel sought to enforce the ban at Oxford. There had already been trouble with the commission at Oxford, one of the proctors, John Birch, trying to get it dissolved. But the real opposition came when Arundel himself intervened. He first demanded an oath of loyalty. But the university, having long lived under royal protection, protested to the king and threatened the archbishop with excommunication for breaking his oath of loyalty as a member of the university. Arundel's reply was to set out on his own visitation in August. He found St. Mary's Church barred to him and he had to break it open. But before he could go further he was summoned to a conference of the disputants by the king; he left placing the university under interdict. But both his sentence and Boniface IX's bull were withdrawn after the university had agreed to write to John XXIII to revoke it—which he did. This

---

[71] Kibre, *Scholarly Privileges,* 310.

was the closest the university came to humiliation during the Middle Ages.

II INTERNAL DEVELOPMENT

Structure of the University. The absence of any life-and-death struggles for survival is reflected in the internal history of the university. Strife there always was: against the townsmen, among the Northerners and Southerners, and with the friars, to mention only the most prominent. But, as we have said, they lacked both constitutional and ecumenical significance beyond providing the occasions for royal confirmations and grants of privilege. Constitutionally Oxford's most striking contrast with Paris is the omnicompetence of the central officers and organs to exclusion of the nations and faculties. The chancellor, as we have seen repeatedly, had no parallel at Paris. This applied to his internal position as well as externally.[72] As chief officer he came, though not at first, to preside over the university's congregations of both the regent (teaching) and the nonregent masters; in exceptional cases he could summon a congregation of regents— normally the function of the proctors. He announced the decisions (*acta*) and dissolved the meetings. He was, also present at the depositions of masters (i.e., their testimonies to a candidate's suitability) and conferred the license. He was responsible for maintaining discipline and law and order, having power to expel, imprison, excommunicate, and fine offenders; this authority extended to virtually every matter involving a member of the university, except for murder, maiming, and property. In addition to morals, carrying arms, and breaches of the peace, it included the letting of halls, the cession of debts, and the engaging of servants by scholars. The chancellor could also permit students to beg for alms and could grant licenses to practice surgery. He was chosen from the doctors of theology and canon law (decrees) and was elected by all the regents in an indirect vote: the proctors nominated one regent from each higher faculty and

[72] For what follows see H. E. Salter, ed., *Registrum cancellarii Oxoniensis*, and S. Gibson, ed., *Statuta antiqua Universitatis Oxoniensis* (Oxford, Oxford University Press, 1931–2), from which the following account is drawn.

an equivalent number from the arts; election was by simple majority decision. Unlike both chancellor and rector at Paris, the chancellor at Oxford held office for two years. Moreover, in the event of his proving intolerable he could be deposed by decree of the congregation of the whole university following representation to it by the congregation of regents.[73] The proctors, who initiated the process, could then call upon the chancellor to resign. There was thus a constitutional safety valve of the kind not known in Paris. Similarly, the chancellor's expulsion of a master took place in congregation. By far the most noteworthy feature of the chancellor's position was that in becoming the presiding officer of the university—to use Rashdall phrase [74]—he became identified with the university and divorced from the bishop. This can be seen as early as the disputes with bishop Lexington in 1254; it was not the masters versus the chancellor and the bishop, but the bishop against the university, including the chancellor. The chancellor's autonomy came to him as head of the university, not the bishop's representative; it therefore also carried with it the autonomy of the university, so that the two became inseparable.

The effects are to be seen in every sphere of the university. Neither the nations nor the faculties were the independent bodies they were at Paris. There were only two nations in the arts faculty; from the first they lacked the importance of the four Paris nations.[75] They were divided purely into those north and south of the river Nene [76]—the *Boreales* and *Australes*. The

---

[73] In 1322 the university persuaded the bishop of Lincoln to recall his commission from John Lutterel, the chancellor (Salter, *Snappe's Formulary,* 44; Salter, *Mediaeval Archives,* I, No. 60). In December of that year the university passed a statute limiting the chancellor's period of office to two years (Gibson, *Statuta antiqua,* 121–3).

[74] Rashdall, III, 54.

[75] For an account of the nations at Oxford see Kibre, *The Nations,* 160 ff., 163; and A. B. Emden, "Northerners and Southerners in the Organization of the University [of Oxford] to 1509" in *Oxford Studies presented to Daniel Callus* (Oxford, OHS, 1963), 1–30. Mr. Emden has, however, pointed to the pervasiveness of the distinction in almost every aspect of university life—administration, congregations, and colleges.

[76] Emden, *op. cit.,* 5–7, who rejects the traditional dividing line of the Trent.

Scots belonged to the *Boreales* and the Irish and Welsh to the *Australes,* together with anyone from France or elsewhere. Oxford never served the continent in the way that Paris did; the majority of her personnel were from England and Wales. This did not make them any less bellicose, but formal nations were less necessary to the functioning of the university, and their autonomy was not fostered. In 1250 they were barred from celebrating their festivals in the Oxford churches.[77] Although their divisions influenced academic matters, they seem to have had no independent part in them; they were mainly prominent in fighting one another. An outbreak between the Northerners and the Irish in 1252 was so intense that a special treaty had to be made between them, drawn up by twelve commissioners from each party and guaranteed by at least thirty masters from North and South; they, and all entering the university, had to take an oath to keep the peace.[78] Further disturbances followed in 1258, this time between the Scots and Welsh, who belonged to the two different nations. In 1267 a new outbreak led to another treaty, again drawn up by twenty-four representatives; its terms were to be enforced by fines and expulsion from the group to which offenders belonged. They seem to have had no lasting effect, for in 1273 several Irish scholars were killed in a battle between Northerners and Southerners, and four clerks were in 1274 imprisoned in the tower of London by order of the king. This seems to have led in the same year to abolition of the nations as separate organizations. On March 27, 1274, the two nations agreed to unite. The king had already shown his concern at the danger of dissensions in a letter to the chancellor in October 1273, threatening severe measures if the peace were disturbed.[79] As a result of the merger the term nation was no longer used, but the two proctors continued to be drawn from each of the regions. In their brief span the nations had contributed little of the stability to be found at Paris and Bologna; rather, the grouping seems to have been an incentive to strife. Not that it ceased with their dissolution. There were clashes between Northerners and Southerners, brawls and riots throughout the Mid-

[77] Kibre, *The Nations,* 163.
[78] *Ibid.,* 164–5.
[79] Salter, *Mediaeval Archives,* I, No. 23 and Appendix I, No. 1.

dle Ages; notable ones occurring in 1314, 1319, 1334, 1385, 1388, 1389, and into the fifteenth century.[80] At the least they helped to cause the Stamford migration of 1334, and they were a constant source of discord between town and university.

This is not to deny the nations any positive contribution to the university. The two proctors sprang from them, and even when they no longer represented the nations as such they stood for the two main groups that made up the university. The different positions of the nations meant a different role for the proctors. To begin with there were two and not four as at Paris. Then, with no national organization to preside over, they became solely concerned with running the university in conjunction with the chancellor. The absence of a rector meant that they were its executive officers, the earliest that the university possessed. They are first specifically mentioned in 1248 when they appeared before the king at Woodstock to complain against injuries suffered by the university from the burgesses and Jews: they received in reply a charter of privileges, confirmed in 1268.[81] As the representatives of the arts faculty they were responsible for presiding over its congregations and enforcing its statutes. At this time they and not the chancellor appear to have done this for the whole university. Thus in 1252 it was the proctors who were to take an oath for the maintenance of the peace, and in 1257 they were empowered to denounce masters who had infringed the statutes and to suspend them from lecturing.[82] Their range of duties concerned all the public business of the university, including supervising public disputations, summoning the congregations, reporting the agenda to the chancellor, pronouncing the graces, supervising the elections of the chancellor and beadles, and assisting the chancellor in all his judicial and academic functions, as well as being able to depose him. They also enforced the discipline of the university.[83]

There was therefore a direct parallel with Paris in that the proctors came to act for the university by virtue of being the officers of the arts faculty. As at Paris, also, they were initially

---

[80] Kibre, *The Nations*, 165–6.
[81] Salter, *Mediaeval Archives*, I, No. 10; Kibre, *The Nations*, 161; Rashdall, III, 57.
[82] Rashdall, III, 53; Gibson, *Statuta antiqua*, 86, 108.
[83] Gibson, *Statuta antiqua*, 86, 107–8.

sometimes called "rectors" but the term fell into disuse. Whether these common traits derived from Paris is not clear; but in the face of other differences their marked similarity does not warrant Rashdall's opinion that "Oxford may be said to represent an arrested development of the Parisian constitution modified by the totally different relations of the chancellor to the masters." [84] The totally different relation of the chancellor to the masters was not a truncated superstructure set upon the same base as at Paris, but one of the main factors in Oxford's distinctive history. It meant not an arrested constitution, but one in which there was less need for federalism in a more unified whole. That much came from Paris is indisputable; Grosseteste himself, as bishop of Lincoln in about 1240, warned the Oxford masters of theology to follow the practice of the theological faculty at Paris over reading the Bible, an injunction repeated by Innocent IV when he commanded Grosseteste that no one in any faculty was to teach unless examined and approved "according to the Paris manner." [85] Thus the real constitutional difference between the two universities was that the university at Oxford performed many of the functions of the faculty and nations at Paris. At Oxford the higher faculties had no independent organization with their own deans and statutes; their regulations [86] were concerned solely with academic requirements and not the least significant aspect is the way in which they sought dispensations (graces) from higher authority, generally the congregations. This situation was due largely to the arts faculty, which claimed that no grace could be granted without its approval.[87] Even more than at Paris, the arts faculty was the dominating influence in the life of the university; at Oxford it did not remain *de facto* but became enshrined in the university's constitutions. This can be seen clearly in the making of its statutes and in the congregation. Originally both resided in the whole body of masters. The earliest dated statute belongs to 1253; it concerned the license to incept in theology.[88] The first reference to an ordinance by the whole university and chancellor occurs in 1231, stipulating that every

[84] Rashdall, III, 59.
[85] *Chart.*, I, Nos. 127, 154; Gibson, *Statuta antiqua*, XIII.
[86] Gibson, *Statuta antiqua*, CIII–XIII; Rashdall, III, 60–1.
[87] Gibson, *Statuta antiqua*, CXVIII ff. 67, 179.
[88] *Ibid.*, XXI and 49.

scholar shall have his name inscribed on the roll of a regent master (i.e., have matriculated).[89] Regents and nonregents all met in St. Mary's Church, retiring to discuss separately the propositions placed before them. These concerned matters affecting the university as a whole—chests, keeping the peace, litigation, studies, testimonials, scholars' houses, payments and fines, the chancellorship. The regents—as the active and younger body of masters concerned with the day-to-day problems of the schools —soon came to deal with minor questions as well as more formal business. They constituted the congregation of regents: unlike the full congregation of regents and nonregents they only passed ordinances, not statutes. Their earliest dated ordinance is for 1278 dealing with regrators.[90] Others concerned procedure, elections of university officers, the chancellor, proctors, beadles, granting graces and dispensations, studies, administrative matters, and the interpretation of statutes. Unresolved questions went to the great congregation (*congregatio magna*) of regents and nonregents. There was a third congregation composed of regents of the arts faculty (*congregatio artistarum*); it met in St. Mildred's Church and was summoned by the proctors to deliberate on matters coming before the great congregation. As such it expressed the power of the arts faculty within the university from an early date, although the first reference to this deliberative assembly is in 1325.[91] Gradually, by the later fourteenth century the power of the regents' congregation increased at the expense of the great congregation (also becoming known as Convocation). The congregation of the arts faculty for a time sought to assert itself, claiming in 1357 and later in the century the right of veto on motions to be brought before the great congregation. This was rejected by the nonregents and the regents in theology and civil law.[92] The arts congregation—from the fifteenth century known as the black congregation (*congregatio nigra*)—thus remained a deliberative body and declined as the powers of the congregation of regents increased. In the great

[89] *Ibid.*, 107. For what follows—except where specific reference is given—*ibid.*, XXII ff.

[90] *Ibid.*, XXIII, 106.

[91] *Ibid.*, 127–8.

[92] *Ibid.*, 156, 179, 293.

congregation voting was by faculties, the nonregents for this purpose counting as a separate faculty; in 1314 it was decreed that the passing of a statute required the assent of a majority of three faculties, including the faculty of arts, together with a majority of the nonregents.[93] That statute was the result of the dispute with the friars that broke out in 1303, which we must now consider.

The Friars. The friars had settled in Oxford soon after reaching England, the Dominicans in 1221, the Franciscans in 1224. In their early history the Franciscans are the more prominent; for not only do we know them through Eccleston's chronicle of their advent in England,[94] but also because Grosseteste was their first regent master. The Dominicans settled in the Jewry; converting the Jews formed an important part of their activities. The Franciscans took a house in St. Ebbes, receiving a permanent site nearby in 1225. From the beginning both orders were closely connected with the university, at first attending lectures in the schools and in due time being joined by eminent masters like Haymo of Faversham (who had already taken the Franciscan habit at Paris), Adam Marsh, Robert Bacon, and Richard Fishacre. Grosseteste was lecturer to the Franciscans from 1229 or 1230 until his appointment as bishop of Lincoln in 1235. He had, as we have mentioned, been chancellor sometime after 1214; his humility in undertaking such a position is matched only by the devotion with which he must have performed it, for he inaugurated one of the outstanding schools of the Middle Ages; his influence left a permanent mark on the intellectual traditions of the Oxford Franciscans, as we shall see in Chapter Five. He was followed by three more secular masters.[95] The Franciscans were therefore far more indigenous to Oxford; this and the absence of the freak events at Paris in

---

[93] *Ibid.*, XXVI–VII and 118.
[94] *Tractatus Fr. Thomae de Eccleston de Adventu fratrum minorum in Angliam*, A. G. Little, ed. (Manchester, Manchester University Press, 1951). See also A. G. Little, "The Franciscan School at Oxford in the Thirteenth Century," *Archivum Franciscanum Historicum* (AFH) **19** (1926), 803–74, and *Studies in English Franciscan History* (Manchester, Manchester University Press, 1917).
[95] For details see Little, "The Franciscan School," 810 ff.

1229–31 that led to the acquisition there of the Dominican and Franciscan chairs helped to make for amicable relations during most of the thirteenth century. The trouble arose—characteristically—over the university's practice that a candidate for the license in theology had first to graduate in arts. This bore heavily on the friars, who were forbidden to study profane knowledge outside their own houses, but who went to the university to qualify in theology. The first clash occurred in 1253, when a Franciscan, Thomas of York, formally petitioned to be admitted as a master in theology not having previously been through the arts faculty. The university deliberated for a fortnight and decided that on this occasion Thomas's plea should be allowed, but that in future "no one shall incept in theology unless he has previously incepted in arts . . . ," together with certain other provisions about lecturing on prescribed texts and preaching. This now became a statute although dispensations could be, and were, granted by the masters and chancellor.[96] No more was heard of the matter until the Dominicans raised it again in 1311–14. But this time it marked the culmination of a conflict that had begun in 1303.

The precise cause is not apparent. Officially there appears to have been little disharmony, for until the first decade of the fourteenth century mendicants were being admitted to theological degrees without having incepted in arts. But secular resentment against the mendicants had not been confined to Paris; as concessions to the mendicants mounted, so did hostility towards them. It had gathered in a new wave in the last years of the thirteenth century with the publication in 1281 of the bull *Ad fructus uberes* by Martin IV giving the mendicants independent sacerdotal powers in the dioceses and parishes without reference to the secular clergy. In response to the outcry among the latter it was modified in 1300 by Boniface VIII in the decree *Super cathedram*.[97] At Oxford, as at Paris, the great doctrinal condemnations of the 1270's had left their scars; Oxford had also suffered a further visitation by Pecham, archbishop of Canter-

[96] *Ibid.*, 823; Gibson, *Statuta antiqua*, 49.
[97] The decrees are in J. Sbaralea, ed., *Bullarium Franciscanum*, III, 480, IV, 498–500: see also D. Knowles, *The Religious Orders in England* (Cambridge, Cambridge University Press, 1948), 186 ff.

bury in 1284, a Franciscan; Kilwardby, his predecessor in the earlier (1277) condemnations, was a Dominican. Moreover, the waiving of the mendicants' need to graduate in arts directly concerned the prestige of the arts as the predominant as well as the most numerous faculty. These factors were calculated to increase friction between the mendicants and the university masters. The immediate occasion for the outbreak was a series of pinpricks by the university. They began in 1303, when the friars were required to perform their examinatory sermons—decreed in 1253 as a condition of incepting in theology—in St. Mary's, away from their own convents by the river. The friars complained that St. Mary's was too noisy.[98] From this time on it seems also that their applications to proceed directly to a degree in theology were being vetoed by individual masters, unanimous assent of all the regents being necessary. Then, in about 1311, came a further statute [99]: that it was necessary to become a bachelor of theology before being able to lecture on the Bible, a requirement that compelled the friars to lecture first for a year on the *Sentences*.[99a] The reason given was that incompetent persons "had been sowing errors, and causing confusion over the holy scriptures." The Dominicans protested—though why they should have done so is not clear—that they were not equipped to meet these demands which, as we shall discuss in Chapter Three, entailed a philosophical training. One of them, Hugh of Sutton, refused to take the oath of obedience to observe the new decree—a condition of being admitted to a degree. He was expelled from the university. The friars now claimed that they were being attacked and ostracized. In 1311 they appealed to the papal curia. In 1312 a commission of two seculars and two friars was set up. Its verdict in 1313 [100] upheld the statutes but called for impar-

---

[98] Rashdall, III, 70 ff., and Rashdall, "The Friar Preachers and the University," *Collectanea*, II, M. Burrows, ed. (Oxford, OHS, 1890) 195–273, in which his account is taken from the record of the friars' appeal to Rome (*ibid.*, 217–62). Interesting as it is, I venture to think that Rashdall—possibly influenced by the earlier events at Paris—has tended to magnify the importance of the dispute for Oxford.

[99] Gibson, *Statuta antiqua*, 52.

[99a] For curriculum in theology see 161 ff.

[100] Rashdall, *Collectanea*, II, 264 ff.; Gibson, *Statuta antiqua*, CXIV, 116–118.

tiality in enforcing them; a dispensation would not be refused out of "malice or hatred or rancour," but only "for the common utility and honour of the university": any regent voting against a grace had to give adequate reasons which if not sustained had no force. Voting procedure was clarified, as we mentioned earlier, to make a majority consist of three faculties (one of them arts) plus a majority of the nonregents; the Dominicans had earlier complained that two faculties had constituted a majority. In view of the university's ambiguous reply this seems to have been a new development.[101]

This settlement—although confirmed by the king in April 1314 [102]—did not put an end to the dispute. The Dominicans now appealed to the pope. They might as well have spared themselves the effort. Although John XXII in 1317 wrote ordering the abrogation of the provision that the friars must first lecture on the *Sentences* before lecturing on the Bible, and instructed the papal legate to induce the university to comply, it did not.[103] It received strong support from the archbishop of Canterbury, who from 1318 took an active part in mediating between the two sides before agreement was finally reached in 1320.[104] The statutes stood. The pope had been effectively ignored, and the university had been upheld by the king and the church. This points clearly not only to the difference between the universities of Paris and Oxford, but to the papacy in 1250 and 1320. The challenge had been to the university's institutions, not to its survival; neither popes nor friars any longer had the power or standing to make kings bow to them.

Halls and Colleges. The colleges at Oxford were initially of no more importance in the university than they were at Paris; nor was their presence in any way peculiar to it. The university—or at least the schools from which it arose—had been in existence for a hundred years before the first college was founded. Yet, for all their unspectacular beginnings, the colleges were to become

---

[101] Rashdall, *Collectanea,* II, 226, 230.

[102] *Ibid.,* 264.

[103] Salter et al., *Oxford Formularies,* I, 13–28, 36, 39, 40–55, 62–5, 68, 73, for the course of these later events.

[104] Salter, *Mediaeval Archives,* I, No. 55; Rashdall, *Collectanea,* II, 272.

of paramount importance in a way distinctive from any other university except Cambridge. The reason is not to be sought solely in the colleges' subsequent history. The structure of the university, as we suggested earlier, played its part. In being more unitary than federal, it offered less of the autonomous life enjoyed by the nations and faculties at Paris; and correspondingly more scope for colleges to fill the void. As a consequence colleges at Oxford from the first were more self-contained and comprehensive societies, as opposed to the mere hostels that were usually, at Paris, the adjuncts of a faculty or nation.[105] Halls and hostels were the mainstay of the university at Oxford; from their emergence in the thirteenth century to the middle of the sixteenth century they were the normal form of residence for the majority of scholars. Unlike the colleges they were not the result of a specific act of foundation and endowment to support a number of scholars, but fee-paying hostels presided over by a master. They had no elaborate constitution designed to perpetuate the particular behests of a founder, but were open to any member of the university who could afford to pay for his board.

These halls arose naturally from the conditions prevailing at Oxford in the early thirteenth century, where there were probably almost as many scholars—estimated by Rashdall at about 1500—as townspeople. At first the scholars had no separate houses or buildings; they had therefore to lodge with the townspeople and the masters had to hire rooms in which to teach. The need to exercise some control over the scholars both in their fights among themselves and with the populace led, as we have seen, to the progressive growth of the chancellor's jurisdiction and with it the university's. As at Paris this had, so far as its own members were concerned, the twofold object of regulating dealings with the town in matters such as rents and the price of foodstuffs and of maintaining peace and some means of discipline within the university. The bellicosity of the scholars was too easily inflamed by the extortions of the townsmen, two con-

---

[105] For an account of the place of the halls in medieval Oxford see especially A. B. Emden, *An Oxford Hall in the Middle Ages* (Oxford, Oxford University Press, 1927), Chapters 1–3, to which much of what follows is owed; see also W. A. Pantin, "The Halls and Schools of Medieval Oxford" in *Oxford Studies presented to Daniel Callus,* 31–100.

stant factors in the conflicts between them. It is noteworthy that, as we have seen, one of the provisions of the university's first charter—granted by the papal legate in 1214—was for the halving of rents over the next ten years, and that in future they would be assessed by a joint commission of masters and burgesses. This was not the end of the difficulties; Henry III in a letter in 1231 to the mayors and bailiffs of Oxford and Cambridge spoke of "onerous and exorbitant" exactions of rent from scholars and warned of the consequent danger that they would go elsewhere.[106] Subsequent interventions by the king until 1290 frequently had rents as one of their subjects. After that they seem to have lost their contentiousness, probably because of the growth of halls, and the regularization of the system of letting. During the thirteenth century it became accepted that once lodgings had been rented to a university clerk they could not be let to laymen while clerks continued to want them; the only layman allowed to live in them was the owner.[107]

Often, of course, the trouble arose from unruly students, as Henry III recognized in his letter of 1231. The first university statutes of 1231 sought to control scholars by requiring each one to be enrolled (matriculated) by a master, and every master to keep a record of attendance at lectures.[108] The penalty for a student failing to satisfy the academic and moral requirements was excommunication. The system of entrusting discipline to the masters in the schools did not prove effective because it did not extend to the areas of a student's life where trouble was most likely to arise. It was the halls that were to provide the discipline.

Rashdall's theory that the halls originated as democratic societies was exploded nearly forty years ago by A. B. Emden.[109] What evidence there is for their early history indicates that—as at Paris—they began as boarding houses under masters. The

[106] *Callendar of Close Rolls* (*1227–31*), 586–7, quoted in Emden, *An Oxford Hall,* 13.
[107] Emden, *An Oxford Hall,* 17.
[108] *Ibid.;* Gibson, *Statuta antiqua,* 107.
[109] Rashdall, III, 169 ff. and repeated by Sir Charles E. Mallet, *A History of the University of Oxford,* I (London, 1924), 41; Emden, *An Oxford Hall,* 19 ff., points out that it derives no support from the evidence at Paris, where the regulations of 1245 show conclusively that they were under the control of a regent master; *Chart.,* I, No. 136.

earliest regulations for them probably belong to the later thirteenth century.[110] They provided for the conditions of the
principal's tenure and duration of office; laid down stringent penalties for the buying and selling of headships of houses; and
forbade the holding of more than one principalship. Headships of
a hall or hospice and of a school were moreover treated in the
same context. As Emden concluded, the regulations leave no
doubt that these were not self-governing communities of scholars
but under the authority of a master or bachelor who was directly
responsible to the university for holding and running the premises. This was not the same as being appointed by the university,
but consisted in recognition which enabled the principal to enjoy
security of tenure. The master could be expelled for not paying a
deposit on rent by September 9 (the feast of the birth of the
Virgin); and each year on this day the principals renewed their
security or caution before the chancellor or his officer in St.
Mary's Church.[111] This annual ceremony continued throughout
the Middle Ages. The landlord from whom the principal rented
the house was responsible for repairs.

The first known occasion when the principals of the halls were
required to enforce discipline was after the outbreak between
the Northern and Irish scholars in 1252. The principals were to
take part in an annual inquisition of all scholars at a certain
appointed place to discover who had broken the peace or had
committed any other transgressions.[112] They were again enlisted
in 1303 in new measures against wrongdoers; every principal or
his deputy, of both halls and rooms, had within fifteen days of
the beginning of each academic year to state on oath before the
chancellor or one of the proctors that he would report within
three days the name of any member of his society who had committed an offense.[113] The university was thus attempting to
bring not only halls but ordinary lodgings within its net as well;
it did not succeed with lodgings, and eventually suppressed
them in the fifteenth century. But the halls had by then become
an integral part of the university's authority.

Moreover, they gradually became more than places of resi-

---

[110] Emden, *An Oxford Hall*, 23; Gibson, *Statuta antiqua*, 78–81.

[111] Emden, *An Oxford Hall*, 25.

[112] *Ibid.*, 27–9; Gibson, *Statuta antiqua*, 88–9.

[113] Emden, *An Oxford Hall*, 29; Gibson, *Statuta antiqua*, 110, 111.

dence presided over usually by a master; by the fourteenth century they also gave instruction. The original schools and lecture rooms had been in separate buildings; because of the shortage of lecture rooms an early statute had provided that once a building was used as a school or for teaching purposes it should continue to be used as such.[114] As more halls were built this was no longer a consideration. Little, however, is known of teaching in the halls before the fifteenth century; in our period it seems plain that it was never more than supplementary to the public lectures in the schools. The halls also displayed another feature of Oxford life: the comparatively greater role of the nonregents in it. Not all hall principals were regent masters; they included even some manciples (or college caterers), although this was prohibited probably before the middle of the fourteenth century.[115]

The very lack of dependence on a benefactor made the life of a hall much more flexible than that of a college. It also exposed it more to the vagaries of taste or fashion or reputation; a scholar who did not like one could go to another, as seems to have happened frequently before 1412, when it was decreed that a scholar expelled from one hall was not to be admitted elsewhere before the chancellor had been told and the offender punished and supported by sureties for his future conduct.[116]

Catering was in the hands of the manciples, on whose honesty the well-being of the members depended. Each member paid a weekly sum for the hall's commons, ranging from eightpence to more than one shilling, as well as for payment of the manciple and the servants at a rate based on these charges; the servants were to take an oath at the beginning of every term to serve the masters and scholars faithfully, and not buy food to sell or for the use of regrators but only for the needs of members of the hall.[117] The biggest difference among halls was between those of the artists and the legists. The former included those who had graduated in arts and were now studying for higher degrees;

[114] Emden, *An Oxford Hall*, 35; Gibson, *Statuta antiqua*, 79—unless occupied by a master who lectured there.

[115] Emden, *An Oxford Hall*, 37; Gibson, *Statuta antiqua*, 183.

[116] Emden, *An Oxford Hall*, 39; Gibson, *Statuta antiqua*, 210–11.

[117] Emden, *An Oxford Hall*, 40–1; Gibson, *Statuta antiqua*, 153.

they were accordingly interfaculty societies. The legists were the only other faculty that contained enough scholars to form halls drawn from its members alone; they were probably also wealthier. The halls of the two faculties were mostly concentrated near their schools, those of law near St. Edward's Church and in the two neighboring parishes of St. Aldate and St. Frideswide; those of the artists were found in Schools Street, to the north of the west end of St. Mary's, in the northern and eastern parishes. The majority of halls probably had four to eight living rooms, most being two-storied buildings.[118] The one Oxford hall surviving from medieval times is St. Edmund's Hall.

Although many of the details are missing, there can be little doubt about the prominent place of the halls in Oxford during the thirteenth and fourteenth centuries. They were to the university then what the colleges were to become from the sixteenth century. They seem to have been much closer to the university —though not more strictly regulated—than at Paris, just because the link was a direct one and not through nations or the faculties; that there were schools for members of each faculty was not the same as the schools coming under faculty jurisdiction.

It is in the context of the halls that we must consider the colleges. As at Paris they were for a minority, originally the poor scholar who could not support himself. But unlike Paris these were mainly for graduates. This almost certainly accounts for the other notable difference from Paris by the fourteenth century: their academic eminence. The colleges were for those who could benefit from support; they therefore produced many bright scholars who made their intellectual mark while doing postgraduate work in an equivalent way to that in which research is done today. Thus, as we shall see in Chapter Five, Oxford intellectual life in the later Middle Ages came to be associated with a number of illustrious circles of scholars in particular colleges—Merton, Queens, Oriel—in a manner distinct from continental universities. In that sense the colleges made a contribution that was out of proportion to their numerical or institutional importance within the university.

The founding of the individual colleges is a subject in itself.

---

[118] Emden, *An Oxford Hall*, 42, 50–1.

and one amply documented in the many college histories and record collections that have been published over the past seventy and more years. We shall confine it here to a brief enumeration of the more important foundations in the thirteenth and fourteenth centuries.[119] They were of two main kinds: those that were the result of individual benefactions and the monastic colleges. To take the latter first, the monastic colleges had begun to appear at Paris by the middle of the thirteenth century and, besides increasing the fears of the seculars in the theological faculty, they set an example for an academic community that—as Rashdall surmised—may have influenced the founders of secular colleges. At Oxford they came later, although the mendicants had settled there in the 1220's. The first college for monks was Gloucester College,[120a] in 1283, for thirteen monks from St. Peter's Monastery in Gloucester; but after protracted negotiations it was opened in 1298–9 to Benedictines from convents throughout the province of Canterbury, and the connection with St. Peter's in Gloucester was broken. It was not, like the other colleges, a corporate body, being under the dual control of the abbots of Malmsbury and the presidents of the college. In 1336 this control became even more amorphous when Benedict XII, as part of his monastic reform, united the provinces of Canterbury and York into one, thereby making the college accessible to monks from over the whole of England.

Gloucester College was followed soon after by Durham College, the building of which was begun in 1289 by Richard of Hoton, prior of the Durham Benedictines. Richard de Bury, the notable fourteenth century bibliophile and patron of scholars, bequeathed to it his library. Other monastic colleges included Canterbury Hall, founded by the monks of Christ Church, Rewley—the Cistercian *studium*—about 1280 and much later, in 1435, St. Mary's College for the Augustinian canons.

None of these played a particularly notable part in the intellectual history of the university. This was left to the secular

[119] For what follows see Rashdall, III, 169–235; and Mallet, *op. cit.*, I, 83–137.
[120a] Rashdall, III, 185, and especially editor's note 3, 185–6.

foundations, preeminent among them Merton,[120b] commonly accepted as the earliest Oxford college. In the words of Rashdall, "Balliol existed before it, we may say *de facto,* but not *de iure,* and University [college] *de iure* but not *de facto.* Merton alone existed both *de iure* and *de facto* in 1264." [121] It was founded by Walter de Merton with the object of providing for eleven bachelors preparing to become masters of arts. After they had obtained the degree they could remain in the college as regent masters or go on to study theology or—in limited numbers—law. Here then was a conception of supporting more mature students to become masters and to enter one of the higher faculties. To this end Merton gave his estate of Maldon in Surrey to the college. The eight scholars—nephews of the founder, the numbers to be increased to twenty from later descendants—were to live in the same hall and have a uniform. By the initial statutes the warden was not to live with them but to act more as a protector. The date of the statutes, 1264, the year of the battle of Northampton, probably accounts for the omission of a place of study. At that time secession was in the air and Oxford's future as the home of the university far from assured; in fact Merton bought a house at Cambridge for his college in 1269–70—an indication of the uncertainty over Oxford at this time.[122]

Further statutes were issued in 1270 and 1274; in 1276 the archbishop of Canterbury became visitor of the college. Apart from the higher age level than among the earlier Paris colleges—as bachelors they were likely to be at least nineteen [123] —the college was also to enjoy a much greater degree of autonomy compared with the halls at Oxford and Paris. Admissions were controlled by the warden and a number of the seniors— thirteen in 1264, seven by the 1274 statutes. The warden himself was to be elected unanimously—if necessary through starving

[120b] For Merton, in addition to Rashdall and Mallet, see especially the valuable introduction by J. R. L. Highfield to his edition of *The Early Rolls of Merton College* (Oxford, OHS, 1964).
[121] Rashdall III, 193.
[122] *Ibid.,* 194.
[123] *Ibid.,* 196, editor's note 4; not seven or eight years old as Rashdall unaccountably says in the text.

the electors into a decision by "subtraction of victuals." Again in contrast to the bursars of the continental colleges, the scholars were part of a landowning body, deriving their income from the revenues from their estates as opposed to receiving pensions from others.[124] They could continue in that state until such time as·they took up some more lucrative position in the church or law. Merton also acquired advowsons so that fellows of the college could be appointed to benefices. Another feature of the Oxford colleges seen in Merton was the importance given to the chapel, and with it the distinctive ecclesiastical character of its architecture. Merton was preeminent among the Oxford colleges in the later thirteenth and fourteenth centuries, having among its alumni six archbishops of Canterbury: they included Winchelsey, Bradwardine, and Islip.[125]

Of the other early colleges, Balliol [126] was first founded in 1266 but did not receive a legal charter until 1282 through John de Balliol's widow, Dervorguilla. It was unlike the other Oxford colleges in being originally only for artists who could not continue there after becoming masters. Government of the college was in the hands of external procurators, a Franciscan and a secular member of arts. Balliol came more into line with the other Oxford colleges when six theological fellowships were established in 1340; in 1364 the original fellowships were also extended by papal bull to allow the study of theology; in that year also the college received new statutes from Sudbury, bishop of London.

The bequest for University College [127] was made in 1249, before any other, by William of Durham, a master at Paris and prelate. On his death in that year he left 310 marks to support ten or more masters of arts studying theology, the money to be invested in rents. The university put the money into a chest, spending 160 marks of it for its own purposes and never repaying them; the remainder was used to buy houses that yielded eighteen marks annually. How it was spent in the years before 1280 is not clear: perhaps on supporting scholars, in which case

[124] *Ibid.*, 197.
[125] Mallet, *op cit.*, 121–2.
[126] Rashdall, III, 180 ff.; Mallet, *op. cit.*, I, 97 ff.
[127] *Ibid.*, 175 ff.; Mallet, *op. cit.*, I, 84 ff.

University would have been the oldest college. But it was not until about that year that the university formally established Great University Hall for four masters studying theology and appointed by the chancellor and masters in theology; when any fellow was promoted to a benefice worth more than five marks a year, he was to be replaced by a new fellow. The remaining fellows were to have a say in the election of new ones, but the university had extensive supervision over the fellows, including power to remove them. Other scholars who were willing to pay might board with the four foundation members. In the fourteenth century the legend grew up, supported by forgeries, that University College had been founded by King Alfred.

The other colleges founded during this period were Exeter (1314–16), Oriel (1324), Queens (1341), and New (1379); Oriel and Queens shared with Merton much of the university's academic distinction. There was also an unsuccessful attempt to found Canterbury Hall as a college for both regulars and seculars in about 1361. John Wyclif, the reformer, as a secular master had been appointed warden in 1365; but an appeal to Rome by the monks of Canterbury led to the foundation becoming wholly monastic after 1371.[128] After New College, the most munificent of all these foundations, there was no further college until Lincoln was established in 1429. During the thirteenth and fourteenth centuries, therefore, the colleges formed only a fraction of the total complement of the university. If they were already gaining at the expense of the halls which they began early to absorb, their real importance was to come after the Reformation. At Oxford as at Paris the life of the university for the first 250 years centered on the schools, halls, and faculties.

[128] Rashdall, III, 211–12, especially editor's notes; and W. A. Pantin, *The Constitutions of Canterbury College* (Oxford, OHS, 1947).

THREE

The Curriculum at Paris and Oxford

Academically, the universities institutionalized higher learning. They did not entirely supersede the earlier forms or activities of education. Cathedral and monastic schools continued in existence. History was still written, grammar still taught, style still cultivated, though never as university subjects in the ways in which they had been practiced during the eleventh and much of the twelfth centuries. Nor—and this was even more important—was the long-established hierarchy of subjects displaced. Indeed, it was enshrined in the university's division among faculties. Nevertheless, in every case, the university gave a new content to traditional subjects and a new framework for their pursuit. Learning now became an independent professional activity, available to all those who had the means or resolution to join a *studium generale* and find themselves a teacher; its regulation lay with the masters who taught it; its end was not abstract understanding but training for a profession. That it is not to say that the ideals of Anselm or the love of learning of an Abelard or Gilbert de la Porrée had by the thirteenth century become debased; they had their counterparts in Grosseteste, Bonaventure, Aquinas, and a host of others. Nor was theology dethroned as the queen of the sciences nor the propaedeutic value of profane knowledge renounced. Rather these ideals were no longer the driving force behind education; they became—if they ever had been more—the preserve of a minority within communities where the intellectual aspirations and activities of a majority were governed by the demands of the curriculum and the prospects to be derived from meeting them. In that sense university education was vocational: to qualify its members for benefices or service in the church, the law, medicine, or teaching. The successful outcome of a university career was a license to practice the skill gained there: the *ius ubique docendi,* which was the hallmark of attainment accepted far and wide.

Accordingly the analogy between medieval and modern universities is closer than might appear at first sight. In both of them studies followed a series of graduated stages; in both of them their organization occupied a large part of the time and energies of the teachers; and in both cases the great majority of those involved were concerned with either mastering or imparting existing knowledge as opposed to engaging in original work. Here, however, the parallels must be qualified by different conceptions of what constituted pure knowledge or rather by the lack of such a conception in the Middle Ages so far as it related to man's natural experience. All truth was regarded as supernatural; reason could only elucidate what had been revealed by faith and dogma. Consequently the search for truth in the Middle Ages was not through research in the way it is now understood, but in the texts that contained it. Even when in the fourteenth century attention was turned increasingly toward mathematical and scientific problems, to be solved by deduction and experiment, this was not conceived in terms of the search for original knowledge. It is an anachronism to make a distinction in the Middle Ages between teaching existing knowledge and discovering new knowledge. At most we can point to the contrast that has always existed in universities between the professional teachers and thinkers and the majority of members who studied to equip themselves for a career. The universities canalized this knowledge into society. They can therefore be said to have made learning professional in two respects: on the one hand by making it the preserve of qualified teachers and transmitted through courses leading to the grant of the license; and on the other by training men for the main professions. The magnitude of this step is to be measured by the universal monopoly of higher education—though not learning—by the universities from the thirteenth century onward. Whereas in the twelfth century an independent master could set up a school and take pupils, and a cathedral school like Chartres or Laon could dominate the study of philosophy or the Bible, in the thirteenth century this was no longer possible. These other forms—as we have said—continued to coexist; but as subsidiaries, no longer in the main stream.

At the same time, however, just because the universities monopolized higher education they also took over the tradition they absorbed. We shall consider the content of the arts course later. That it was radically different from the earlier conception of the liberal arts should not blind us to the fact that the universities came to perpetuate it. This sense of continuity is as striking as the innovations that accompanied its preservation. The entire faculty structure, especially of the northern ecclesiastical universities, was based on the belief that the seven liberal arts were the foundation of all higher knowledge. These had long been divided into two groups of the *trivium* (grammar, logic, and rhetoric) and the *quadrivium* (arithmetic, geometry, astronomy, and music) a division going back to Boethius, who had in turn taken it over from Varro (c. A.D. 400). It had underlain the educational reforms of Alcuin and his associates, under Charlemagne, and had been carried down into the revival of learning in the eleventh and twelfth centuries. Rudimentary and perfunctory as the teaching of many of these subjects had been, the subjects themselves were invested with a divine aura as providing the indispensable prerequisite to the study of theology, the summit of all knowledge. This attitude was still strong in the earlier thirteenth century, when many sought to defend them as traditionally understood. Various chancellors of the university at Paris continued during the first part of the thirteenth century to compare the seven liberal arts with seven gifts of the Holy Spirit.[1] They were not an end in themselves but the necessary preparation for theology, especially the *trivium*. "The sword of God is forged by grammar, sharpened by logic, and burnished by rhetoric, but only theology can use it." [1a] Nevertheless by this time such opinions had become merely pious hopes. Neither

[1] For examples see C. H. Haskins, *Studies in Mediaeval Culture* (reprint, New York, Ungar, 1960), 44 ff.
[1a] *Ibid.*, 46.

the *trivium* nor the *quadrivium* in its traditional meaning was any longer of relevance to the new learning. The sum of knowledge had changed. By the time we read the first syllabus for Paris in Robert de Courçon's statutes of 1215, dialectic and philosophy had virtually displaced all the other liberal arts. The change had come about during the second half of the twelfth century. It had been caused not by the university, but by the very conditions that had helped toward the organization of university studies: namely, new knowledge and new modes of expressing it and increasing pressure on higher education as preparation for a career. Let us consider these aspects in turn: the first bears on the nature of the courses in arts and the three higher faculties; the second on the training they entailed.

I THE BACKGROUND

So far as both Paris and Oxford were concerned, theology was queen, even though the number of students studying it was not so great as in the other subjects. Its pre-eminence at once accounts for the close convergence academically and intellectually of the two universities and for their position in Christendom. Theology not only stood alone in value, it was confined to a handful of universities in the thirteenth and fourteenth centuries, requiring a special license from the pope to be taught. There was a faculty of law, on the other hand, in every university, even it did not include both canon and civil law. The reasons for the discrepancy were doctrinal and practical. Theology remained the closely guarded preserve of the papacy which strictly controlled it. Law was the most lucrative of the professions and in universal demand. Although both canon and civil law were taught at Oxford, at Paris civil law was banned in 1219 by Honorius III, probably at the behest of Philip II, who did not want the incursion of Roman principles of government on the customary law of his kingdom.[2]

These factors had a direct bearing on the arts course, especially at Paris and Oxford. They meant the direct orientation of

[2] *Chart.*, I, No. 32; Rashdall, *Universities*, I, 322, 437.

the subjects traditionally comprising the seven liberal arts toward the subject matter of theology; they also meant the need to adapt its requirements to the demands of law. Thus, at one and the same time, arts as the point of departure for the higher subjects had to serve the speculative needs of theology and the practical needs of law and also medicine. Inevitably, therefore, those parts of the seven liberal arts that had no direct connection with these higher studies became excluded, or subordinated, to those that had. In effect this led to the enthronement at Paris and Oxford of dialectic (logic) and philosophy, at the expense of grammar, and the transformation of rhetoric into preparation for that branch of law concerned with the drawing up of letters and documents (*ars dictaminis*). Of the subjects of the *quadrivium* Oxford, always the more scientifically orientated university, prescribed books and periods of study specifically for each of them. But at Paris metaphysics was dominant.

This change away from grammar and rhetoric to logic and philosophy was the most striking development in the arts course during the thirteenth century. It dates back to the twelfth century, when the study of both logic and theology underwent something like a transformation. This was the result of two main developments. The first was the influx, steadily increasing in tempo as the twelfth century went on, of a mass of translations of the works of Aristotle, of Greek science, and of Arabian and Jewish thinkers and scientists. The second was the predominance of dialectical methods in the study of these works. The first development changed the content of knowledge, the second the mode of treating it. Although neither can be made the direct cause of the other, they interacted on one another. The rediscovery of the greater part of Aristotle's works by 1230, as well as introduction to the new world of Greek and Arabian science and thought, altered the terms of reference for both the validity of arguments and knowledge. At the same time the work of biblical exegesis in the cathedral schools of Laon and Paris and the law schools of Italy had led to the employment of the dialectical form of question and disputation that became universal in the universities. Gratian's *Decretum*—the basis of canon law—and Peter Lombard's *Book of Sentences*—after the Bible the textbook of the theological course at Paris and Oxford—were the supreme early examples of this method; each was written within a decade either side of the middle of the twelfth century (*Decretum,* c. 1140; *Sentences,* c. 1160), before the full effect of the new translations had been felt. Peter Abelard had been the supreme popular exponent of the same dialectical approach and did more than anyone else to give it currency especially in the schools of St. Geneviève. By then enough of Aristotle's logic was known to make dialectic an instrument of discussion that, properly used, could carry all before it. But there is ample evidence of its vogue in the eleventh century among masters like Anselm of Besate, Berengarius of Tours, and Roscelin. It is also to be found among members of the school of Chartres, above all Gilbert de la Porrée, where it was not directly related to biblical and exegetical problems in the manner of Laon and Paris, but part of the wider tradition of the seven liberal arts.

The rise to prominence of dialectic was thus the accompaniment of the renewal of learning and speculation in the eleventh and twelfth centuries rather than a sudden and disruptive incursion. Until the middle of the twelfth century it coexisted with the study of grammar and rhetoric as one of the dominant *trivium,* the subjects of the *quadrivium* being generally neglected save at Chartres; after that it increasingly overshadowed grammar, whereas rhetoric succumbed to the demands of law. Already in the second half of the twelfth century these changes were being lamented at Paris. By then Paris overshadowed the other French cathedral schools in theology and dialectic. It was the conjunction of these two disciplines that more than anything else accounts for the rise to dominance of dialectic among the liberal arts. Not only was the method of theology dialectical, with questions raised and solved by the juxtaposition of arguments *pro* and *contra;* but it was increasingly drawing on the new knowledge to support its tenets. By the last two decades of the century works of a new speculative kind were appearing—such, for example, as those by Alan of Lille and Hugh of St. Victor—which made use of metaphysics and natural knowledge within a Christian context. This was to be the broad highway of philosophy and theology for the next hundred years, attracting the greatest speculative minds of the epoch along it and to Paris.

The chief sufferer in the process was grammar; for whereas

rhetoric was adapted to the study of law, and the practical arts
of the *quadrivium* received new outlets in medicine and, at Oxford—and later Paris—metaphysics, grammar was effectively excluded from the two universities as an independent subject.
There was no room for it. At Orleans, where theology was not
one of the higher subjects, grammar continued to flourish into
the middle of the thirteenth century.[3] The strength of Paris as a
center of theology more than anything else accounts for the early
demise of grammar. Its conjunction with the early development
of the scholastic method of question and disputation directly
affected grammar itself, not at first in excluding it but in changing its content. There is ample evidence that many classical
authors were being studied in the last two decades of the twelfth
century: Virgil, Juvenal, Lucan, Horace, Ovid, Sallust, Cicero,
Livy, Seneca, and many others. But the death throes of the study
of grammar in the first decades of the new century can be seen
in its last representative at Paris, John of Garland.[4] He taught
grammar at the university until his death in 1252, writing a large
number of grammatical treatises; but they lacked the spirit of
John of Salisbury and the earlier grammarians. In works like the
Morale scolarium [5] he fought a losing rearguard action in defense of the classics. It is noteworthy that it was to Orleans that
he looked for support, not to his own university. The defeat of
grammar by arts at Paris is expressed clearly in the allegorical
French poem *The Battle of the Seven Arts,* written about 1250:
Grammar, from Orleans, the defender of the humanists and classical authors, is worsted in battle with Paris and goes into hid-
ing. The author, Henry of Andeli, consoles himself that grammar
will re-emerge when the next generation sees the folly of logic
and returns to the study of letters [6]—vain hope. The poem also
speaks of the competition from physicians and surgeons.

There was at the same time inherent in the medieval attitude
a marked strain of distaste for the profanity of classical litera-

---

[3] L. J. Paetow, *The Arts Course at the Mediaeval Universities* (Champaign,
Illinois, 1910), 13 ff. and *passim.*

[4] *Ibid.,* 16 ff.

[5] Edited by L. J. Paetow, in *Two Medieval Satires on the University of Paris*
(Berkeley, 1927).

[6] Paetow, *The Arts Course,* 19.

ture. How influential it was as must remain a matter of conjecture; but it was undeniably present at Paris.[7] More than anything else, however, as we can discern from John of Salisbury's *Metalogian*, there was the sheer growth of the current toward logic and speculative philosophy. Like so many such movements it defies any precise analysis. A point was reached at which the old was superseded, at which, in John of Salisbury's world, Cicero was rejected for Aristotle, just because men had become carried along by the momentum of the change. The rationale for the change was there in the new, exciting possibilities opened up by dialectical reasoning in theology and philosophy; but in embracing it not every man's motive is susceptible of rational explanation. The change did not happen without protest. Men like Peter of Blois and John of Salisbury, who were sympathetic to dialectic as well as being humanists, lamented the preoccupation with logic. Stephen, bishop of Tournai, complained of "beardless youths [who] sit in the chairs of the old professors . . . Neglecting the rules of the arts and discarding the books of good authority, with their sophistications they catch flies of senseless verbiage as in webs of spiders." [8] Alexander of Neckham (d. 1217) was another upholder of the seven liberal arts who shared this view of the Paris dialecticians and deplored the decline in the study of literature.

If the twelfth century marked the parting of the ways between the old and new learning, it also saw the coming of the new grammar.[9] Until that time the basis of its teaching had for centuries been the textbooks of Donatus and Priscian. Donatus, a Roman teacher of grammar (c. A.D. 350), had written two books, the *Ars minor*, a primary grammar, and a larger work the *Ars grammatica*, the third part of which, the *Barbarismus*, alone continued to be read widely. Priscian taught grammar at Constantinople (c. A.D. 500) and wrote a grammar in eighteen books

---

[7] *Ibid.*, 20–1. Paetow cites the examples of Peter Comestor, chancellor of Notre Dame in 1164, Alexander of Villedieu in 1199–1202 and Jacques of Vitry. But I doubt whether it qualifies as one of his five main causes for the decline of the classics.

[8] Translated by Paetow, *The Arts Course*, 31; *Chart.*, I, Introduction No. 48.

[9] For what follows see especially Paetow, *The Arts Course*, Chapter 2.

published from his lectures. Intended for advanced students, the first sixteen books dealing with the parts of speech were known as *Priscianus maior;* the last two as *Priscianus minor,* the subject of which is syntax. Together with other manuals, they had taught the rules of Latin through the earlier Middle Ages, with only minor adjustments to meet the needs of the monastic and cathedral schools. These books, however, were designed for those whose native language was Latin; they provided little in the way of general syntax. The new grammar books introduced syntax, adapting their explanations to the vulgar tongues of those learning them. One of the curious features of these new grammars, whose principles were taken over in the Renaissance and have survived beyond it, was the verse form in which many of them were composed. They began to displace Priscian because his work was in prose; to remedy the defect his work was versified.[10]

Beyond these developments within the subject, which introduced a much-needed flexibility into it, there was the impact of scholasticism, which transformed grammar into a new subject entirely. It did so by making it speculative, subjecting it to the rules of logic instead of style. In these circumstances Priscian was otiose. As the words of a gloss to one of the new textbooks put it, Priscian "gives many constructions without assigning reasons for them, relying solely on the authority of the ancient grammarians. Therefore he should not teach, because only those should teach who give reasons for what they say." [11]

Two new grammars especially were of the first importance: the *Doctrinale* of Alexander of Villedieu and the *Graecismus* of Eberhard of Béthune. These, written in 1199 and 1215 respectively, gradually influenced the study of grammar in the universities. Apart from John of Garland, however, who sought to replace them by his own *compendium,* only Roger Bacon seems to have concerned himself with reforming the study of grammar and extending it to oriental languages. As we shall see when we consider the textbooks for the arts courses at Paris and Oxford, grammar rated low in the syllabus, and its teaching was largely

[10] Paetow, *The Arts Course,* 35. Paetow draws attention to a *Priscian maior* in verse used at the Sorbonne.
[11] *Ibid.*

in the hands of separate grammar masters as well as grammar schools, largely outside the universities.[12] In contrast, at the southern French universities grammar occupied a separate faculty.

The position of rhetoric also changed, but in a different way from grammar.[13] In Roman times it had been the art of eloquence taught as a training for public life. It had little relevance to the semiprivate life of the earlier Middle Ages; it hardly entered into the activities of the church, where God's word eternally stood, or of lay society, where custom and rights were not susceptible to the arts of persuasion. In the universities logic came before eloquence. Consequently rhetoric as a formal discipline lacked a defined place, its functions frequently becoming merged with grammar as in the *Graecismus* of Eberhard of Béthune. By the thirteenth century at Paris it was losing its formal identity, as can be seen from the comparatively minor role assigned to its study in Robert de Courçon's statutes of 1215. Together with grammar, it continued as an adjunct to the main subject of philosophy. That, however, was not the sum of its influence. As we have already said it went into the training for letter writing, as the art of composition (*ars dictaminis*). It had always been associated with writing; but in Roman times cultivation of style in writing had been subordinated to that in speaking. In the Middle Ages there was far more scope for the written word. Throughout the earlier Middle Ages Roman law was taught as part of rhetoric. When law became independent, as one of the higher studies, the *dictamen* became in turn a part of law. As might be expected it first grew up into a separate branch of legal studies in Italy. Initially *dictamen* denoted the art of composition in prose or poetry; but in the Middle Ages it came to be associated with letter writing and the drawing up of legal documents. As both ecclesiastical and lay government developed, the need for trained notaries in the numerous chanceries enormously increased from the eleventh century; the Investiture Contest with its flood of documents provided a great stimulus at

[12] See R. W. Hunt, "Oxford Grammar Masters in the Middle Ages," *Oxford Studies Presented to Daniel Callus*, 163–193.

[13] For rhetoric and the *ars dictaminis* see Paetow, *The Arts Course*, Chapter 3; also Haskins, *Mediaeval Culture*, 170–192.

both the papal and imperial courts as well as among the developing cities of Lombardy and Tuscany. Inerius, the first great name in the school of Roman law at Bologna, wrote among his other works a treatise for notaries.[14] But it was Alberich, a monk of Monte Cassino,[15] who in the second half of the eleventh century put the subject on a permanent footing with the first proper manuals of instruction in his *Rationes dictandi*. As it developed subsequently more and more attention was given to illustrations taken from collections of real letters, thereby among other things preserving important documents for posterity. This element increased as the manuals sought to meet the practical needs of those training for the profession. Instruction also became more elaborate with the inclusion of the charter-hand, as distinct from book-hand, and the *cursus*—the rules for rhythmic phrasing—in the twelfth century.

In Italy Bologna was the great center of the *ars dictaminis,* and Boncompagno (c. 1165–c. 1240) its most celebrated exponent there. For him the *dictamen* was a subject in its own right, the art of arts.[16] Although not the first to teach it, he raised it to a new status; his numerous works treated the *ars dictaminis* as the art of rhetoric itself. But it did not long outlast him as an independent discipline, because its *raison d'être* was as an ancillary to the law. As the demands of the latter became more technical, so the manuals of letter writing became more practical, in the mid-thirteenth century turning into the separate faculty of the *ars notaria* at Bologna. Outside Italy the teaching of the *ars dictaminis* was widespread, although only at Orleans did it enjoy a comparable standing. It had no official recognition at Paris university, but there is good evidence for its practice there as well. In 1215 the chapter at Notre Dame demanded of its cathedral school teacher an ability to write letters from the chapter. Giraldus Cambrensis tells of learning meter and the *dictamen* there; John Garland wrote a textbook on it, the *Parisiana poetria*.[17] This shows that, although not taught at Paris as an individual discipline, letter writing formed part of grammar

[14] Paetow, *The Arts Course,* 72.
[15] For Alberich see Haskins, *Mediaeval Culture,* 171 ff.
[16] Paetow, *The Arts Course,* 75.
[17] For these examples, *ibid.,* 85–6.

and rhetoric. Hence for John it went together with the writing of verse. It also finds a place in the *Battle of the Seven Arts* as the "Lombard dame rhetoric," showing at least a contact with men trained in it in Italy, who may have taught it at Paris. Accordingly, although never receiving official recognition as part of the arts course, it must have been in existence, if only on an irregular basis. There are no traces of it at Oxford. But here, as at Paris, the large number of surviving formularies as well as collections of student letters leaves no doubt about the widespread importance of letter writing not only in public affairs but in matters of private life, which in the case of students centered on their recurrent requests for money from home.[18]

II THE TRANSLATIONS

We come now to the core of the arts course, logic and philosophy as they became based on Aristotle's works and interpretations of them. If institutionally the universities are the great new fact in the academic life of Christendom from the thirteenth century onward, intellectually it consists in the coming of the Greco-Arabian corpus of knowledge and ideas. The far-reaching doctrinal and theoretical ramifications of their advent will be considered in the following chapters. Here we are concerned with the educational effects on the structure of the arts, which were no less far-reaching. They transformed the physiognomy of the arts in two primary respects. The first was to enthrone dialectic or logic as the arbiter of discussion and demonstrative validity, reducing it to the rules of the syllogism. The second was to make Aristotle's works the mainstay of the study of arts, so that whereas the *trivium* was effectively reduced to Aristotle's logic the old divisions of the *quadrivium* became largely subsumed under his different scientific works; at Paris, where the influence of the *trivium* was greater than at Oxford, the separate subjects of the *quadrivium* were not even formally retained.

The impact of Aristotle was not confined to the arts faculty; the diffusion of his writings had already begun to change the

[18] On these student letters see the amusing first chapter in Haskins, *Mediaeval Culture*, 1–35.

modes of thinking of the twelfth century. But the arts faculty—
above all at Paris—became the stronghold of Aristotelianism
from the middle of the thirteenth century. It came to exist there
in such a strong solution that it threatened the very Christian
tenets which, in a more diluted form, it had helped to flower into
new systems. For that reason the trends in the arts faculties of
Paris and Oxford took on an ecumenical significance in the
1260's and 1270's, as we shall later see.

The translation of Aristotelian and Arabian works into Latin
began in earnest from about the first third of the twelfth century.[19] The two main regions from which the translations came
were Spain and Sicily. From Spain, especially at Toledo, came
the new learning of the Arabs in works on mathematics, astronomy, medicine, philosophy. But Sicily, North Africa, and Syria
were also important. In the first part of the thirteenth century
Frederick II's court was a center of Arab learning, and the important translator Michael Scot spent his later years there.
Arabian science and philosophy were themselves derived from
the Greek heritage the Arabs had taken over with the territories
of Syria and North Africa in the seventh and eighth centuries.
They translated and absorbed the works of Aristotle, Ptolemy,
Euclid, Hippocrates, Galen, and other Greek thinkers into their
own culture. This stimulated not only the growth of Arabian science and medicine but also the great philosophical systems of,
among others, Alfarabi, Avicenna and Averroes; such thinkers,
above all Avicenna, combined the pursuit of philosophy with science, medicine, or law.

In the twelfth century Spain began to attract a stream of in-
vestigators and translators from the Christian world: Adelard of
Bath, Plato of Tivoli, Robert of Chester, Hermann of Carinthia,
his pupil Rudolph of Bruges, and Gerard of Cremona. Within
Spain itself were Dominicus Gundisalvi (or Gundissalinus),
Hugh of Santalla, and the Jewish scholars Petrus Alphonsi, John
of Seville, and others. The translators originally worked from diverse places on each side of the Pyrenees; but Toledo became the
chief place of translation some time after 1126—largely because
of the patronage of archbishop Raymond of Toledo and bishop

---

[19] For these translations see Haskins, *Mediæval Science,* especially 1–19 for
those that refer to Spain.

Michael of Tarazona. The translations were mainly of works on astrology, astronomy, and mathematics. Adelard of Bath was earliest in the field; he also went to Syria and southern Italy. His translation of astronomical tables dates from 1126. He also translated Euclid's *Elements*. Between them, these translators made accessible to the Latin world a wealth of Greek and Arabian and Jewish works including Avicenna's *Metaphysics,* Avicebrol's *Fons vitae,* Alfarabi's classification of the sciences, Algazel's philosophy. Gerard of Cremona alone made seventy-one translations, among them Aristotle's *Posterior Analytics;* he died at Toledo in 1187.

In the earlier thirteenth century Alfred the Englishman, Michael Scot, and Hermann the German were the principal translators from the Arabic; they were all working in Spain during those years and were especially concerned with the writings of Aristotle and Averroes. They and other translators were often aided by Jewish interpreters, who turned the Arabic texts into Spanish for them to render into Latin.

The diffusion of the new knowledge that came from these translations is to be seen especially in England during the twelfth century because of the close connection with many of the translators who were English. Adelard of Bath was probably the most influential, though not the first to have utilized the Arabian science.[20] His translation of the astronomical tables was known by 1138; there are also from this time references to other Arabian works including those of Alkindi, as well as treatises on geometry, algebra, the astrolabe, numerous astronomical tables, and a philosophical work by Daniel of Morley, another of the translators, to explain the teaching of Toledo to John, bishop of Norwich, in the last quarter of the century. The writings of Alfred Sareshel, the Englishman, cited Aristotle's natural philosophy and metaphysics, which were to be the most important aspect of the new learning.

The formative part played by translations made direct from the Greek has come to be recognized.[21] Although it is true that the Arabian works were at first the main intermediaries between

---

[20] Ibid., 113 ff. Adelard was not the first; Walcher, prior of Malvern, began to utilize the new learning at the end of the eleventh century (*ibid.*).

[21] *Ibid.*, Chapters 8–11.

the learning of Greece and the Latin world, knowledge of the original Greek sources was as important. The main points of contact were Sicily and the Norman kingdom of southern Italy. Both had belonged to the Byzantine empire, contact with which and with the Greek language and customs was retained. There were Greek libraries, chiefly of theological and biblical writings in the monastery of St. Basil, and a more comprehensive one at Palermo. As the meeting point of the three cultures of Greek, Arabic, and Latin, Sicily offered a unique advantage for translation, each of the languages being used in royal charters and among officials at the king of Sicily's court. Translation was directly fostered for over a century by the Sicilian kings from Roger II in the earlier twelfth century to Manfred the last of the Hohenstaufen in the mid-thirteenth century. Under William I the two principal translators, Henry of Aristippus and Eugene the Emir, were both court officials. Aristippus, *inter alia,* was the first to translate Plato's *Meno* and *Phaedo,* and his version of Aristotle's *Meteorology,* fourth book, was used until the Renaissance. Scientific works of Euclid, Proclus, and Hero of Alexandria, as well as Ptolemy's *Almagest* (c. 1160) were also translated by the Sicilian school.

There were in addition to the translators at Palermo Latins who had learned their Greek at Constantinople, such as James of Venice, Burgundio of Pisa, and Moses of Bergamo, who were active in translation from the first third of the twelfth century. James of Venice, in rendering Aristotle's *Topics, Analytics,* and *Elenchi* into Latin from the Greek, could be said to have revived the "New Logic," as it was called, which came to be known sometime after 1121 and before about 1158. But in fact Boethius had translated these works in the fifth century and, despite contentions to the contrary, it seems that it was his versions that now began to be used. Certainly contemporaries regarded them as by Boethius, and why they should have lain dormant for so long is not clear.[22]

North of the Alps the works of the pseudo-Denys were brought to the abbey of St. Denis at Paris by a future abbot, William, and translated; the most important part of them was

---

[22] For a discussion of this problem, *ibid.,* Chapter 11, especially 230 ff.

done by John Sarrazin, one of the few Greek scholars in France.

By 1200 the main corpus of Aristotle's logical, physical, and metaphysical works had become accessible to the West in Latin versions. (The *Politics, Ethics, Rhetoric,* and *Economics* were not translated until the first third of the thirteenth century). These early versions from the Greek were strictly literal, to the extent of providing the means to reestablish the original Greek text from them. This was done deliberately to preserve the exact meaning. Ultimately, compared with the translations from the Arabic, they had authenticity on their side. In retrospect this search for the new learning—or rather the rediscovery of the old and the unknown—was one of the most remarkable episodes of the Middle Ages. It deserves to be put in the forefront of the historical events of the epoch, as far-reaching in its own more rarefied way as the silent colonization of the wastes in the eleventh and twelfth centuries; each was an indispensable condition for the subsequent flowering that followed it. If the growth of new systems of thought in the thirteenth century lacks the palpability of new towns and trade in the twelfth century, it represents no less a change in kind that came near to being a revolution. New concepts, new problems, new alignments, new modes of thinking were the outcome. If these were not the results merely of the autonomous working of ideas—which cannot be compartmentalized—they derived much of their force and impetus from the new knowledge that engendered them. The handful of scholars who sought out the heritage of ancient Greece and who penetrated to the novelties of Islam succeeded where the Crusades for all their spectacle utterly failed; they annexed the achievements of a more advanced society. The importance of their undertakings will be seen in what follows. By 1200 the most important works translated were: [23] the New Logic of Aristotle, namely the *Topics, Analytics,* and *Elenchi,* which, added to the Old Logic of the *Organon* (the *Categories* and *De interpretatione* together with the commentaries of Porphyry and Boethius) made his logical works complete;

[23] For a summary of the question, see F. van Steenberghen, *Siger de Brabant d'après ses oeuvres inédites,* vol. II (Louvain, 1942), Chapter 2, translated into English as *Aristotle in the West* (Louvain, 1955) without notes. I have used the translation here.

a large part of the works on nature (*libri naturales*) translated from the Arabic by Gerard of Cremona, including the
Physics, the *De generatione,* the *De caelo,* the first three books
of the *Meteors;* the fourth book of the *Meteors* and the *De
generatione,* both translated by Henricus Aristippus (d. 1162)
from the Greek; also from the Greek were the *Physics,* the *De
anima,* the *Parva naturalia,* Books 1 to 4 of the *Metaphysics* (the
Metaphysica vetustissima), and part of the *Nichomachean
Ethics* (*Ethica vetus*), both the latter so called to distinguish
them from subsequent translations.

In addition to the works of Aristotle there were the commentaries that had become inseparable from them. Porphyry's
Isagogue (an introduction to the *Categories,* which had stimulated the early disputes between the realists and nominalists of
the later eleventh and earlier twelfth centuries) translated by
Marius Victorinns (A.D. after 280–c. 365) and Boethius (c.
480–524 or 525); the commentaries of Boethius on the *Categories* and on *De interpretatione;* the commentary of Themistius
on the *Posterior Analytics.* There were also the important Arabic
works of Alfarabi and Avicenna on Aristotle, but perhaps most
momentous of all was the work called the *Liber de causis,* falsely
ascribed to Aristotle; this was in fact a commentary on extracts
from the *Institutio theologica* of Proclus, the third century Neoplatonist, and it did more than anything else to confound Aristotle with Neoplatonism. Translated by Gerard of Cremona from
Arabic into Latin before 1187, it brought to the West a confused—we might say polluted—image of Aristotle, which was
only clarified when Thomas Aquinas recognized Proclus's author-
ship from his confrère William of Moerbeke's translation of the
Institutio theologica.

The Neoplatonic element that accompanied the translation of
Aristotle was not confined to the *Liber de causis,* nor to the
translations made from the Arabic—mainly, as we saw, in Spain
—although these undoubtedly accentuated the influence of Neoplatonism on the Christian thinkers of the thirteenth and fourteenth centuries. There were also the works of the Neoplatonists
themselves and of Arabian and Jewish thinkers. Their combined
influence can hardly be exaggerated. It was not, of course, new.
St. Augustine had fashioned his Christian system from largely
Neoplatonic elements; the most original thinker of the early

Middle Ages, John the Scot Eriugena, had been almost a pure Neoplatonist; the speculation of St. Anselm and the members of the school of Chartres in the late eleventh and the twelfth centuries were similarly inspired by Neoplatonist notions. Aristotle did not come to have a formative part in the Christian outlook until the thirteenth century, and then primarily as an adjunct to a Neoplatonic framework. It is far from the truth to regard the Middle Ages as being under the dominance of Aristotle, and more true to say that until the time of Thomas Aquinas Aristotle supplied the mechanism but not the direction to Christian thought. His place was with technicalities of logic and nature; when he was taken further, into metaphysics, he became a threat to the accepted Christian values, in the way we shall examine in Chapter Four. Neoplatonism, on the other hand, could be regarded as the mainstay of a Christian outlook; it provided the means for harmonizing the created and the divine, the oneness of God and the multiplicity of creation. It is not accidental that all the main doctrinal condemnations principally concerned Aristotelian or naturalistic conceptions; and that the pre-Aristotelian age (before the translation of his physical and metaphysical works) was free from the doctrinal and intellectual discord that followed it.

Among the Neoplatonic works that became known to the West by 1200 were those by the pseudo-Dionysius, Apuleius, Chalcidius, and Macrobius, and the *Institutio theologica* of Proclus already mentioned. Of Plato's writings only the *Timaeus* in a fragment, the *Phaedo,* and the *Meno* were known, and those of the greatest of all the Neoplatonists, Plotinus, not at all. Beyond these overtly Neoplatonic and long-established authors, however, was the whole new corpus of Arabian writing. It was here, above all, in the vast assemblage of mathematics, natural science, astronomy, medicine, and philosophy that the strongest element for change is to be found. The formative works in the new thinking of the West during the first half of the thirteenth century were those of Avicenna and the Arabian and Jewish Neoplatonists like Alfarabi, Alkindi, Algazali, and Avicebrol. The most important of those translated by 1200 were Alkindi's *De intellectu,* Alfarabi's *De scientiis, De ortu scientiarum,* and *Distinction,* on Aristotle's natural works; Isaac Israeli's *Liber definitionum* and *De elementis;* Avicebrol's *Fons vitae* and large parts of Avicenna's encyclopedia of philosophy, the *Book of Healing* (*Aš-Sifa*), known to the Latin word as *Sufficientia;* as a paraphrase of Aristotle's philosophy the book was important in diffusing it during the twelfth century.

With such an array of books before them it is hardly surprising that both arts and philosophy should have taken on a new content in the thirteenth century, especially in their strongholds of Paris and later Oxford. Aristotle's logic provided the universal key to knowledge, and his scientific writings and metaphysics, vastly augmented, provided a comprehensive basis for a *Weltanschauung* that revolutionized previous views of the world. The speculations of Anselm, or of Chartrains like Bernard of Silvestris or Thierry of Chartres, the logic and epistemology of Abelard and Gilbert de la Porrée, for all their daring, had lacked a common metaphysical foundation. The concept of being had remained a purely ideal one; it had not gone beyond the contraposition of categories such as genus, species, essence, substance, relation; thus even Abelard, who had done more than anyone to distinguish between a word—man—and an individual being—Socrates or Plato—had not attempted to locate their connection in terms of actual being. Questions of the relation of a being's form or general nature—humanity—to the individual man or tree in which it was embodied were treated in purely logical and psychological terms of the difference between genus, species, and individual and the way the mind grasped them. The manner in which a form or nature inhered in a material subject was not broached. This had to await knowledge of the structure of being, together with the metaphysical categories of form and matter, potentiality and act, which sought to explain being. This only came with the Greco-Arabian translations. Accordingly, their diffusion among Christian thinkers introduced an entirely new scientific and metaphysical element into philosophy. If Aristotle's logic now became the arbiter of discussion, Greek, Arabian, and Neoplatonic ideas and science provided its content. In the face of them, the traditional categories of the *quadrivium* were submerged; even when, as at Oxford, the divisions were retained, the sciences they represented became transformed, just as most aspects of speculative theology were.

We shall leave initial doctrinal reactions to the new learning until the next chapter, and pass on to the second phase of its transmission to the West later in the thirteenth century. Before doing so, however, it is important to recognize that there were three prohibitions at Paris by 1231 of the works of Aristotle and his Arabian commentators on natural science and metaphysics and that these must be accounted partly responsible for the neglect of these subjects in favor of logic and ethics. The theological conservatism of the cathedral authorities at Paris held back the development of science and metaphysics there in striking contrast to Oxford, where Grosseteste fostered them; hence the different relations of Paris and Oxford to ecclesiastical authority had also important intellectual repercussions.

Among other things, these early condemnations cannot have included Averroes; the first quotations from his works do not occur until after 1230 in the *De universo* and *De anima* of William of Auvergne, composed probably between 1231 and 1236. From that time evidence of Averroes multiplies. It is found in the writings of Philip the Chancellor (of Paris, 1218–1236) between 1232 and 1236, and Albert the Great's *Summa de creaturis,* written in about 1240, which contains some eighty references to Averroes in the first two parts, including the commentaries on the *Metaphysics, De anima,* and *De caelo,* but none yet to the *Physics, De generatione,* or *De meteoris.* The accession of Averroes represents a new phase in the translations. It seems clear that Michael Scot translated the *De caelo* of Averroes after 1217, working on his subsequent translations at Frederick II's court in Sicily, between 1228 and 1235. Scot [24] had, as we saw earlier been at Toledo, where he is first mentioned in 1217 as having completed his translation of an Arabic work of Alpetragius on the sphere. After going to Bologna in 1220 he gained the favor of Pope Honorius III and Pope Gregory IX, who both sought benefices for him.[25] Shortly after 1230 Frederick II sent some of Scot's translations of Averroes to universities in Italy; they reached Paris at about the same date. Although Scot owed his main fame to his own writings on astrology—he was described as an astrologer to Frederick II—and Roger Bacon criti-

---

[24] See Haskins, *Mediaeval Science,* Chapter 13, "Michael Scot," 272–98.
[25] *Ibid.,* 274; *Chart.,* I, Nos. 48, 54.

cized him for his translations of Aristotle,[26] there can be little doubt that he had an important part in the transmission of Averroes's work; he translated at least his commentaries on *De caelo* and *De anima* and may also have rendered those on *De generatione*, Book 4 of *Meteors*, and the *Parva naturalia*.. Other of Averroes's works were translated by William of Luna who did the paraphrase of Porphyry's *Isagogue;* by Master Theodoric, who was responsible for the prologue to the commentary on the *Physics;* and especially by Hermann the German, from whom came the translation of the "Middle Commentaries" on the *Nichomachaen Ethics* in 1240 and on the *Poetics* in 1256. Thus between 1230 and 1240 the greater part of Averroes's works became known to the West.[27]

The effects of Averroes's advent were among the most far-reaching in the intellectual history of the thirteenth century. But they were not alone. The translation of his works was accompanied by others of the first importance. These included the *De animalibus* of Avicenna by Michael Scot at the court of Frederick II about 1230; the *Guide to the Perplexed* by Maimonides, at a comparable date; and the works of the pseudo-Dionysius and the *De orthodoxa fide* of John Damascene. At the same time the rendering of Averroes's works went together with the translation of the accompanying texts of Aristotle on which they were commentaries. In that way Aristotle's *De caelo, De anima, Nichomachaean Ethics, Rhetoric,* and *Poetics* were all translated by Michael Scot and Hermann the German in the process of translating Averroes on these books. Even more, however, came the translation of many of Aristotle's works directly from the Greek. These Greek translations had already begun in the twelfth century. But from the 1240's they received a new impetus. Between 1240 and 1243 Grosseteste undertook the first complete translation and revision of the *Nichomachaean Ethics* from the Greek; he also translated the first two books of *De caelo.*

[26] *Opus tertium* in *Opera_quaedam hactenus inedita,* J. S. Brewer, ed. (London, 1859), 91; Haskins, *Mediaeval Science,* 283.
[27] For the coming of Averroes, see above all, R. de Vaux, "La Première entrée d'Averroës chez les Latins," in *Revue des sciences philosophiques et théologiques,* **21** (1933), 193–245. He has shown that MS. Latin 15453 (Bibliothèque Nationale, Paris), dated 1243, contains the whole of Averroes's corpus (*ibid.,* 223).

The greatest of all the Greek translators, however, was William of Moerbeke, the Flemish Dominican (1215–86) who provided his confrère Thomas Aquinas with many of the first properly authenticated texts. His most important work was not in the field of science and metaphysics as heretofore, but in his scarcely less momentous translations of the *Politics* (1260) and the works of the Neoplatonists, including the *Institutio theologica* of Proclus. The coming of the *Politics* radically affected political thinking, even if it did not destroy the traditional assumptions, and the writings of Proclus, together with those of the pseudo-Dyonisius, helped to generate a new stream of speculative mysticism in the Rhineland that was to dominate much of the outlook of the fourteenth century. William also translated the commentaries of Simplicius and Alexander of Aphrodisias on different works of Aristotle's, that by Alexander on *De anima* in particular being of fundamental importance for theories of cognition.

These developments formed the context for the academic and intellectual life of Paris and Oxford. They did not take place suddenly, nor did they give rise to clear-cut reactions. On the contrary—and this is of key importance for an understanding of the epoch—they created a ferment. Far from the emergence of defined schools of thought, eclecticism reigned, certainly until the 1260's. Moreover, it is equally difficult to make a firm distinction between arts and theology, because so many of the same works bore upon both. Although it is true that the faculties of arts and theology had their own separate syllabuses and texts, many of the same thinkers went from one to the other, read Aristotle, Avicenna, Averroes, Boethius, and Ptolemy in common and were confronted by the same body of logic and metaphysics and later physics in their speculations, with what effects we shall consider in Chapter Four.

III THE REGULATION OF THE FACULTIES

The regulations of the faculties alone cannot provide more than a superficial glimpse of the intellectual content of the courses. This is especially true of theology, which was based on two books—the Bible and the *Sentences*. Only by reading the disputations and the commentaries on them is it possible to know the issues and doctrines that arose out of their study. Accordingly we must beware of locating the influence of the Greco-Arabian corpus too exclusively in the faculty of arts. Although it is possible to learn from the syllabus which texts were being read, it does not of itself tell us the use to which they were being put. The connection will only operate the other way: a knowledge of which books were current can enable us to know when certain influences could have been at work, but not whether they were nor with what effect.

Arts. The first regulations of the arts faculty were drawn up, together with those for the faculty of theology, by Robert de Courçon in 1215.[28] We have had occasion to refer to them before in this and other contexts. The main requirements as they affected the study of arts concerned the ages for the different grades, the conditions to be observed, and the books to be read. Twenty-one years was the minimum age at which a man could begin to lecture in arts, and six years the minimum period of study. We also meet one of the distinctive features of the system at both Paris and Oxford—the obligation, when licensed and admitted as master by the other masters (inception), to remain teaching in the faculty for at least two years afterward. This period of necessary regency was not peculiar to arts, for it was the means of maintaining a supply of teachers; it was, however, particularly important in arts as the most numerous and fluid of the faculties. For the majority the arts were mainly a stepping stone either to a higher faculty or to a career in the world. Unlike the faculty of theology, the chairs were not limited; the danger was from demand for teaching in arts outrunning supply. The master in order to teach needed only to hire a room in a school in the Rue du Fouarre or elsewhere. It is probable that the two-year period of teaching was not strictly enforced, certainly not after the reforms of Cardinal d'Estouteville at Paris in 1452.[29] The books to be lectured on, as we have just said, do not give any indication of the state of studies within the different arts subjects save for confirming the predominance of dialectic by 1215. They comprised the New and Old Logic of Aristotle, both parts of

[28] *Chart.*, I, No. 11; Thorndike, *op. cit.*, No. 15.
[29] Rashdall, I, 465.

Priscian's grammar (*Priscianus maior* and *Priscianus minor*), the third book of *Donatus's Ars maior* (the *Barbarismus*), the first four books of Aristotle's *Ethics,* and the fourth book of the *Topics.* In addition, moreover, to these prescribed texts, the papal legate also renewed the ban of 1210 on Aristotle's metaphysical and physical works, together with any summaries on them, as well as those of David of Dinant (condemned for pantheism in 1210) and the "heretic, Amaury or Maurice of Spain." [30] Which Arab thinker was meant by the last allusion is not clear. Whoever it was, what is significant in this list is, first, the preponderance of Aristotle's logic in the complete works; second, the subsidiary place of grammar, which is reduced to compulsory lectures on only one part of Priscian, and the even smaller place of rhetoric; third, the complete absence of any of the practical sciences of the *quadrivium;* and finally the attempt to exclude Aristotelian and Arabian metaphysics and science from the course. We are thereby shown the extent to which the arts faculty had departed from an education based on the seven liberal arts while at the same time drawing back from the new learning. As it stands, the document is hardly an advertisement for the advanced thinking of university; it did not, however, last for much more than a decade if it was ever wholly effective; for Gregory IX, after repeating the ban on Aristotle's works in 1228 and with qualifications in *Parens scientiarum,* in 1231 ordered a commission of French ecclesiastics to expurgate them, "so that, what are suspect being removed, the rest may be studied without delay and without offence." [31] The next known regulations, for the bachelors of the English-German nation at Paris in 1252, evinces little change in the books prescribed. We should be hard put to tell from them that virtually the whole of Aristotle's works, except for the *Politics* and *Economics,* as well as a large part of Avicenna's and Averroes's, were now known in the West, together with a vast body of Greek and Arabian science. The only additions to the list of 1215 are the *Six Principles* of Gilbert de la Porrée (a logical treatise on the first six of Aristotle's ten *Categories*), from the twelfth century, whereas, as a concession to

---

[30] *Chart.,* I, No. 20.
[31] *Chart.,* I, No. 87; Thorndike, *op. cit.,* No. 20.

the problems of psychology, *De anima* was to have been heard
in lectures once. This was, however, the first step along a path
that led ultimately to the great condemnations of 1277; for it was
in Averroes's commentary on *De anima* that his theory of a single intellect for all men was posited: a view that became the
hallmark of so-called Latin Averroism.

It is only three years later, in 1255, that the full impact of the
new learning is officially revealed in the syllabus of the arts faculty. There have now been added Aristotle's *Physics, Metaphysics, De animalibus, De caelo et mundo,* the first book of *Meteors,
De generatione, De sensu et senato, De somno et vigilia, De
memoria et reminiscentia, De morte et vita,* and the pseudo-Aristotelian *Liber de causis* (by Proclus), *De differentia spiritus et
animae* (by Costa ben Lucca), and *De plantis.* These works represented the full complement of Aristotle's then known works together with those ascribed to him, above all the *Liber de causis.*
Their study was now integrated into a strict timetable which, it
is true, did not allow more than a few weeks for the reading of
many of them. But the important thing was that Aristotle had
now effectively become the arts course; the arts course was now
a training ground not only in Aristotle's logic (together with the
commentaries of Boethius, Porphyry, and Gilbert de la Porrée)
but in pagan philosophy. This more than anything else accounts
for the doctrinal conflicts that culminated in 1277; for it now
meant, as we shall see clearly in Chapter Four, that philosophy
had lost its propedeutic character. Aristotle and Proclus and the
Arabian systems based on them had no connection with Christian conceptions; they did not represent doctrinally neutral facts
like the principles of grammar or indeed logic. They were a self-
contained and potentially antithetic world view which at best
was independent of Christianity and at worst challeneged it.
One was inherent in the other, as 1277 proved.

How, we may ask, did this seeming transformation come
about in the curriculum of the arts course in a mere three years?
The answer seems to be that it was not so sudden. To begin with
there is the tenor of the faculty's decree, which makes no attempt to explain or justify its new regulations but treats them as
merely designed to tighten up lecture discipline and time-keep-
ing; the list of works is introduced not as an announcement of

prescribed texts but by the words "that all and single masters of our faculty in future shall be required to finish the texts which they have begun on the feast of St. Remy [October 1] at the times below noted, not before." Too much should not be made of this casualness; it might have been a deliberate attempt to create a *fait accompli;* but it cannot at the same time be entirely discounted, especially when there was no reaction from the pope or ecclesiastical authorities.

There are other indications, too, that the 1255 syllabus was not a bolt from the blue. A Barcelona manuscript discovered in 1927 by the late Martin Grabmann [32] contains an anonymous guide to the courses in the arts faculty, written probably between 1230 and 1245. Designed as a help to passing examinations it gives the order of topics and the most common questions asked by the examiners. There is a digest of each of the textbooks together with model answers. The handbook begins with a general introduction to the subject of philosophy, the author adopting the customary division, dating from Boethius, between rational, natural, and moral philosophy. More important are the textbooks listed. There are the *Liber de causis,* here treated as the third part of Aristotle's *Metaphysics;* Ptolemy's *Almagest,* though it is not clear whether the writer thinks them both to be by separate authors; and Plato's *Timaeus* and Boethius's *Consolation of Philosophy* included under ethics. The *Physics* of Aristotle are also there. Neither they nor the *Metaphysics,* however, are treated as examination texts. The chapters on Logic, Ethics, and Grammar (although only about one-third the length of those devoted to Logic) are analyzed textually and accompanied by examination questions, but the *Physics* and *Metaphysics* are treated only in general terms. This shows indisputably that they were not officially taught in the arts faculty at the time, but that they were in circulation, if only clandestinely. A knowledge of them was considered inseparable from the arts course. Being wise after the event, we may also surmise that they were the more exciting, if

[32] M. Grabmann, "Eine für Examinazwecke abgefasste Questionensammlung der Pariser Artistenfacultät aus der ersten Hälfte des 13 Jahrhunderts," *Revue néoscolastique,* **36** (1934), 211–29; "I divieti ecclesiastici di Aristotele sotto Innocenzo III e Gregorio IX," in *Miscellanea historiae pontificae,* V, No. 7. (Rome, 1941), 113–127.

not immediately more useful, for being forbidden. The document also reveals one other telling fact about the influence of Aristotelian philosophy. Study of the *Ethics*, which as we saw had been prescribed by the 1215 statutes, had already led to the contraposing of natural and supernatural standards. One of the questions raised was whether the body was made to enjoy happiness in the way that the soul was. The reply was that although from a theological standpoint the body enjoyed the same felicity as the soul through its resurrection, this was by means of a miracle that had no bearing on natural laws.[33] It therefore had nothing to do with philosophers. Here, thirty or more years before Siger of Brabant's condemnation, autonomy was already being claimed for philosophy, even when, as in this instance, it meant ignoring an article of Christian faith.

When we turn to Oxford over the corresponding period we meet a very different situation. Here, mainly owing to Grosseteste's influence, the *libri naturales* were early accepted and never had to go underground. This led to two differences of the first order from Paris. The first, and more long-term difference, was in the emergence of the foremost school of science north of the Alps in the thirteenth and much of the fourteenth centuries. The fact that it owed more to Grosseteste than to Aristotle, and through Grossetese remained closer to traditional Augustinian philosophy on the one hand and Neoplatonic mathematical speculation on the other, is further evidence of the comprehensiveness of the new learning. Aristotle was but one element, if the most formative philosophically; but there were other lines of development in the Greek and Arabian scientific writings that did not entail a clash with Christian belief and that could lead to the most fertile intellectual results, as we shall consider in Chapter Five. The other difference was that the banning of the *libri naturales* at Paris helped to accentuate the predominantly logical and later philosophical bent of the arts faculty at Paris. Not until the age of Buridan in the middle of the fourteenth century did a scientific school at Paris grow up to rival that at Oxford; but

[33] M. Grabmann, "Der lateinische Averroismus des 13 Jahrhunderts und seine Stellung zur christlichen Weltanschauung," *Sitzungsberichte der Bayerischen Akademie der Wissenschaften Philos-Hist. Klasse* (Munich, 1931) 76.

even so, it never, save for Nicholas Oresme, had the same mathematical bent. The question on the *Ethics* we have just instanced indicates how early and deep-seated the speculative tradition at Paris was. It went back to Abelard and the logicians who followed him. We must not therefore exaggerate the effect of the decrees against Aristotle's scientific works; their important consequence was in helping to harden the traditional trend by feeding speculation into logical and philosophical, rather than scientific, channels.

Tradition also played an important part in Oxford's cultivation of mathematics and optics in the thirteenth and fourteenth centuries. In England, as we have earlier mentioned, knowledge of Arabian scientific writings is evident from the 1120's. It came from a line of English translators and scientists that included Adelard of Bath, Alfred of Sareshel, Daniel Morley, Roger of Hereford, Robert Cricklade, and William of Chester.[34] Cricklade was associated with Oxford as prior of St. Frideswide's from before 1141 until about 1172, and probably came into direct contact with the scholars at Oxford.[35] Roger of Hereford wrote during the last quarter of the twelfth century a series of scientific treatises that showed acquaintance with a wide range of Aristotle's scientific and metaphysical works.[36] His *De motu cordis* was dedicated to Alexander of Neckham, an English master who studied and taught arts at Paris also in the last quarter of the century; he later returned to England as a canon at Cirencester, becoming prior in 1213 until his death in 1217. He is credited with being the author of an anonymous list of books dating from his time at Paris, probably in the 1180's.[37] It is interesting for the range of knowledge it displays of Greek and Arabic works. Among them, in addition to the standard texts of the Old and New Logic and the textbooks on grammar, were Aristotle's *Metaphysics, De anima,* and *De generatione at corruptione.* There are a number of Arabian books on medicine and Ptolemy's *Canons* and a compendium by Alfragenus on astronomy. But the list is weighted heavily in favor of the traditional subjects of the *tri-*

Haskins, *Mediaeval Science,* Chapter 6.

Rashdall, III, 28.

Haskins, *Mediaeval Science,* 129.

Ibid., 365. Haskins devotes Chapter 18 to a study of it.

vium, with a wide selection of classical authors including Cicero, Livy, Lucan, Statius, Martial, Petronius, Suetonius, Juvenal, Horace, and Ovid. How genuine or representative this learning was we do not know; and it is always dangerous to read the mores of an age or society into one fortuitous survival. What it does show is the comparative sparseness of scientific works, especially Arabian astronomy, studied at Paris as compared with England during the same period. The list is in many ways more reminiscent of the twelfth century humanism of Chartres than of Paris or the threshold of scholasticism.[38]

The early development of Aristotelian and scientific studies at Oxford however is no more clear than that of the university.[39] Roger Bacon credited Edmund of Abingdon with being the first officially to study the *Sophistici elenchi* there, and a Master Hugh with having made the first commentary on the *Analytics*.[40] This would put them in the first decade of the thirteenth century, a little before Grosseteste's commentaries on the *Organon*. From John of Garland we learn that his teacher John of London had taught and "read" (i.e., studied) the "philosophers" at Oxford, which must have been before the 1209 dispersion from Oxford. John Blund, a contemporary of St. Edmund, was a master in the arts, first at Paris in about 1205 and later at Oxford from about 1207 to 1209. From a description of him by Henry of Avranches in 1232 he would seem to have been one of the first to have commented at Paris on Aristotle's scientific works, which he then introduced into Oxford.[41] In his treatise on the *De anima*, Blund, although citing Plato, Cicero, St. Augustine, Boethius, and John of Damascene, drew principally on Algazel and especially Avicenna, whom he used in conjunction with Aristotle. Averroes was not mentioned. Blund later taught theology from 1229 until his death in 1248.

[38] *Ibid.*, 370, for a comparison with the *Heptateuchon* of Thierry of Chartres.

[39] For what follows see D. A. Callus, "The Introduction of Aristotelian Learning to Oxford," *Proceedings of the British Academy,* **29** (1943) 229–81.

[40] *Ibid.*, 238–9, citing Bacon, *Compendium studii theologii*, H. Rashdall, ed (Aberdeen, British Society for Franciscan Studies, 1911), 34.

[41] *Ibid.*, 242: *Primus Aristotelis satagene perquirere libros,/Quando recente eos Arabes misere Latinis.*

By far the most important influence, however, was Grosseteste; to his career in the faculty of arts belong his glosses on the *Sophistici elenchi* and the *Posterior Analytics,* made during the first decade of the thirteenth century before he migrated to Paris, together with Edmund of Abingdon, John Blund, and other masters, in the dispersion from Oxford.[42] The commentary on the *Posterior Analytics* was of seminal importance in Grosseteste's later work, as we shall consider in Chapter Five. It was also of influence on studies at Oxford and at Paris. He also wrote a brief introduction in praise of the seven liberal arts; this may well have helped their establishment in the Oxford curriculum, of which they remained—formally at least—the basis. Here, too, Grosseteste's early tendencies were borne out by his subsequent career as a scholar. He upheld the study of grammar and languages and adhered to the older expository methods rather than to dialectical discussion, just as he seriously studied the sciences —although in his early treatise he strangely neglected mathematics.[43] Grosseteste described the seven arts as attendants (*ministrae*) on the philosophy of nature and ethics. Grammar and logic provided true reasoning; rhetoric by stirring the emotions helped moral philosophy in the task of desiring the good and rejecting evil; music and astronomy ministered to the philosophy of nature. Music Grosseteste considered to be a universal art; it was concerned at once with sounds, the harmony of all celestial and noncelestial beings, and with time and movement; hence with the inner structure of things. Astronomy was necessary for nearly all activities involving nature, whether they concerned vegetables or minerals or the curing of diseases.[44] The breadth of Grosseteste's sympathies here fits Gerald Cambrensis's description at this time of his remarkable learning, "built upon the sure foundations of the liberal arts and an abundant knowledge of literature." [45] These were qualities Grosseteste imparted to his successors at Oxford.

---

[42] D. A. Callus, "Robert Grosseteste as Scholar," in *Robert Grosseteste: Scholar and Bishop,* D. A. Callus, ed. (Oxford, Oxford University Press, 1955), 12 ff.
[43] *Ibid.,* 18.
[44] *Ibid.,* 16–17.
[45] *Ibid.,* 18.

Institutionally they can be seen in the preservation of the seven categories in the arts course. Thus the regulations of 1431 for the license and inception list the prescribed books under their headings.[46] They were as follows.

For Grammar:	*Priscian Major* or *minor*—for one term.
Rhetoric:	Aristotle's *Rhetoric*, or Book 4 of Boethius's *Topics*, or Cicero, or Ovid's *Metamorphoses*, or Virgil—three terms,
Logic:	*Peri Hermeneias*, or Books 1–3 of Boethius's *Topics*, or Aristotle's *Prior Analytics* or *Topics*—three terms.
Arithmetic and Music:	Boethius—one term each.
Astronomy:	Aristotle's *Physics*, or *De caelo*, or *De proprietatibus elementorum*, or *Meteors*, or *De vegetabilibus et plantis*, or *De anima*, or *De animalibus*, or one of the other small books of Aristotle—three terms.
Moral Philosophy:	Aristotle's *Ethics*, or *Economics* or *Politics*—three terms.
Metaphysics:	Aristotle's *Metaphysics*—two terms.

Coming so long after the formative years of the first half of the thirteenth century, these books tell us nothing about the sequence in which they came to be included. They can therefore throw no additional light on the formation of the arts course at Oxford. From the circumstantial evidence we have of its origins and of contemporary events at Paris, it seems almost certain that the *libri naturales* of Aristotle, as well as Arabian scientific writings, after reaching Oxford in the last decades of the twelfth century, were thenceforth openly read. There was no ban on them as at Paris. This, together with the concomitants of an established scientific tradition in England in the twelfth century and the influence of Grosseteste, led Oxford to an outlook that, as we shall see, diverged from that of Paris in important aspects. On their respective examination requirements and degrees, however, the two universities came very close to one another as we now consider.

---

[46] Gibson, *Statuta antiqua*, XCIV–V, 234–5.

The first regulations for the arts faculty at Paris, by Robert de Courçon, prescribed nothing beyond requirements of age and reading. The first mention of what can be called degrees comes in the statutes of the English-German nation in 1252. Compared with those of 1215 they are remarkable for their fullness; the contrast is between a still inchoate faculty structure and a highly elaborate one. In 1215 there seem to have been no intermediate grades or tests before examination for the license in either of the two faculties of arts or theology for which the papal legate made provision. The later key words [47] "responsion," "determination," "inception," "bachelor," and the kind of exercises to be undergone are all missing. Nevertheless the 1215 statute suggests them in a rudimentary form. Thus after five of the eight years of study necessary for the license in theology, the student can give public lectures, a division that corresponds to the baccalaureate later; in the arts faculty we are told of the *principia* and responsions and oppositions, which indicate the determinations or disputes that a bachelor had subsequently to undergo. In both cases, therefore, we see implicit the basic division in the course of study at a medieval university between the initial period when a student had solely to study and the second period when he was able to teach under supervision. This corresponded closely to the general notion of apprenticeship gradually leading to an intermediate phase of journeyman or pupil-teacher, still under a master. When successfully completed it led to the granting of the license that made the graduate eligible to be received into the association of masters—inception. Historically, as Boyce has pointed out,[48] the license came first, followed by the inception (the mastership) and the determination (the bachelorship) with its preliminary examination (the responsions). These all become enunciated for the first time in the 1252 statutes for the English-German nation and were formally adopted by the arts faculty in 1275—though they had by then long been practiced.

Before considering the requirements for each of these grades or degrees it is important to know how they evolved. Taking them in their chronological order again, originally the license had been the one requisite for teaching. It had, in the cathedral

[47] For the more technical terms see Note (pp. 182–4) on Lectures, etc., at the end of this chapter.
[48] Boyce, *The English-German Nation*, 75.

schools, been granted by the chancellor to any clerk considered worthy of it. It was therefore for a directly practical end; it entailed no formal authorization from a recognized body. The multiplication of masters, however, created a professional association evolving its own rules and regulations, at first by custom. At Paris, as we have abundantly seen, the masters took issue with the chancellor over the granting of the license, the conditions for which they sought to control. But beyond the masters' claim to have the right of examining and passing or failing candidates, they had a further power of admitting or refusing entry to their association. Hence, as we saw, they fought for recognition—given by Innocent III—of their claim to be able to expel and readmit masters to their guilds. In consequence, even when the license had been bestowed and the recipient had thereby graduated with the right to teach, he was still not a master. He had yet to be formally accepted by the masters as one of them; this took place through the ceremony of inception. Inception—induction into the masters' guild—therefore followed the license, the latter coming to signify a candidate's eligibility for the mastership. At both Paris and Oxford from the middle of the thirteenth century it entailed a series of exercises by the candidate for admission—the inceptor—which we shall discuss shortly; when they had been performed he was then formally admitted to the mastership, signified by having a cap put on his head (the symbol of his master's status) and receiving the insignia of his office, a ring and an open book. He then had to deliver a formal lecture and inaugurate a disputation, which he followed by giving a celebration in a tavern. Together with the cost of gifts and fees, expenses for inception were heavy and many inceptors never incepted or delayed doing so; William of Ockham—the Venerable Inceptor—is the most eminent of them, although, as a friar, in his case the reasons were not financial. License and inception thus expressed a division of powers between the chancellor and masters: one was more than the formal complement of the other; it meant recognition by a separate body. Inception probably went back to the earliest days of the masters' gatherings when they were entirely unofficial and customary bodies. It became recognized at Paris during the first two decades of the thirteenth century in their struggle with the chancellor.

Determination first emerges as a definite examination in the 1252 statutes of the English-German nation at Paris.[49] As set out there it entailed the delegation by the proctor of two electors who then appointed three examiners; they were to swear to act impartially toward both the candidates and the masters who presented them. Before they could be admitted to determine—dispute over the whole period of Lent (i.e., for forty days)—they had to satisfy the examiner that they had fulfilled an extensive series of requirement. These were of two kinds: first, a minimum age of twenty years and a minimum attendance at courses in the arts faculty of at least four years (or five years if the candidate had come from another university). Second, the academic attainments included having listened to lectures on the prescribed books for the prescribed periods: the Old Logic, twice in a course of ordinary lectures (*ordinarie,* which were given by masters and involved exegesis and the raising of philosophical problems) and once in cursory lectures (*cursorie,* usually given by bachelors and confined to a purely literal running commentary of the text); Gilbert de la Porrée's *Six Principles* at least once in ordinary lectures and once cursorily; the New Logic, twice in ordinary lectures and at least once cursorily, or otherwise three times ordinarily; *Priscian minor* and the *Barbarismus* twice ordinarily and at least once cursorily; *Priscian maior* once cursorily; and Aristotles *De anima,* to be heard once. The preponderance of Aristotelian logic has already been noticed. Of more immediate interest here is that the candidate for determination had to swear that he had diligently attended the disputations of the master for two years and had himself taken part in sophistical exercises (*sophismata*) in class during the same period. Any of these conditions could be waived—and were for many students, according to Robert de Sorbon in his *De conscientia,* certainly when it came to the chancellor's examination [50] —if the examiners regarded a candidate as sufficiently well qualified to be admitted. Another of the nation's statutes at this time made the passing of a preliminary examination to determining [51]

[49] *Chart.,* I, No. 201.
[50] *De Conscientia et de tribus dietis,* F. Chambon, ed. (Paris, 1903), 2; Haskins, *Mediaeval Culture,* 51–2.
[51] *Chart.,* I, No. 202.

—responsions—compulsory. It consisted in responding to questions put by the master who presided in the exercises prescribed by the statutes. The candidate had thereafter to participate in public disputations under a master and also in the determinations of the bachelors—during Lent—as a respondent (*respondens*). By the faculty of arts statutes of 1275 [52] this period of disputation had to be completed by the Christmas before the Lent in which determination took place. Both the candidate and his master had to swear on oath that he had fulfilled these requirements; only after the examiners had considered and sanctioned his application at a preliminary examination of his credentials could he then go through to the determination. It was not until that stage had been reached that he was in a position to begin the examination proper. Failure on the part of master or bachelor in any of the intermediate stages meant ineligibility.

Determination itself consisted in a series of disputations. By the 1252 English-German nation's statutes they were to begin immediately after the first week in Lent (*Brandones*) and continue until the middle of Lent, unless a special dispensation was granted. But by 1275 the faculty of arts had increased their duration to the whole of Lent, unless a substitute was employed.[53] They normally took place in the schools in the Rue du Fouarre, one of the provisions in 1252 being that a determiner should swear that he had the schools of a regent master in which to determine; normally he determined under his own regent master. The fees for the examinations were to be collected by one of the appointed examiners. After determination had been completed the student had, as one of the conditions, to continue to respond in disputations for a further year.[54] The reason was that it did not in itself signify the end of the course or the award of the license. Many students indeed went down after determination, having received a written testimonial from the nation sanctioned in full congregation and authenticated with its seal. It was not

[52] *Ibid.*, No. 461.
[53] *Ibid.*
[54] *Ibid.*, No. 201. "*Item per annum integrum a principio unius quadragesime ad principium alterius det fidem quod responderit de questione*" (p. 228).

the same as a diploma but had to be initiated by petition from the determiner.[55]

This raises the problem of his status immediately before, during, and after determination: at what stage did he become a bachelor and what if any were the different grades of bachelor in the arts faculty? There, unlike the theological faculty, the distinctions were never made precise. The statutes of 1252, 1275, and 1279 all use the word bachelor for the student who determines. Rashdall defined the bachelor as one who had "been duly admitted to determine and to give cursory lectures"; he went on to say that "Determination thus played the same part in the admission to this new degree that inception played at the final stage of his career." [56] Boyce commented on this passage to stress that "the word *bachellarius* does not mean one who has yet received a degree but rather one who was about to present himself for the examination which would, if successfully completed, make him a bachelor in the technical sense"; [57] he proceeded to draw attention to the change in terminology that came in the mid-fifteenth century: whereas previously those who had passed the determination were called determiners they now became bachelors. Rashdall's editor complicated this already somewhat exiguous additional evidence by a further piece taken from a document of 1508. Both of these appear to have little to do with the real issue, in my view correctly stated by Rashdall, that a man admitted to determine—that is, one who had passed the preliminary scrutiny of his credentials including his performance in responsions—became a bachelor in status. By that test he had been judged sufficiently advanced to present himself for the examination (determination) that led on to the license. Sometime after having passed the determination—perhaps when he had fulfilled the obligation of lecturing cursorily for a year—he became a full-fledged bachelor. These two stages within the same grade correspond to the distinction we meet in the 1275 statutes of the arts faculty between bachelors and licensed bachelors. They are both allowed to lecture *cursorie* (i.e., literally or text-

---

[55] Boyce, *op. cit.*, 95–6.
[56] Rashdall, III, 454.
[57] Boyce, *op. cit.*, 80, note.

ually) only if they have first, *inter alia,* taken an oath of obedience to the rector and proctors.[58] The division can only be between those who have determined and those who have not. This is supported first by the wording of the 1252 statutes which throughout call the candidate, who has to undergo the preliminary tests of age, reading, and responsions, bachelor. His acceptance depended as much on age and standing as on performance, which in any event would be put to the test in the determination. The books prescribed applied to the course as a whole, not—as the editor of Rashdall's first volume believed— merely to the preliminary examination. Having satisfied the examiners first that he had read them, the candidate then in the course of determining had to show that he understood them well enough to dispute on questions they raised. The student permitted to do so had reached a higher stage at which he was no longer a mere tyro.

Bachelors are first mentioned at Paris in a bull of Gregory IX in 1231, which indicates that they were lecturing in the theological faculty.[59] They are first mentioned in connection with the arts faculty in 1245, when Innocent IV prescribed the hours and days for cursory lectures there. Their practice of lecturing was therefore well established by the middle of the thirteenth century, and must be accounted one of the attributes of a bachelor. The fact that it was permitted for both licensed and unlicensed bachelors by the 1275 statutes suggests that it initially denoted a degree of maturity and attainment before it came to be associated with a specific examination. This is confirmed by the fact that we hear of bachelors lecturing at least twenty years before we hear of the determination. By 1252 what had originally been a customary division became a regulation. But enough remained of the earlier honorific conception of the bachelorship as a status—a status not confined to universities—which ultimately led to differentiation into licensed and unlicensed bachelors by 1275. These gradations have their counterpart, as we shall see, in the theological faculty.

At Oxford there were the same preliminary requirements for

[58] *Chart.,* I, No. 461, p. 531.
[59] *Ibid.,* No. 71.

determination.[60] The student had to be on the roll of a regent master, from whom he heard at least one ordinary lecture every day. After three years, the last of which was spent in disputation and sophistical exercises, as a sophister, the student had to undergo responsions. In the following Lent he had to respond to questions with a determining bachelor, becoming then a questionist. The latter was a status as I have suggested it was at Paris. In these four years the student was supposed to have heard all the books of the Old Logic and the New Logic, the *Prior Analytics*, the *Topics* and *Elenchi* twice, and the *Posterior Analytics* at least once. Those who had not publicly responded in sophistical exercises (*de sophismatibus*) had to hear the *Posterior Analytics* an additional time. In grammar they were to have heard the *De constructionibus* of Priscian twice and the *Barbarismus* of Donatus once. In natural science Aristotle's *Physics*, *De anima*, and *De generatione et corruptione* were the set books. Candidates for determination, having applied for admission to the examination, had to appear before four regent masters who had "to satisfy themselves as to their knowledge and morals." [61] When doubt arose they had to refer to the body of the regents. Those who passed this scrutiny were admitted by the chancellor in the presence of the proctors to lecture on any prescribed book in the arts faculty. Determination, which took place in Lent in the school of a regent master, began at latest on the Monday of the second week in Lent and continued to within three days of the end of the masters' lectures before the Easter vacation (*cessatio magistrorum*); the determiners were to engage in logical disputations whenever possible except for the first and last Fridays.[62] Celebrations and potations were to be kept to a minimum. Four masters were to admit those determiners who had proved themselves suitable; and the chancellor was only to license those approved by the examiners.

There was a fundamental similarity between the requirements

---

[60] Gibson, *Statuta, antiqua*, lxxxviii–xci, 24–30.

[61] *Ibid.*, XC, 28.

[62] *Ibid.*, 27–8. The editor speaks of these exercises as "immediately preceding determination" (*ibid.*, XCI), but I find nothing to support this in the passage cited, nor does it seem to make sense, because it was during this very period that the determiner was disputing.

at Oxford and Paris, but it must not be pressed too far because the first full statutes at Oxford date from the first decade of the fifteenth century. This no doubt accounts for their greater definition especially over the divisions in the different phases of a student's career before determination. Although he does not come to be called bachelor until he has determined, there is some rise in status after being admitted to determine, as at Paris; for the determiner is now authorized to lecture, which at Paris, certainly from 1275, was open to unlicensed as well as licensed bachelors. His sanction to do so was through the same process of a formal preliminary examination, the chancellor and proctors at Oxford also being present. From this it is apparent that determination both at Paris and at Oxford came, from the middle of the thirteenth century, to constitute the first degree in arts: in Boyce's words, the student who had reached this stage was a full-fledged bachelor.[63]

To receive this degree entailed the kinds of ceremony and oath that pervaded every official act of a medieval university: the candidate had to swear to obey the statutes, the rector, and proctors; not to reveal the university's secrets; to wear and not to wear certain clothes—for example, not to have a mitre on his head under his bachelor's cap out of doors; to accompany the funerals of scholars and the congregations of his nation; not to procure students; to observe the feast days; to attend the required masses of his nation on Saturdays unless he had a legitimate excuse to be absent; not to permit a bachelor to determine against the custom and statutes of the university; to maintain strict impartiality in examinations; to pay three burses, one to the university, one to the nations, and one to the beadles; and to make a present to the nation.[64]

Those who remained in the faculty could, as we have seen, lecture cursorily; but these lectures could, at Paris, only be on any book in which the bachelor had attended lectures—once at least at Paris or twice anywhere else: [65] the university seems to have treated seriously its title of "Parent of the Sciences." They had also to take an oath that they would obey the rector and proctors. In oaths dating probably from before 1350 bachelors

---

[63] Boyce, *op. cit.*, 85.
[64] E.g., *Chart.*, I, No. 202.
[65] *Ibid.*, No. 461, the statutes of the arts faculty of 1275.

being licensed to lecture in arts had to swear—doubtless as a result of the 1277 and subsequent condemnations—that they
would not dispute on theological questions such as the Trinity or
the Incarnation.[66]

For those who remained the next object was the mastership.
As we have seen, it was not an automatic accompaniment of the
license; nor was the license gained without a further series of
exercises and ceremonies. Their successful completion, unlike determination, directly concerned both the faculty and the chancellor. Now at Paris there were, as we have briefly mentioned
earlier, two chancellors, one at Notre Dame and the other at St.
Geneviève-on-the-Mount. The arts faculty had early started going to St. Geneviève for the license in order to escape from the
control of the chancellor at Notre Dame. In 1259 Alexander IV
regularized this by decreeing that four masters, one from each
nation, should be appointed to examine for the license at St.
Geneviève.[67] The four examiners followed certain agreed procedure: by a statute of 1288 [68] they promised to license not
more than forty-eight bachelors a month; the case of any un-
worthy candidate who slipped through the net and received the
license was to be reported to the faculty of arts, and the masters
responsible punished. No bachelor who had not determined at
Paris or elsewhere was to be licensed, nor could his master be
one of the examiners. There were usually three or four monthly
auditions for candidates, but occasionally as many as six.[69]
There was no set rule to guide candidates to which of the two
chancellors they should apply; but from the time of the Great
Schism (1378–1418) the English-German nation refused to recognize the authority of the chancellor of Notre Dame, who supported the rival pope; accordingly their students went to the
chancellor at St. Geneviève almost exclusively. There were also
altercations from time to time among the nations themselves, as
in 1370 when the Picards and the English claimed that they
were being victimized by the French examiner.[70] On the whole

---

[66] *Ibid.,* II No. 1185, p. 675; Boyce, *op. cit.,* 95.

[67] *Chart.,* I, No. 346.

[68] *Ibid.,* II, Nos. 544, 545; Boyce, *op. cit.,* 100.

[69] Boyce, *op. cit.,* 102–3.

[70] *Ibid.,* 104–5.

it is remarkable that there was not more discord in so contentious an arena.

From the records of the English-German school we can gain an idea of what being licensed entailed.[71] The prospective licentiates had first to come before the nation and take their oaths to the manifold allegiances enumerated above. To the assembled faculty of arts they swore their probity in all matters affecting the illicit giving or taking of money. They then presented themselves to one of the vice-chancellors—normally at St. Geneviève —where they repeated many of their earlier undertakings, but also had to vouch for their scholastic attainments since determining. In addition to the prescribed books previously cited, the books they had to have studied by now included Aristotle's *Physics, De caelo, De anima,* the *Parvos libros naturales,* and Books 1 to 4 of the *Ethics,* together with Boethius's *De consolatione philosophiae.* They were also to have heard certain lectures on mathematics. Those approved by the vice-chancellor were assigned a day on which to appear before him to deliver their lectures (*collationes*) as the last formal exercise; the lectures were followed by a final oath, after which candidates were allowed to receive the license. The formality of the *collationes* is shown by the fact—in the fifteenth century and by implication for the fourteenth as well—that "it was enough that one from each nation sufficed to perform this task," being chosen from those whom the chancellor believed to be the most capable.[72] During their performance the lecturers could be questioned in the same way as during a disputation or a master's inception. This participation by the chancellor or his deputy distinguished the procedure for candidates in the arts faculty from that in higher faculties over the award of the license. Among the latter, examination by the chancellor, probably never more than a formality, had likely disappeared by the end of the thirteenth century. The difference was sanctioned in the bull of Innocent III in 1213, which provided for six masters to examine candidates before the chancellor,[73] and again by Gregory IX in 1231, when he decreed that the artists were to undergo examination by the

[71] *Ibid.,* 105 ff.; *Chart.,* II, No. 1185.
[72] *Chart.,* IV, No. 2690, p. 725; Boyce, *op. cit.,* 107.
[73] *Chart.,* I, No. 16; Rashdall, I, 457.

chancellor. After the *collationes* came a final oath in which the candidate promised that if he should incept in the arts faculty he would lecture for two years and dispute for forty days unless given a special dispensation; he also undertook to give honest testimony to the vice-chancellor, when required, on bachelors being presented for the license. He further promised not to exceed the sum fixed for his inception banquet, and to complete all unfinished lectures and readings before it took place. Finally the candidate, having sworn on the Bible, knelt before the vice-chancellor and received "the licence for lecturing, reading, disputing and determining, and for exercising other scholastic and magisterial acts in the faculty of arts at Paris and elsewhere in the name of the Father and the Son and the Holy Spirit. Amen." [74]

Only inception now remained. For this the candidate had to present himself to the masters and gain admission as one of them. This, too, consisted mainly in a number of formal acts, namely a solemn disputation the night before, known as Vespers from the time at which it was held, attendance at certain religious services, the delivery of an inaugural lecture as the formal act of inception (*principium*)—a practice rooted in Roman law. The proceedings ended with the new master acting as host to his new colleagues at their favorite tavern or other place of celebration. The length of the entire undertaking from entry into the schools to inception varied, not least because, at Paris, there was no fixed interval—contrary to Rashdall's assertion that it was six months [75]—between receiving the license and inception. It could be on the same day or years later or sometimes not at all. The actual course at Paris, however, for the license in arts was between five and six years. In the regulations of 1215, Robert de Courçon set it at six years; a determiner had, as we saw, to be a student of four years' standing; if anything the time required became shorter: by the second half of the fourteenth century it had come down from five years to four and a half years. [76] Even so, we must marvel at the fortitude of the medieval student at Paris;

[74] *Chart.*, II, No. 1185, p. 679; quoted from Boyce's rendering, *op. cit.*, 108–9.

[75] Rashdall, III, 461 (Boyce's point, *op. cit.*, 109–110).

[76] *Chart.*, I, No. 461; and Boyce, 96 ff.

if many of his numerous oaths to preserve peace and maintain amity among the nations were broken, he nevertheless had to persevere along an exacting path, which was rarely free from obligations to prove himself either morally or dialectically; he had, unless specially dispensed—as in the case of the subdeterminer who could not afford to pay the fees for determining in his own right [77]—to regard his master not only as a teacher but as rent and fee collector who supported himself and ran his school by the payments he received from his students. Other considerations apart, that this could tend undeniably toward procuring students and even financial irregularities is seen by the elaborately repetitious oaths against such possible misdemeanors. With such expenditure of effort, time, and money it is not surprising that only a minority ever stayed the full course.

At Oxford inception came three years after determination, thereby pointing more clearly than at Paris to the distinction between the two examinations. Indeed, in contrast with Paris, it was not necessary to have determined previously; those who wished to incept and had not determined had instead to spend an additional year in arts—for a total of eight years—and to have heard all the prescribed books. The provision seems to confirm Rashdall's surmise that determination did not itself constitute an examination; [78] once the chancellor had conducted the preliminary inquiry into the candidate's *bona fides*—the deposition—and had licensed him to lecture on any book used in the arts faculty, he appears to have become a bachelor: which would confirm what has already been said about the corresponding preliminary stage at Paris. We do not hear of the special category of licensed bachelor in the way it occurs in the 1275 statutes of the Paris arts faculty; the word "license" must be used with caution because it was applied universally to any case in which permission of some kind had been granted. The difference in the university's attitude to the determination is reflected in the examination for master, which becomes synonymous with inception. The prescribed texts were given on page 146 above; these were in addition to the books the candidate was to have heard in the arts faculty for determination—even if he had not him-

---

[77] Boyce, *loc. cit.*
[78] Rashdall, III, 141.

self determined. The bachelor admitted to incept had to hear at least two lectures a week from the regent master with whom he had enrolled.[79] Before being allowed to incept he had to lecture publicly on a book of Aristotle—expounding the text, raising any pertinent questions in the manner of an ordinary lecture given by masters, and also to take part in public disputations of bachelors and masters, responding at least twice [80] to a master in a solemn disputation. He had to continue disputing and responding for a year. Having fulfilled these obligations the candidate supplicated for his degree and received a grace allowing him to be admitted.[81] For this fifteen regent masters testified to the candidate's fittedness, nine of them and the master presenting him having to speak from personal knowledge and five from belief. The depositions were made before the chancellor and proctors. The candidate then swore that he had performed his obligations, would keep the peace, would not incept elsewhere than at Oxford and Cambridge or study at Stamford (a relic of the migration there), would not spend more than 3000 livres tournois on his inception banquet, and would incept within a year. He further undertook to lecture at the beginning of the next year on the seven arts and three philosophies—evidence, as we have seen, of the stronger hold of the liberal arts at Oxford—and that he had a school in which to do so for a year. He also paid the university a fee of a commons. After 1412 his oaths also included a promise not to maintain Wyclif's heresies.[82] The chancellor then licensed the inceptor to lecture, dispute, and do all those things that pertain to a master in the faculty of arts. The newly licensed master went round the schools inviting the masters to attend his inception. This was in two parts, as at Paris: first came the holding of Vespers, to be followed the next day by the master's inaugural lecture, the *principium*. There were disputations, at both, set on teaching days, the *principium* being on a day for disputations (*dies disputabilis*). At both Vespers and the *principium* the questions to be debated were announced previously in congregation; before the inceptor's own

[79] Gibson, *Statuta antiqua*, XCV ff. and 32, 33, 34, 147, 247.
[80] For the statutes of 1340; once in the earlier statutes, *ibid.*, 32, 34.
[81] *Ibid.*, XCVI ff., 29 ff.
[82] *Ibid.*, XCVII, 222.

lecture he was presented with his master's insignia. The entertainment that followed, together with other payments, made it a very costly business, which was sometimes mitigated by wealthy inceptors standing the cost for the poor ones.

Once having incepted, the new master had to promise to dispute for forty consecutive disputable days and to teach for a period of two years (necessary regency). Beyond his routine duties of attending congregations, inceptions and funerals—which were often unpopular and tended to be evaded—his principal task was to give—as at Paris—ordinary lectures on the seven arts and the three philosophies. In the regulations for 1333 he could charge fees of one shilling in logic and eighteen pence in science.[83] To cover the course the regents—from at least 1431— were divided into groups, the juniors (together with the supervisors of grammar) lecturing on grammar, the seniors on the arts and the philosophies.

There was thus a basic affinity between the arts course at Paris and Oxford, with certain noteworthy differences. In the first place the more tranquil institutional histry of Oxford is once again to be discerned in the greater integration of the faculty and the university represented by the chancellor and proctors. There was no separate chancellor's examination for the license, even a formal one, beyond the deposition of the candidate's eighteen sponsors. In the second place inception and mastership became virtually inseparable, the one leading directly to the other under university auspices, for although the inceptor summoned the masters to his *principium,* the beadle did the same on behalf of the master who was to preside over Vespers.[84] Otherwise similar obligations and similar exercises were demanded at both universities, though Oxford seemed more prepared to waive its formal examinations.

Theology. When we turn to the faculty of theology we see the same basic structure but more elaborate and on a fuller scale. This is partly because more of the writings from the theological faculties of both universities have survived, partly because of the nature of the subject, partly because its members were older and

[83] *Ibid.,* C, 131–2.
[84] *Ibid.,* XCVII, 36, 37, 39, 142.

spent over twice as long there as in the arts faculty, and partly because of the nature of the course. To take these in order, the vast number of disputed questions and commentaries that lie in the libraries of Europe enables us to form a much fuller picture of the nature of the disputations and the different kinds of questions and academic phases to which they corresponded. Whereas in the arts faculty only a relatively small number of *sophismata* provide the main testimony to the questions debated, those from the theological faculty fall into at least five main groups, as we shall consider shortly. This amplitude is the direct result of the nature of theology as a study. Instead of the heterogeneous collection of texts that made up the books of the arts course, it consisted basically of the Bible [85] and the main theological questions systematized in Peter Lombard's four books of the *Sentences:* on God, Creation, Christ, and the Sacraments. Together these formed the textbooks of the course, continually in use until the end of the tenth year. This applied above all to the Bible. Reading its books was inseparable from reading the fathers and the saints. Everything outside the canon of the sacred authorities, however authoritative, was an adjunct. The Lombard's *Sentences* involved the same canon and shared the same themes. They were the culmination of over fifty years of dialectical treatment of the article of faith: of posing the matters they raised as questions to be disputed and resolved. Their influence on the exercises of the theological faculty was decisive: early in the thirteenth century it can be seen in the works of theologians like Stephen Langton, Stephen of Tournai, Prepositinus of Cremona and Simon of Tournai. Nor at first were the Lombard's *Sentences* the only such work used in the theological faculty: for a time the *Historia scholastica* of Peter Comestor was also studied both at Paris and Oxford.[86] But one such book was enough and it came to be the Lombard's *Sentences*. It comprised a separate part of the course concerned with speculative problems; to it were added other such questions and commentaries, making up a vast literature of its own. The same occurred in

[85] By the Paris statutes of 1366 students in the theological faculty had, for the first four years of the course, to carry with them to lectures a copy of the Bible. *Chart.,* II, No. 1189 (14), p. 698.

[86] E.g., *Chart.,* I, No. 57; Gibson, *Statuta antiqua,* 49.

Peter Lombard composing the *Sentences*.

commenting the Bible: [87] the expositions and postillae (literally *post illa verba*) were added to the standard authorities like St. Augustine on particular books of the Bible, so that any student coming to the book of his choice was confronted with an array of other works on it. The very fact that it involved a common body of doctrine and was based on a book, or rather series of books—the Bible—gave the theological faculty's work a coherence that must be lacking in the diversity of the arts course. It meant among other things a vast output of works by masters of the faculty that, like the successive commentaries on the *Sentences* from the time of Alexander of Hales in the 1230's, became part of the material of the course; to read the works of such eminent masters on either the *Sentences* or the Bible became as much a *sine qua non* of success in examinations as to read the

[87] For a discussion of the literature used in the faculties at Oxford and Paris see A. G. Little and F. Pelster, eds., *Oxford Theology and Theologians* (OHS, Oxford, 1934), 26 ff.

important articles and books is today. Thus a theological student's notebook for 1243 at Paris contained extracts from William of Auxerre's *Golden Summa*, St. Augustine's *83 Questions,* and Philip the Chancellor's *De bono.*[88] Although it would be untrue to deny any originality to the arts faculty, there was little scope for it there other than in logic; arts provided the critical dialectical and speculative instruments for grappling with the questions of substance that, at Paris in the heyday of scholasticism in the thirteenth century, were almost entirely theological. At Oxford, especially in mathematics and scientific problems, the subjects of the old *quadrivium* received a new significance from the work on Grosseteste and his school. But for the most part philosophical questions—on the nature of being or movement or form or matter—arose out of theological disputations, not least the free discussions (*quodlibeta*) held there twice a year. Thus the commentaries and disputed questions of thinkers like Henry of Ghent, Duns Scotus, William of Ockham, produced while in the theological faculty, also contain most of their philosophical concepts for they arose in a theological context.

That so much of the intellectual activity of the period came under the rubric of theology was not only because of its universality as the queen of sciences; it was also the outcome of the greater age and maturity of its members, the longer time spent in the theological faculty, their fewer numbers, and the consequent high ratio of quality to quantity. To go on to one of the higher faculties in itself entailed a master's degree in arts—or exemption from it, in the case of the mendicants and, at Oxford, some seculars. In theology the number of chairs, or regent masterships, was strictly limited, probably not going beyond twenty in the later thirteenth century and the first two decades of the fourteenth century.[89] Although masters were licensed in theology normally only every two years, competition was keener for the correspondingly fewer students and still further sharpened by the rivalry between seculars and mendicants. Law and medicine were both lucrative professions; theology could lead to the

[88] P. Glorieux, "Les Années 1242–7 à la faculté de théologie de Paris," *Recherches de théologie ancienne et médiévale,* **29** (1962) 237.
[89] See P. Glorieux, *Répertoire des maîtres en théologie de Paris au XIII*ᵉ *siècle, I* (Paris, 1933), tables at p. 388.

highest honors, but it also attracted the purest thinkers, those who were prepared to spend a large part of their lives debating and speculating on abstract questions that had no direct relevance to a calling outside the university or religious *studium*. If the theological faculty—certainly at Paris with its strong ties to the cathedral—was the center of conservatism, it also gave much freer reign to speculation and innovation, as the roll of names from Albert the Great and St. Thomas to Duns Scotus and Ockham testifies. At Paris, above all, the theologians were the pacemakers until the third or fourth decades of the fourteenth century. At Oxford speculation was from the first more scientifically orientated, but it still drew its inspiration from the more traditional Augustinian outlook in theology.

Taken together these different factors made the theological faculty, especially at Paris, the doctrinal and intellectual nerve center of Christendom until the later fourteenth century. Directly or indirectly all its main developments and tensions were registered there. For that reason alone we hear much more about the ways in which they came about.

So far as Paris was concerned, we have already said that the length of the course was double that of the arts course. How long precisely is not certain in the early years. Robert de Courçon in 1215 decreed "that no one shall lecture at Paris before his thirty-fifth year and unless he has studied for eight years at least, and has heard the books faithfully and in classrooms, and has attended lectures in theology for five years before he gives lectures himself publicly." [89a] To what status does lecturing after the eight years refer? Rashdall took it to mean on becoming a doctor of theology (the equivalent of master in the arts faculty); [90] Denifle implied that it meant a bachelor,[91] but he understood this to refer to the total years spent in both arts and theology. Neither interpretation as it stands is tenable. Denifle is surely correct in taking the provision to refer to bachelors (a) because it mentions a period of only five years in theology, which, had it been for a master, would have been less than the

---

[89a] *Chart.*, I, No. 20.

[90] Rashdall, I, 472.

[91] Denifle, *Entstehung*, 100–2; the word he used was Lehrer (as opposed to Professor).

six years required by the statutes for a master in arts, and (b) because the lectures are clearly those of a bachelor: "none of these shall lecture before the third hour on days when *masters* [my italics] lecture," an unmistakable distinction between these lectures and masters' lectures. Yet the eight years of previous study necessary before they can be given cannot meaningfully include the period in arts as well as the five years in theology. In that case the bachelor would be barely twenty-five years old, having ten years to go before he could incept as a master. It both makes more sense and is more consistent with subsequent developments to see the eight years as referring to theological study in addition to the requisite six years in the arts faculty. With twenty-one years as the minimum age for a master of arts, another two years of necessary regency in arts would bring up the age at which a man could enter the theological faculty to twenty-three years; a further eight years at least before becoming a bachelor would mean that he would then be not less than thirty-one years of age—far closer to the requisite thirty-five years. Many in fact went to the study of theology after holding benefices and so would have been older. It would seem therefore that Rashdall was correct in making eight years the necessary period of study in theology but that Denifle had reason on his side when he took the statute to be for bachelors, not doctors, of theology.[92]

During the thirteenth century the course gradually lengthened until it came to be sixteen years by the reform of 1366, which it remained until the statutes of cardinal d'Estouteville in 1452 when it was shortened by one year.[93] The complexity of its ma-

---

[92] Rashdall's editor (I, 472, note 1) cites a statute of Benedict XII in 1335 (*Chart.*, II, No. 992) that invokes seven years as the minimum for a bachelor at the Paris university as favoring Denifle's interpretation. If this refers to the theological faculty—as seems most likely—it also undermines Denifle's contention that only eight years were required in all.

[93] Rashdall, I, 474 ff.; Glorieux, *Répertoire des maîtres en théologie*, 21. The earliest statutes date from two fourteenth-century collections in *Chart.*, II, Nos. 1188 and 1189 (appendix). The Paris customs are known most fully from the 1364 statutes of the theological faculty at Bologna, which were modeled on Paris. See F. Ehrle, *Statuta facultatis theologiae Bononiensis* (Bologna, 1932). New statutes were issued for all the faculties by Urban V in 1366; *Chart.*, III, No. 1319.

terial doubtless accounts for the steady increase, as we can see from the monumental commentaries and exhaustive disputed questions of many theologians. The first six years (seven for a secular before 1335) of the course were spent in hearing lectures, four years on the Bible and two on the *Sentences* of Peter Lombard. At the end of this period, if he was already twenty-five years of age and had attended the prescribed lectures, the student could petition the faculty for his first course, that is, to be made a bachelor; on presentation of his *bona fides* he was examined by seven doctors and if passed by them he was formally admitted to the first course and became a bachelor. He made his entry into his new status with a public exercise, the *principium*, before 1250 called the *introitus*. It had its parallel in the various inceptory acts that we remarked for the arts faculty. Having performed it the bachelor now lectured on the Bible for two years, at Paris, taking a different book for each year, usually one from the Old Testament and the other from the New. At Oxford, as we saw in the dispute there between the university and the mendicants, the *Sentences* came before the Bible; hence the mendicants were compelled to engage in philosophical activities if they were to be allowed to lecture on the Bible. In this period of biblical lecturing, the bachelor was called a *cursor*, from the cursory lectures he gave. The mendicants and regulars, on the other hand, lectured ordinarily (*ordinarie*) in view of their previous theological training in their own *studia;* they were not required to lecture on a different book in each of the two years. During his two years as a *cursor* the bachelor had to gloss the text according to "the ancient and approved mode," not covering more than one chapter in a lecture; he had also to respond at least once in disputes at the inception of a master—the Vespers and the *aula,* which we shall discuss presently—and to deliver one sermon.

Having completed his two years as *cursor,* he now became a bachelor of the *Sentences* (*Baccalarius Sententiarius*). Originally this was also for a period of two years. Before a student could attain to it he had to have taken part once at least in a disputation called a *tentative,* that is, acting as respondent to the question posed by a master and opposed by senior bachelors who then together judged the adequacy of the candidate's performance. If he passed muster and had completed nine years in the-

ological study he could go on to read the *Sentences* (the mendicants and other religions were exempted from the provision).
By the fourteenth century the period for the *Sentences* had become one academic year, nine months. This contraction was undoubtedly owing to the pressure of the mendicants who, as we
saw at Oxford, wished to devote themselves to the study of the
Bible. In that one year the activities of the bachelor of the *Sentences* centered on a solemn introduction (*principium*) to each
of the four books, together with questions from each of the
books. The statutes of the later fourteenth century stressed the
need to cover all four books and not stop at the prologue and
book one.[94] This had clearly become the common practice as
can be seen from the many commentaries on the *Sentences* of
the time; it was also decreed that the reading of the *Sentences*
should have been completed in the vacation before the bachelor
was admitted to the third and final phase of his bachelorship:
that of the "formed bachelor" (*baccalarius formatus*). It dates
from the second half of the thirteenth century. By the regulations of 1335 it was to last for four years, having earlier been five
years.[95] During this time the bachelor was not to be away from
Paris for more than two months in any year without special permission from the faculty. He was to take part in public disputations both ordinary and extraordinary (*quodlibeta*) twice or at
least once a year; he had to deliver one university sermon annually in one of the places customarily used on these occasions,
such as the convent of the Dominicans at St. Jacques or at St.
Bernard's, the house of the Cistercians; he had also to assist at
the sermon or address (*collatio*) of another bachelor once a year
but not more; he was to attend university congregations properly
dressed. Altogether he had to respond to questions in the public
disputations of other bachelors at least five times before he could
be licensed, including the inception disputes of Vespers, *principium* and the *aula* in the Sorbonne. These were also the exercises he had to perform at his own inception.

We must now consider these different disputations.[96] They
can be divided into two main categories: (a) the ordinary or

[94] *Chart.*, II, No. 1189, art. 37.
[95] E.g., *Ibid.*, Nos. 822, 1093.
[96] For what follows see especially Little and Pelster, *Oxford Theology,*
31–56.

public or solemn or magisterial disputations—they are synonymous—and (b) the extraordinary or quodlibetal disputation.
There were also the private disputations (*collationes*) held by a
master in his own school for his pupils, which we shall briefly
mention.

The ordinary public disputations grew naturally out of the
twelfth- and early-thirteenth-century disputations. As in the arts
faculty, they were presided over by a master who put the question (e.g., Whether the act of willing presupposes the act of
understanding); [97] an appointed student (*respondens*) attempted to reply (*respondere de questione*); he also had to answer
objections put by the master or others. At Oxford—whose practices we shall consider afterwards—respondents did not have to
be bachelors. At the end the master would sum up at least
briefly (determine), even if this was only to confirm what the
respondent had said; it did not, however, have to be a formal
determination in which all the points raised *pro* and *contra* were
resolved. In the fourteenth century, probably because of the increasing frequency of disputation, the latter became distinguished from a formal determination by a master, in the statute
of the theological faculty at Bologna.[98] At Oxford, too, one did
not necessarily entail the other; thus, in the agreement between
the university and friars in 1314, they were treated as separate.[99]
The determination to a dispute could, however, be made on
another, later occasion, as was the custom in the "resumptions"
of quodlibetal questions and the new master's own subsequent
reply to the public debate (*aula*) at his inception.

The disputes connected with the inception were the most
solemn of all. They followed the testimony of the masters (the
deposition) to the candidate's morals and learning, which we
have already observed in connection with the licensing of a master in arts. The disputes went back equally far in the theological
faculty, having been mentioned first by Gregory IX in 1231 and
then by Alexander IV in 1255.[100] At Paris they were probably
preceded by the special examination of the *disputata tentativa*,

[97] *Ibid.*, 318.
[98] *Ibid.*, 41.
[99] *Ibid.;* Gibson, *Statuta antiqua*, 118.
[100] *Chart.*, I, Nos. 79, 247.

An examination in progress.

which was followed by the granting of the license subject to ful-
filling the requirements of inception. Unlike the granting of the
license in the arts faculty, in the higher faculties there was not
even a formal examination by the chancellor or his deputy. The
inception as we have said consisted in the two distinct disputations of Vespers and the *principium*. The latter as we have seen
went back very early and was first mentioned in Robert de Courçon's statutes. It occurs again in the Paris masters' letter of 1252;
and three years later Alexander IV asked the chancellor, who
had given the license to Thomas Aquinas, to arrange for the
holding of the *principium*.[101] At Oxford it dates at least from
the time of Grosseteste, one of whose lost treatises was called *In
vesperiis Ade* [102] (probably of Adam Marsh).

The first description of these acts comes from the Bologna

---

[01] *Ibid.*, Nos. 20, 200, 270, 280.
[02] A. G. Little, "The Franciscan School at Oxford," AFH **19** (1926), 828,
cited in Little and Pelster, *Oxford Theology*, 45.

statutes of 1364 which were modeled on those of Paris. The name Vespers was, as we mentioned, taken from the time at which they were held, which except during Lent was in the afternoon.[103] The second part of the dispute, following the *principium,* was called the *aula* at Paris because it was held in the bishop's hall. When these disputes were held other lectures and disputations had to be postponed to allow all masters and students to attend. The candidate for the license (the inceptor) had to choose four questions, two to be disputed at Vespers, and two to be disputed in the *aula* on the following day. The disputation at Vespers was presided over by a master, normally the one who had presented the candidate for the license. The *respondens* was usually a bachelor: he proposed the solutions to the first question posed (the *expectantia*); the presiding master then made the first objections, followed by those of the bachelors attending. The responding bachelor then concluded this first disputation by replying to the master's objections. The disputation on the second question followed immediately. This time the licentiate was the respondent; after one of the masters had introduced the question with one or two arguments for and against, the licentiate (also called vesperiand) proposed his thesis and gave proofs for it; this was countered with a number of arguments by the same master. The licentiate replied only to two of them— there were ordinarily four or five; he was in turn replied to by another master, and so it went on for two or three times more before the presiding master orated in praise of the Bible, and of the candidate, and announced the time, place, and book with which the licentiate would begin his lecture at the *aula.*

The *aula* was held in the morning at about tierce, no other lecture or disputation being permitted. The licentiate sat among the chancellor and masters. The presiding master (*magister aulator*), as in the ceremony for inception in arts, placed the master's hat (*biretta*) on the new master's head; the new master after a short speech praising holy scripture, performed the first action of his office by presiding over the disputation which began with the third of the four questions which he had chosen for his inception. After a bachelor—probably a formed bachelor—had replied

[103] For what follows, see Little and Pelster, *Oxford Theology,* 45 ff.

with three or four conclusions the new master produced arguments against them, the same procedure of reply and counter-reply being observed as over the two questions of the previous evening. The new master was in turn followed by the presiding master and the chancellor—or his representative—acting as opponents. The fourth question was disputed only by masters. The proceedings ended with the new master summing up (determining) the third question over which he had presided. The full and final determination followed in his first lecture (the *resumptio* or *resumpta*) held soon afterwards on one of the lecturing days. In it he completed his *principium*—the opening address in praise of scripture—made at the *aula* and went on to deal with the second question, in which he had been involved as respondent, and the third question, over which he had presided. He had then to enter a two-year period of necessary regency. *Resumptio* was also the term for a disputation that took place when a master who had been a regent wished to resume teaching.[104]

We come now to the *quodlibeta,* or free questions. The literature from these is extensive, nearly every important thinker from about 1260 to 1320, certainly at Paris, having produced them.[105] As we have already seen, formed bachelors were obliged to take part in them during their four years before being eligible for the license. They were held twice a year, in Lent and in Advent. Their great merit—and historical interest—is that they could be on any topic. Accordingly they tended to reflect the questions of the day with an immediacy not found in the more formal exercises of the schools: this does not of course apply to special lectures or treatises, such as those written in times of crisis, as for example in the disputes between seculars and mendicants by William of St. Amour, Bonaventure, and Thomas Aquinas. The other aspect of their freedom was that anyone could participate. They were therefore occasions both for airing important matters and for verbal dexterity; occasionally, too, they were a means of paying off scores by attacking a particular master's opinions on a subject. Only a few entered them more than once during the

[104] *Ibid.,* 52–3; Gibson, *Statuta antiqua* 37, 53–4.
[105] See P. Glorieux, *La Littérature quodlibètique,* vols. I and II (Paris, J. Vrin, 1925–36).

year. On the days when they were held all the schools closed
the masters and scholars gathering in the place where they were
to be held—the church of the Mathurins or St. Jacques or the
bishop's *aula*. The number of participants was great. Roger Marston recounts the famous occasion when Aquinas was virtually
arraigned before the theological faculty in one such disputation
over his doctrine of a single substantial form: according to him
twenty-five masters were present.[106] The quodlibetal disputes
began early in the morning; the subjects were not announced in
advance, so that it was for anyone present to raise a question.
They thus provided an outlet for the more contentious and un-
quiet spirits. The range of subjects was great, including the
debates on Averroism—and their doctrinal aftermath on the nature of the soul, plurality forms, the will, and intellect—the mendicants' privileges granted by Martin IV, the suppression of the
Templars, and so on.

The quodlibet was not confined to the theological faculty
though, for reasons suggested earlier, it reached its fullest expression among the theologians. It was to be found in all three
other faculties: in medicine especially more importance attached
to disputations than lectures. At Oxford, however, the Dominicans prohibited any brothers who were not doctors of theology
from disputing quodlibetically, and when they did so, it had to
be in places approved by the order.[107]

The main object of the quodlibet from a pedagogical point of
view was to help train the student in argument; formally it was
an exercise in pure dialectic, though in content it often produced
ideas of fundamental importance. Instead of one respondent
there was a succession who followed one another in the course
of the debate; the first *responsialis* was a bachelor. The presiding
master—it was a magisterial disputation—could act as chairman
or himself enter the lists and take an active—indeed, exclusive
—part in sustaining a thesis. To him belonged the right of reply.
Gradually, however, after about 1320 the masters seem to have
lost interest and ceased to dominate it; by the later fourteenth
century it had become principally a bachelor's exercise. Certainly

[106] See 228 below.
[107] *Ibid.*, II, 23.

after the first two decades of that century the stream of quodlibetic literature dries up. To a large degree this must reflect the changed circumstances at Paris; it was no longer the doctrinal nerve center of Christendom or the indispensable meeting point for the finest speculative minds. This in turn was due to the mendicant orders' loss of impetus and the growth of independent centers of learning, a process greatly accentuated after the middle of the fourteenth century by the outbreak of the Hundred Years' War.

In structure the quodlibet consisted of two phases: the *disputatio* and the *determinatio*. The *disputatio* was the occasion of the general debate on anything (*de quolibet*) and by anyone (*a quolibet*). Inevitably such a discussion lacked the order and unity of an ordinary disputation: many points were raised that did not fall within the same theme; there was no set sequence of questions that had to be followed; hence no immediate possibility of giving them coherence. A second session was therefore held on a separate day soon after the first, in which the presiding master alone determined, drawing together the threads of the general disputation. This is the form in which the quodlibets were written—as the determination of a number of diverse questions by a single writer. If in the interests of intelligibility many of the original arguments were omitted, the writings contain enough often to throw light on the disputants involved as well as to take us along doctrinal paths that would otherwise not be so clearly known.

Finally, there were also the private disputations held in a school or religious house by its members. These were called *collationes* (a term that was also used for a short university sermon or formal lecture such as St. Bonaventure's on the *Hexaemeron*). As found in Duns Scotus's *Collationes Oxonienses*, the collation represents a practice disputation by the students themselves. Such exercises had been decreed in the Dominicans' statutes as early as 1259; they took place in the houses of the religious orders at Paris and Oxford. The celebrated fifteenth-century disputations at the Sorbonne held on Saturdays among members of the college—the *Sorbonica*—were modeled on these collations.[108]

Little and Pelster, *Oxford Theology*, 54–56.

Many of the features discussed here were to be found at Oxford, as a number of the examples quoted show. There were two
main differences between the course there and at Paris. The first
which we have repeatedly had occasion to stress, was that the
order between the biblical bachelor and the sententiary bachelor
was reversed. At Oxford he lectured on the *Sentences* before he
could lecture on the Bible; hence he did not become a bachelor
(BD) until he had completed lecturing on the *Sentences*. This
meant that the provisions for disputing were different: they
made length of study, not status, the test of when a student
could respond and oppose, as he began to do so before he had
been made a bachelor. Thus in the first half of the fourteenth
century, at the latest, the statutes prescribed at least four years
attendance at lectures in theology before a student could be an
opposer and at least six years to be a respondent. For those who
were not already masters of arts the minimum period was six
years for an opponent and eight years for a respondent. Another
decree stipulated that responsions should not begin until one
year after the completion of lectures on the *Sentences*.[109]

The second feature of the Oxford course was that it became
shorter while that at Paris lengthened. By the mid-fourteenth
century the Paris statutes demanded a period of at least fourteen
years.[110] At Oxford [111] a master of arts entering the theological
faculty had to spend seven years before he could become a
bachelor, that is, begin lecturing on the *Sentences*. Of these
seven years, the first four were taken up with attending lectures
mainly on the Bible; in his fifth year he could oppose in disputa-

[109] *Ibid.*, 33–5; Gibson, *Statuta antiqua* 48, 50; Salter, in *Registrum an
nalium collegii Mertonensis* (Oxford, OHS, 1921) XXVII, attempts to estab
lish that *opponens* denoted the defender of the thesis by taking *opponere* t
mean "to open." This is not the etymological sense given by Du Cang
(*Glossarium mediae et infimae Latinatis,* vol VI, 49), nor does it correspon
the facts. Technically it was the presiding master who opened the disputa
tion by putting the question. The *respondens* then answered.

[110] i.e. six as a student; two as a bachelor cursor; one as sententiary bach
lor; four as formed bachelor—admission to which could only be after th
tentativa in the tenth year. Rashdall, I, 472, makes the total sixteen year
after the 1366 reform of Urban V.

[111] Gibson, *Statuta antiqua,* CIX–XIII; 48 ff.; see also Little and Pelste
Oxford Theology 33 ff.

tions and in his seventh year respond. For those who were not masters of arts the period was longer: six years of theological study for opponency and eight for responsion. Before he could go on to read the *Sentences,* admission to which constituted becoming a bachelor (BD), he had, after 1419, to have taken part in a solemn disputation and receive masters' depositions. By the 1253 statutes, as we saw earlier. Peter Comestor's *Historia* had been an alternative to the Bible, but by a statute of 1310 this provision had been replaced by making it obligatory to read the *Sentences* for one year for the bachelorship. After completing them he had to spend a further two years opposing and responding in all the theological schools, to preach publicly, which after 1303 included a sermon in St. Mary's, and to lecture on any book of the Bible or the *Sentences.* If, on the testimony of the regent masters, he had performed these exercises satisfactorily he was then eligible for the license. As we have said, because of the reversed order of *Sentences* and the Bible, he could only lecture on the Bible after he had done so on the *Sentences.*

There is plenty of evidence from the surviving literature for the same kind of disputed questions and solemn inception disputations—Vespers, *principium, aula,* and *resumptio*—at Oxford as we have already enumerated for Paris.[112] The evidence is particularly striking from the discord with the Dominicans in the first decade of the fourteenth century. In the Dominican appeal to the pope in 1314 their proctor, Laurence of Warwick, complained that the regent master of the Dominicans, Hugh of Sutton, had found the day on which Hugh had arranged to dispute taken by two other masters, Henry of Harclay and the Carmelite Robert of Walsingham; this went against the established custom for ordinary disputations, in which two could not take place under different masters on the same fixed day. The time of the disputation had been proclaimed publicly in the schools by the beadles who had invited the other masters to attend.[113] In the medical faculty, similarly, it was decreed that disputations should be held weekly, the masters following one another in rotation, or, if there was only one regent master, the disputations

---

[112] Little and Pelster, *Oxford Theology,* 36 ff.
[113] *Ibid.;* Rashdall in *Collectanea,* II, 239 ff.

were to be fortnightly.[114] In the arts faculty, as we have seen, a master newly incepted had to dispute on every "disputable day" for forty days continuously. That the frequency of disputations was even greater in the theological faculty is suggested not only by the extant literature and the close parallels with Paris practice, but also from a statute sometime before 1350 that permitted two masters to dispute on the same day. As Pelster has suggested, it may have originated from the Dominican dispute.[115] This is further supported by the number of times certain Oxford masters are known to have disputed in the same year: Roger Marston at least eight times, Richard Knapwell and Robert Winchelsey at least six times.[116]

The compromise of 1314 between the university and the Dominicans, as well as the statutes, also provides evidence for a similar procedure for inceptions as at Paris: the Vespers of Dominican licentiates had until two years previously been held in the Dominican house, but they had now to take place in St. Mary's; the same must have applied to the Franciscans.[117] The statutes provided that the holding of Vespers was not to extend to a second day; they could be held on any day when there were lectures in the arts faculty, but for inception a "disputable day" was needed. The regent masters presiding at Vespers had to announce the questions in advance at a congregation where they were discussed. It also appears that nonregents could hold Vespers, because some had to be invited. At the Vespers themselves the senior master was to act as the opponent of the licentiate, who was the respondent. At the inception the new master had to give an introductory lecture and then state the questions to be disputed; we have also the order of disputants for both questions, the new master giving a partial solution to the question with at least one argument. The rest would follow in a separate determination later. It was, as we have seen, separated in time from the disputation, and considered always as a solemn and public act.

---

[114] Little and Pelster, *Oxford Theology*, 38; Gibson, *Statuta antiqua*, 42.

[115] Little and Pelster, *Oxford Theology;* Gibson, *Statuta antiqua*, 51.

[116] Little and Pelster, *Oxford Theology.*

[117] For what follows see Little and Pelster, *Oxford Theology*, 48–50; Gibson, *Statuta antiqua*, 36–40 and 116.

For seculars the two years of necessary regency began immediately after inception, continuing for the whole of the remainder of that year and the following year. During that time the regent master had to lecture throughout every term; he was also, as a member of congregation, involved in the affairs of the university. Regulars, according to a late statute of 1478, had to lecture for the twenty-four months following inception but remained members of congregation only until a new member of their order incepted; the latter then succeeded his confrère. Generally among the Dominicans and the Franciscans one friar from each order incepted every year so that both had two regent masters but only one member of congregation.[118] Many masters, both seculars and regulars, however continued to lecture and dispute afterwards: for example Thomas Docking, Nicholas Trivet, and Thomas of Sutton, to mention only three. As we have mentioned nonregents were allowed to hold Vespers, and they may also have presided at ordinary disputations.[119] Whether secular or regular, the expenses for inception were heavy, even if the course had been some four or five years shorter than at Paris.

Law and Medicine. Neither law nor medicine had the same importance for Paris and Oxford as arts and theology. It was from the latter that their international standing sprang. This is not to deny the place of law and medicine in the studies of either university, but to point to their more limited ramifications. The homes of both disciplines lay elsewhere, at Montpellier, Toulouse, Bologna, and Padua. We shall accordingly only touch on them briefly here, remembering that the same kinds of principles and practices applied as in arts and theology.

At Paris,[120] as we have said, the study of civil law was proscribed by Honorius III. How effective the ban was may be doubted; the fact, however, that civil law could not be taught officially and openly inevitably hobbled the pursuit of canon law. The periods of study varied from time to time; but in the fourteenth century the course came to be six years for a bachelor and about another five years for the license. Law attracted the

---

[113] *Oxford Theology*, 233; Gibson, *Statuta antiqua*, 54, 290.
[119] *Oxford Theology*, 234; Gibson, *Statuta antiqua*, 37.
[120] For law at Paris, see Rashdall, I, 473–9.

wealthiest students as well as promising the most lucrative returns. This, as Rashdall observed, no doubt accounted for the frequency of legislation against sham students and abuses such as bribery. The course followed closely that of Bologna: its basis was the study of Gratian's *Decretum,* the subsequent collections of canon law in the Decretals,[121] together with certain books on the sacraments and the extensive literature of authorative glosses. In that sense there was an affinity with theology in a canon of a few basic texts that afforded almost limitless scope for examination and commentary.

At Oxford there were faculties of both canon and civil law; [122] and the study of civil law was obligatory for a doctorate in canon law. As in the other higher faculties it was possible to be a doctor without being already a master of arts; but in the case of canon law the scales were weighted even more strongly against the candidate who was not already a doctor of civil law: before he could lecture extraordinarily (cursorily) in canon law he had to swear that he had attended courses in civil law for three years, in addition to having spent two years on the *Decretum* and studied the Decretals completely. Admission to lecture extraordinarily—following Bolognese terminology—constituted becoming a bachelor; it was not preceded by any set examination, beyond having satisfied the chancellor and regents in the faculty of these qualifications. There was no fixed time from admission to lecture to receiving the license: it entailed for those not doctors of civil law another year's study of the *Decretum* besides giving a course of extraordinary lectures on any one book of the Decretals and opposing in the school of a regent master on any two of the three tractates ("causes") of the *Decretum: De symonia, De consecratione,* and *De poenitentia.* Early

---

[121] For their growing importance, see E. Fournier, "L'Enseignement des décrétals à l'Université de Paris au moyen âge," *Revue de l'histoire de l'église de France,* **26** (1940), 58–62.

[122] Gibson, *Statuta antiqua,* CVI–VIII; 45–7, 177, Rashdall, III, 156–8. I am indebted for what follows on canon law at Oxford to L. Boyle, "The Curriculum of Canon Law at Oxford in the First Half of the Fourteenth Century," *Oxford Studies Presented to Daniel Callus,* 135–62. My only criticism of an admirable account is his habit—explained but hardly justified—of calling the bachelor a licentiate; in the context of the accepted terminology, this can only confuse.

on in the fourteenth century the new decretal collection known as the Sext—sixth book—promulgated by Boniface VIII became an important additional text; by 1333 it was joined by the study of Clement V's collection—the Clementines—promulgated in 1317. By then the Decretals had become an ordinary text to be lectured on. To meet the many demands made on teaching this new body of canon law, the faculty for a time resorted to the practice of quasi-ordinary lectures. Both doctors in civil law and mature bachelors—who had already heard civil law for three years, the *Decretum* for two years, and the Decretals complete —were eligible. Only a few bachelors could have been among those chosen to help out; the majority were probably doctors of civil law, and they lectured quasi-ordinarily on the Sext. Doctors of civil law had neither to take an oath before being admitted to extraordinary lecturing nor to have spent more than two years on the *Decretum* nor to have studied the Bible for two years before they could incept. Together with nondoctors in civil law they had to lecture ordinarily for each regent in turn beyond their other lectures and disputations.

In 1333 came a new arrangement for covering the syllabus, with the introduction of a two-year cycle of lectures. All regents had to swear that the books of the Decretals covered in that year had been read *ordinarie* and the Sext quasi-*ordinarie;* these were now divided into different ones for each year: in the first year of the two-year cycle Books 1, 4, and 5 of the Decretals and the Clementines were lectured on, in the second year Books 2 and 3 of the Decretals and the whole of the Sext. The penalty for not doing so was a fine of £5. Thus Decretals had displaced the *Decretum* as the basic ordinary text. The license to incept came after the bachelor had completed his requirements of lecturing and disputing; whether it was preceded by a formal examination is unclear. At Bologna the candidate for the license had to comment on selected passages from the *Decretum* and Decretals and answer objections from the doctors, who afterwards pronounced on his suitability. At Oxford four regents had to pass the candidate, who had, among other things, to promise to incept within one year. Doubtless they did so only if he had given formal evidence of his competence. After inception—which only a small number ever reached—the licentiate had to undergo a period of necessary regency: it was reduced from two years to one sometime before 1333.

To become a bachelor of civil law entailed four years of study if the candidate was already a master of arts; otherwise six; it was followed by extraordinary lectures on the *Volumina* (the *Digestum novum* and *Infortiatum*) as a bachelor. For inception he had also to have lectured on the *Libellus institutionum* and to have taken part in similar disputatory exercises to those in canon

In medicine the license carried with it the right to practice; hence it also conferred a public position on the recipient. Much of the history of the medical faculty at Paris [123] was, as we mentioned earlier, occupied in trying to put down charlatans. The structure of the course was similar to that of the other faculties, with disputations, lectures, and examinations. The earliest statute, about 1270–4, required about four years (thirty-two months) of study for a bachelorship and five and a half years for the license if the candidate was already a master of arts; otherwise six years. Later this period for the license was increased to fifty-six months and sixty months respectively.[124] The texts used, as we might expect from our earlier discussion, drew heavily upon the Greco-Arabian tradition: the whole corpus was known as the *Ars medicinae*—the collection of texts by Constantinus Africanus that brought together the works of Hippocrates; Galen; the *Urinis* of the Byzantine Theophilus; the *Viaticum* of Al-Djezzar; the *Books of Isaac* (Israeli ben Salomon), that is, the *Urines, Fevers,* and *Diets;* the pharmacopeia of Nicholas of Salerno, called the *Antiodarium;* the medical verses *De urinis* of Giles of Corbeil, physician to Philip II of France; and the *Theoretica* and *Practica* into which the *Opus pantegni* of Ali ben Abbas was divided.[125] By the end of the fourteenth century—1395—the treatises of Avicenna, Averroes, and their Italian and French adherents had also entered the canon. In Paris and the northern universities medicine remained a predominantly theoretical discipline almost entirely dependent on the Arabian tradition.

[123] Rashdall, I, 435–7; S. D'Irsay, *Histoire des universités françaises et étrangères,* I (Paris, 1935), 162–3.
[124] *Chart.,* I, Nos. 452, 453; *ibid.,* II, No. 921.
[125] *Ibid.,* No. 453; Rashdall, I, 436; D'Irsay, *op. cit.,* 104–7.

At Oxford [126] much the same curriculum was followed. Nothing is said in the statutes of the course for a bachelor. A new stage was entered when the student, having heard lectures on medicine for four years, and been successfully examined, was admitted to practice. For masters of arts the total period to inception was six years, eight years for those who were not MA's. After inception a doctor of medicine had to dispute for forty consecutive days on "disputable days" and to lecture for the rest of his year of inception and for two years after that. Disputes among regents had to be held weekly, but if there was only one regent, then at least once a fortnight—an indication of the small numbers involved.

IV CONCLUSION

This account of academic life can leave no doubt that medieval universities, for all their turbulence, were places of study that made exacting demands on those who wished to succeed in it. If, from the great numbers who came and went, only a comparatively small core of scholars persevered to the end and beyond, that was not peculiar to medieval universities. The rigor of the courses and the intensity of the exercises are to be seen in the vast output of treatises, questions, and commentaries that has survived. Even if there was a premium on dialectical and speculative skill—where words and ideas were all—the product of this training is impressive. The most indifferent scholastic writing has a precision and an edge often lacking in later times. Much of it was directed to seemingly pointless ends, but that should not blind us to the questions of real substance to which, in the heyday of scholasticism at least, an education in the schools gave rise. Nor does it seem true, as Rashdall thought, that it all declined into mere aridity and logic-chopping in the later Middle Ages. Certainly there was not later the great galaxy of talent that had filled a few universities in the 120 years or so until about 1340. But this was as much the effect of the gradual shift in intellectual interest and the intellectual centers as it was

---

[126] Gibson, *Statuta antiqua*, CIII 39–42.

cause; Paris, at least, had enjoyed a unique glory as the focus of speculative thought, which was not to recur. Genius is always hard to evaluate, but scattered among the growing number of universities and professions there was probably as much intellectual activity as in the thirteenth century, and of a comparable standard. The difference was that it was now channeled into criticism and empiricism, of their nature less positive and uplifting, and, in the context of what had gone before, destructive of the very foundations of scholastic thought.

V NOTE ON LECTURES, DAYS, TERMS, DEGREES AND DISPUTATIONS

Ordinary Lectures. Formal lectures (*lectiones ordinarie*) delivered by masters in the mornings at fixed hours and for a fixed period of the year, usually from October to Lent. They were normally more analytical and speculative, raising philosophical or theological questions as well as expounding the text. They could begin as early as 6 A.M. and could continue until 2 or 3 P.M.

Cursory Lectures (Lectiones cursorie). Usually but not exclusively given by bachelors. They could not be held in the official hours for ordinary lectures in the morning; they frequently took place in the afternoon, but they could also be at any time when ordinary lectures were not taking place and on days when lectures were allowed. They could be delivered outside the schools and out of term. As their name suggests, they were more rapid than the ordinary lectures, and not supposed to be more than a running commentary on the text, leaving the deeper questions to those qualified to deal with them.

Legible and Disputable days (dies legibiles, dies disputabiles). The days when lectures and disputations were permitted. Disputations—apart from inceptions—were usually in the afternoons and evenings.

The Academic Year. At first there were four terms running from October to mid-September; in 1231 Gregory IX decreed a long vacation of one month.[127] Gradually the terms became three, from October 1 to the beginning of July. The feast of St. Remigius (October 1) always marked the new academic year when the courses began. The period from October until Easter was called the Grand Ordinary; and the period from Easter until the end of June the Little Ordinary. A few days' holiday were given at Christmas and Easter, but this was compensated by the numerous festival days that were nonlegible and nondisputable.

Regent Master. One officially lecturing in the schools.

Nonregent Master. One not officially lecturing but who could still do so.

Responsion. A preliminary examination to determination.

Determination. The point at which a student became a bachelor in the arts faculty by being admitted to dispute for forty days during Lent under a regent master.

Inception. Admission to the mastership.

Necessary Regency. The obligation to lecture in the schools originally for two or (in law) more years after having incepted.

Disputatio Ordinaria. Formal public disputation held regularly in the schools, presided over by a master.

Vespers. The first part of the inception disputation, held in the evening at the hour of vespers, in which the first two of four questions were debated.

The Principium. The opening lecture given by an incepting master or by bachelors beginning a book of the Bible or the *Sentences.*

The Aula. The second part of the inception disputation, which took the remaining two questions left over from Vespers the night before; it followed the inceptor's *Principium.*

The Resumptio. The first formal lecture of a new master, in which he summed up (determined) the questions of his disputation.

---

[127] *Chart.*, I, No. 79.

Determinatio. The public summing up by a master of a disputation held previously—usually a few weeks at most.

Quodlibeta. Free general discussions held twice a year, in which any question could be raised by anyone. Presided over by a master who determined separately at a second public session the next day.

Collatio. Either a short sermon usually delivered at inception, or a private discussion within a school or a religious house among students, or a course of lectures or readings.

Part Two

DOCTRINAL AND INTELLECTUAL

FOUR

Paris: Doctrinal and Intellectual Developments during the Thirteenth and Fourteenth Centuries

There is a parallel between the distinctive histories of the universities at Paris and Oxford and thir doctrinal and intellectual histories—not that it must be overemphasized at the expense of their common tradition and evolution. Both shared the same major phases in thought, as they shared the same institutions and academic structure; many of their thinkers—certainly English ones from Alexander Neckham and Alexander of Hales to Duns Scotus and Ockham—were members of both *studia*. Above all they worked within the same universal framework of Christian faith confronting the Greco-Arabian corpus of philosophy and science. Their ends, if not their means, were identical. Nevertheless within this common foundation there were secondary variations that it is equally important to recognize if we are to do justice to each. Oxford to a great extent belonged to itself; Paris belonged to Christendom: it was the direct concern of the papacy for its doctrines as much as its institutions. Whatever happened there had European-wide ramifications, as we saw in the conflict between seculars and mendicants. Its debates, like its struggles, were on an ecumenical scale. Oxford's, on the other hand, were of more domestic proportions and rarely resounded outside academe. They were nevertheless of comparable importance, certainly in the long term.

187

Nothing could be more misconceived than to see scholastic Oxford as the mere reflection of scholastic Paris. If there were echoes from across the channel, as in the case of the 1277 condemnations, they were not all from one direction. As Oxford benefited in its institutional history from not being the center of attention so it did also doctrinally and intellectually. Aristotle and the Arabian thinkers were not—until 1277 and fleetingly in 1284—the explosive presence that they were at Paris; there was none of the conflict over poverty and Joachist prophecy; the impact of Ockhamism was not so disruptive. Traditionalism in theology went with more radical innovation in science; there was a continuity in outlook reaching down from Grosseteste to Bradwardine that warrants our speaking of an Oxford school in a way that it is impossible to do of Paris.

Paris had all the glories and miseries of being a public figure never able to perform a private action. It attracted to it all the greatest minds (in theology and philosophy) and most of the great controversies. There was not therefore the homogeneity that there was at Oxford. We shall accordingly consider the intellectual developments at Paris under a number of different aspects; [1] the contrast with Oxford will become plain in Chapter Five when we come to treat the intellectual developments there over the same period.

I ARISTOTELIANISM

I use this term for the corpus of doctrines and knowledge associated with Aristotle and his Arabian and Jewish commentators. In one sense therefore it is imprecise because it includes much that was not Aristotelian at all. In another sense, however, I have chosen it just because, in their impact on Christian thinkers, these different elements were inseparable; not only was the *Liber de causis,* one of the most formative works in the Arabian and Jewish systems, taken for Aristotle's (usually as part three of

---

[1] To prevent the footnotes becoming unwieldy, they have been restricted to the more essential references. A full bibliography will be found in Gilson, *A History of Christian Philosophy in the Middle Ages* (London, 1955), which also provides the standard account of what follows.

his *Metaphysics*) until Aquinas recognized it as by Proclus, but it can be said that the main phases of speculative thought from the end of the twelfth century to the beginning of the fourteenth century largely corresponded to the alternating influence of Aristotle, Avicenna, and Averroes. This was not a simple matter of one thinker outrunning the others, to be overtaken in his turn. Nor, as the older nineteenth century historians—Jourdain, Haréau, and Renan among others—thought, was it because Aristotle gradually became released from the Neoplatonic garb of the Arabic-Latin translations in which he first appeared to the West: we have already seen how important early on, from the middle decades of the twelfth century, the translations of Aristotle's works direct from the Greek became. It was in fact far less a case of the true Aristotle being rediscovered—and even less of his being ousted in his turn by Averroes—than of his metaphysics displacing the older Neoplatonic tenets that prevailed among Christian theologians until the middle of the thirteenth century. That is to say, the change was as much a change in attitude toward Aristotle's metaphysics and moral and natural philosophy—primarily on the part of Albert the Great and Thomas Aquinas—as it was in any sudden new knowledge of Aristotle. It was this adoption of an Aristotelian rather than a Neoplatonic metaphysics as the foundation of a theological system that marked the great revolution in medieval thought in the thirteenth century. It entailed a twofold movement: a true knowledge of Aristotle's outlook, freed above all from the influence of the *Liber de causis;* and a desire to employ it to underpin a natural theology or Christian philosophy. The first was the prerequisite for the second, but not its cause. Until Albert the Great, and far more until Thomas Aquinas, theologians had jibbed at embracing Aristotelian principles to establish Christian tenets, such as proofs for the existence of God. It took more than Aristotle purified from the interpretation of Avicenna's encyclopedia (The *Sufficientia*) to make him acceptable; and it is of overriding importance for the intellectual history of the thirteenth and fourteenth centuries that to the majority of theologians, both before and after St. Thomas, Aristotle represented an alien outlook, although in matters of logic and natural philosophy his authority was universal.

This antinomy was the heart of the problem of Aristotle in the thirteenth and fourteenth centuries. On the one hand he provided the indispensable foundations of knowledge of the natural world and of logic on which all other intellectual activities were built; on the other he denied and—if the opposition were pressed—threatened the tenets of Christian belief. He was at once both necessary and abhorrent. He and his commentators thus crystallized the latent conflict between natural experience and revelation in any attempt to harmonize them. It was this that made the place of reason in faith one of the central themes of the period until, with the fourteenth century, under the combined influence of Ockhamism and mysticism, nature and supernature were increasingly left to follow their own separate paths.

There are three main phases in the history of Aristotelianism during this period, all within the thirteenth century, and all centering on Paris. The first is from 1210 until 1231, when the teaching of Aristotle's natural and metaphysical writings was banned in the faculty of arts. Included with them also were the works of Avicenna, John Scotus Eriugena, David of Dinant, and Amaury of Bène, which raises the problem of the connection—if any—between them. In this period knowledge of Avicenna becomes evident. The second phase is from about 1230 to about 1260, when Aristotle's metaphysics and natural philosophy were no longer under ban, even if only tacitly permitted. The growth of Aristotle's influence can be seen on all sides, among the theologians as well as the artists, culminating in the writings of Albert the Great and St. Thomas Aquinas; it was accompanied by new translations of Aristotle's works and the transmission of those of Averroes.

The third phase was from the 1260's until 1277, the years of heterodox Aristotelianism among the arts faculty, the so-called Latin Averroists under Siger of Brabant. It led to renewed condemnations of Aristotle in 1270 reaching a climax in 1277. Both tendencies—the Christian Aristotelianism of St. Thomas and the heterodox Aristotelianism of Siger of Brabant—came under attack; the hostility to Aristotle always latent in the theological faculty was released in an unprecedented list of over two hundred condemned propositions.

The fourth and last phase was the aftermath; from one point

of view it could be said to have lasted until the fifteenth century. The attempt to harness Aristotelian metaphysics to theological truths was discredited; Averroes lay under a shadow; and it was to Avicenna with his much more strongly Neoplatonist outlook that some of the greatest thinkers of the later thirteenth and earlier fourteenth century—Henry of Ghent, Duns Scotus, Meister Eckhart—turned. But by 1320 the era of the great systems —which had come about under the impetus of the new knowledge—was over. Ockhamism reigned instead, bringing, as we shall see, new doctrinal problems scarcely less challenging.

1210–1230. In 1210 and again in 1215 bans were pronounced against the reading of Aristotle's books on natural philosophy, and their commentaries, under pain of excommunication. The two occasions differed in a number of respects. Before considering them it is worth trying to recall the background. This was the circulation at Paris, above all in the arts faculty, of the works of Aristotle and his commentators, especially Avicenna, and the hostility to them on the part of the leading members of the theological faculty. The latter were conservatives deeply distrustful of the new tendencies. Although the dialectical form of the Lombard's *Sentences* was by then generally accepted, the content of theology was still predominantly sacramental and moral rather than metaphysical or speculative. This can be seen from the works that are known. Almost all show a distrust of natural, profane knowledge and a reliance on scripture. Thus Stephen of Tournai inveighed against those who sought truth in the figments of poets, philosophical opinions, the rules of Priscian, the laws of Justinian, the doctrine of Galen, rhetorical speech, the perplexities of Aristotle, the theorems of Euclid, or the conjectures of Ptolemy ". . . The arts called liberal are of great value in sharpening the understanding of scripture . . . but the reading of pagan books darkens, not enlightens, the mind." [2] Peter Comestor, author of the *Historia scholastica,* which, as a sign of older times at Oxford, remained in the thirteenth century the alternative to the Lombard's *Sentences,* also wrote a number of other theological works. None shows any trace of the influence

---

[2] Quoted from M. Grabmann, *I divieti,* 61; and for what follows, *ibid.,* 62 ff.

of the new learning. Their themes were pastoral and sacramental; theology was the "celestial philosophy" which had no need of the adornments of profane knowledge. Prepositinus of Cremona, one of the main figures in the theological faculty and chancellor of the university from 1206 to 1210, for all his profound knowledge gained in Italy of the Old and New Logic of Aristotle, and of grammar and rhetoric, never went beyond them to metaphysics or the natural knowledge brought by the new learning. He, too, spoke of the "vain wisdom which is the eye of the philosophers and dialecticians who with it see clouds and inanities." His predecessor, Peter of Poitiers, likewise displayed no interest in Aristotle's philosophical writings. The same attitude was shared by Stephen Langton, Martin of Cremona, Godfrey of Poitiers, and Robert de Courçon himself, who was to repeat the ban in 1215. De Courçon had studied theology at Paris from 1190 to 1195; he was probably a master in the theological faculty between 1204 and 1210. His principal work was a *Summa theologiae;* like his master Peter the Chanter he too regarded theology as the "celestial philosophy" which consisted in "good rules and faith," concerned essentially with moral and sacramental matters.

To such men the spread of Aristotelian and Arabian philosophy among the arts faculty could only cause growing concern; it threatened to pollute theology at its source in the study of the seven liberal arts. There can be no doubt that their attitude helped to bring about the first ban on the reading of Aristotle's philosophy. In 1210, as throughout the periodic official attacks on Aristotelianism in the thirteenth century, the theological faculty played a leading part. To treat their opposition in terms of interfaculty rivalry or university politics is untenable; as we have repeatedly had occasion to see, the majority of seculars in the theological faculty were also masters of arts and remained in some degree connected with it and their nations. Nor were the seculars more noticeably advanced in their outlook than the mendicants. The root of their opposition to Aristotle lay in the difference in outlook between arts and theology. The artists were concerned with logical and philosophical problems, for all practical purposes to the exclusion of theological considerations; the criteria were philosophical not doctrinal, whereas those of theology were dogmatic. Hence the potential for clashes was always there. They had arisen from the time of the revival of speculative thought in the eleventh century; Berengarius, Roscelin, and Abelard had all met trouble by following reason too far. The difference from 1200 onward was that the path to reason was by the works of Aristotle and his commentators. As a result what had been caused by excessive use of logic now came from the application of non-Christian philosophy; the danger was no longer merely from a clash of terms but from opposed world outlooks.

The first official reaction to this danger—which never became real until the 1260's—was at the provincial synod of Sens in 1210. It was held at Paris and presided over by the archbishop Peter of Corbeil, who had also been a master of theology and canon law at Paris from 1190 to 1198. Thus he also stood for the older outlook of the theological faculty, which was almost certainly represented at the synod as it was in 1215. What was distinctive about the proceeding in 1210 [3] was that Aristotle's works were only one of the objects of anathema; they also included the heresies of Amaury of Bène and David of Dinant. Whereas the ban "on the books of Aristotle on natural philosophy and their commentaries" only extended to their being "read at Paris in public or secret," Amaury's body was to "be exhumed and cast into unconsecrated ground," and the writings of David of Dinant were to be burned; anyone found in possession of them after Christmas was to be considered a heretic.[3a] Some followers of Amaury were named, all clerks, who were to be degraded. The precise nature of both Amaury's and David's teachings is not known, nor is it likely to be discovered because their works were destroyed or disappeared. The one thing that is fairly clear is that they were not related. They were both pantheists. But Amaury's teaching was a debased Neoplatonism in which a man by attaining spiritual perfection became one with God; it also seems to have contained a trinitarian view of history, the ages of the Father, the Son, and the Holy Spirit succeeding one another until, with the ending of the third age of the Spirit, would come

[3] *Chart.*, I, No. 11.
[3a] *Ibid.*

the end of the world. How far Amaury was responsible for the heresy of the Free Spirit, which combined pantheism with amorality, is at the least uncertain; there are echoes of it among the 219 propositions condemned in 1277. But there was no connection between his teaching and Aristotle's. The reason for its inclusion in the synod's proscriptions was probably a revulsion against the whole body of new doctrines the translations had brought. These, as we have said, were not confined to Aristotle's works: not only did they include the *Liber de causis,* but at this time, especially, Avicenna's *Sufficientia.* Avicenna's works, which were the ones almost certainly meant by "the commentaries," were also banned. The *Sufficientia* had been translated by John of Spain and Gundissalinus, as well as the separate parts of it that treated the *Physics,* the *Metaphysics,* the sixth book of *De anima,* and logic—all from the Arabic.[4] There was also from the end of the twelfth or the beginning of the thirteenth century a pseudo-Avicennan work in circulation, *De causis primis et secundis.* Although by a Christian writer, it was thought to be Avicenna's; it faithfully represented his teachings on an active intellect, a separate celestial intelligence emanating from the One or first intelligence, under whose influence individual human intelligences were able to understand. That this and other works had come to the attention of the authorities by 1210 and were included in the condemnations then and in 1215 is suggested in a reference to Avicenna by William of Auvergne, later bishop of Paris from 1229 to 1231. "His condemnation," said William "was the more just for so great a philosopher being able to see beyond such absurdities as the denial of individual immortality and yet neglecting to do so." He accused Avicenna of blasphemies against the Trinity and the divinity of Christ "which we have already destroyed elsewhere." These allusions to Avicenna's condemnation have been justly taken to refer to those at Paris in 1210 and 1215;[5] this is not to exclude other of Aristotle's Greek commentators, especially Alexander of Aphrodisias, some of whose works had been translated by then and who denied the

---

[4] Grabmann, *I divieti,* 13.
[5] *Ibid.,* 35–6; and R. de Vaux, *Notes et textes sur l'Avicennisme latin aux confins des XII*e*–XIII*e *siècles* (Paris, Vrin 1934), 45–52.

survival of the individual soul, as attacked here by William of Auvergne. It may also have extended to Alfarabi's *De scientiis,* translated by Gerard of Cremona, which could also be considered as a *summa* of Aristotle's philosophy, and his *Distinctio Aristotelis de naturali auditu,* a commentary on the *Physics.*[6]

What of Aristotle's own works, the *Libri de naturali philosophia?* There seems very good reason to take these as referring to his writings on natural philosophy as opposed to "rational philosophy" (dialectic and logic) and "moral philosophy" (ethics)—Boethius's three accepted divisions of philosophy, which, as we saw from the anonymous guide to the arts course from about 1230–40, were followed in the arts faculty. The *Metaphysics* would therefore have been included among the *libri naturales,* as they were explicitly in the 1215 condemnations. Now, as we have also seen from the same anonymous treatise, the *Liber de causis* was considered part—the third part—of Aristotle's *Metaphysics,* an attribution also made by the early thirteenth-century logician Adam of Buckfield.[7]

The *Metaphysics* had reached the West by 1210 in two Latin versions: the *Metaphysica vetutissima,* a partial Greco-Latin translation as far as Chapter Four of the fourth book dating from the twelfth century; and the middle translation (*Metaphysica media*), which included the first eleven of the twelve books and was made at Constantinople from the Greek. That it was already known at Paris can be seen from William of Brittany's remark that it was "newly brought from Constantinople and translated from Greek into Latin." [8] Accordingly the natural philosophy of Aristotle and his commentators included a body of both Aristotelian and Neoplatonic writings that together represented a non-Christian outlook; as such they were more than merely the sum of individual errors but a challenge to the Christian tenets upheld by the theological faculty. Whether its members and those of the 1210 synod regarded the heresies of Amaury and David as the outcome of this false philosophy, there can be little doubt that they saw a connection, and that the pro-

---

[6] Grabmann, I divieti, 50.
[7] *Ibid.,* 49.
[8] *Ibid.,* 44.

hibition on its further teaching was an attempt to prevent their recurrence. The relation of David of Dinant's outlook to Aristotle's writings was much more direct than Amaury's was. His materialist pantheism, endowing everything created with the presence of the creator, was combated by Albert the Great and Aquinas in their defense of the true Aristotle. It is from their references to David's lost work, *De tomis,* that we know of his doctrines; Albert, in particular, in his Commentary on the *Metaphysics* saw David's doctrines as the result of his having drawn false conclusions from Aristotle's own work.[9] For that reason the triple condemnation in 1210 of Amaury of Bène, David of Dinant, and Aristotle's natural philosophy must be regarded as all of a piece rather than the fortuitous grouping of a number of separate tendencies: that this is what they were, in the strict sense of not being truly Aristotelian, only emphasizes the ramifications of the new learning. Roger Bacon, writing eighty years later in his *Compendium studii theologiae,* gave as the reasons for these attacks Aristotle's teaching on "the eternity of the world and time." [10a] This was certainly one element found in David of Dinant; and it was to become a central tenet among the Latin Averroists from the 1260's until 1277. But that was after the study of Aristotle in the arts faculty had come to be influenced by the interpretation of Averroes, with whom Bacon bracketed Aristotle in this statement. By then Aristotle's doctrines, unalloyed and separated from any Neoplatonic overtones, were a far greater threat to Christian belief than in 1210. It was the progressive de-Platonizing of Aristotle that, in stripping his doctrine of all transcendentalism, made any reconciliation with Christian belief impossible; that was ultimately the difference between Avicenna and Averroes, just as it was between the Christian Aristotelianism of St. Thomas and the Averroistic Aristotelianism of Siger of Brabant.

There can be little doubt that both bans on Aristotle's natural

---

[9] *Ibid.,* 31. The authoritative account of David of Dinant's doctrine is in G. Théry, *Autour du décret de 1210: 1. David de Dinant, étude sur son panthéisme matérialiste* (Le Saulchoir, 1925).

[10a] Grabmann, *I divieti,* 55–6, citing *Fratris Rogeri Bacon compendium studii theologiae,* H. Rashdall, ed. (Aberdeen, British Society for Franciscan Studies, 1911), 33–4.

philosophy, in 1210 and 1215, were directed against its teaching in the arts faculty. In the first place they were not general, but confined to Paris; and in the second place the injunction of 1210, that his works were not to be "read in public or secret," was in 1215 directly applied to the arts faculty. Since "to read" (*legere*) used in 1210 was the technical term for "to lecture," it must have applied equally to the teaching of Aristotle, and predominantly in the arts faculty. That is to say Robert de Courçon's repetition of the ban in 1215 made explicit what was already contained in that of 1210. It also repeated the anathema on David of Dinant and added the name of Maurice of Spain. Much ink has been spent on trying to identify the latter, none so far convincingly. From this we cannot conclude that the ban on Aristotle's natural philosophy was directed to the artists, but rather that it was not to be included in the syllabus of the arts faculty where philosophy was taught. Nothing was said about his works being read elsewhere, either outside the university or in France; and the fact that the same ban was never applied beyond Paris university makes it clear that it was essentially in response to circumstances there. In happening at Paris, however, it became more than a local matter. Not only was Paris the center of philosophy and theology, but, at least in 1215, Robert de Courçon was acting for the pope as his legate. In his preamble to his statutes he spoke of having had "a special mandate from the pope to take effective measures to reform the state of the scholars at Paris for the better, wishing with the counsel of good men to provide for the tranquillity of the scholars in the future." [10b] He was therefore acting in an ecumenical capacity. Moreover, his references to "the counsel of good men" has been taken, probably rightly, to mean theologians and masters of the theological faculty, many of whom would have been his colleagues when he was a master. [11]

The role of the pope in regulating the affairs of the university has been amply illustrated in Chapter One. It is equally apparent in matters of doctrine. Where Robert de Courçon left off in 1215, Gregory IX resumed in 1228. During the intervening years

[10b] *Chart.*, I, No. 20.
[11] Grabmann, *I divieti*, 65–6.

Philosophy with her daughters, the Seven Liberal Arts.

the ban on Aristotle's natural philosophy was still in force; in fact it was never officially lifted. But even though it was officially adhered to during these years it could hardly be effective when every other place of learning outside Paris was free to read and study Aristotle. In consequence his natural philosophy must have continued to be read there as well; for when Gregory IX returned to the question in July 1228 with a letter to the university it was in a similar tone of hostility to that we noticed among the conservative theologians before 1210. It was also preceded by comparable attacks on the same trends away from the study of the Bible to profane knowledge. We have already mentioned William of Auvergne's attack on Avicenna; analogous assertions of the primacy of faith over the arguments of the philosophers can be found among other masters of the theology at this time. Roland of Cremona, who became holder of the first Dominican chair, wrote a *Summa theologica* in which he stressed the subordination of the liberal arts to theology.

"Philosophy is the handmaid [*ancilla*] of theology; theology is the ruler and queen of all the sciences which must wait upon it as servants . . . Theology is the science of sciences which is raised above all philosophical speculation and surpasses all others in dignity." [12]

The same sentiments can be found among the sermons of the masters in theology. Odo of Châteauroux expressed resentment at the pretensions of the philosophers.

"It is deplorable that the faculty of theology, which is called the republic [*civitas*] of sole truth and understanding, should have to speak in the language of the philosophers, that is, those in the theological faculty who seek to impose upon it an authority taken from the words of the philosophers, as if it was not derived from the highest authority from which all other authority comes." [13a]

John of St. Giles, Roland of Cremona's teacher and first holder of the second Dominican chair, was even more outspoken in directly implicating the arts faculty as the cause of the trouble.

"When such [masters of arts] come to the faculty of theology, they can be scarcely detached from their [profane] knowledge, as some of them show, who, in their theology, cannot be separated from Aristotle . . . posing philosophical questions and opinions." [13b]

Eustace of Ely, in a sermon at St. Victor, inveighed against the "pernicious men" who sought to reduce the ineffable mysteries of the Trinity, transubstantiation and the other theological truths to "our understanding . . . and presume to formulate them according to certain natural and philosophical and logical reasons, seeking to include within the rules of nature what is above all nature [i.e., supernatural]." [14a] Jacques of Vitry, the protector of the Beguines, condemned all the philosophers, save Boethius; among the many false and vain things, they said were

---

[12] *Ibid.*, 81.
[13a] *Ibid.*
[13b] *Ibid.*
[14a] *Ibid.*, 81–2.

Plato's assertion that the planets were gods, and Aristotle's opinion that the world was eternal.

"Hence we must be exccedingly wary in reading the books of natural philosophy lest we err from the excessive inquiry . . . When therefore the theological books suffice for a Christian, he should not occupy himself too much with the books of natural philosophy (*libris naturalibus*)." [14b]

Jacques of Vitry expressed the prevailing outlook among the conservative theologians when he elsewhere stressed the asymmetry between the natural and the supernatural. "The Christian faith embraces much which is above nature and against it." [15] This was the antithesis of what was to be St. Thomas's axiom of Christian Aristotelianism that "grace does not destroy nature but perfects it." For these theologians it was the encroachment of nature upon grace that they saw as the danger. Their fears were to be repeated in more systematic manner in the generation after the 1277 condemnations. Much of what was to be said then had in essence been said in the first three decades of the century. It was at this time very much bound up with the intrusion of the liberal arts into the domain of theology, thereby serving to emphasize how closely it was in turn bound up with the university at Paris. As an anonymous treatise against Aristotle put it: "When by the introductory bridge of the liberal arts they are thrust into the imperial kingdom of the faculty [of theology] they founder on diverse problems and drown in heresies." [16] William of Auxerre was another who saw the source of heresy in the desire to "apply the reasons proper to natural things to things divine, as though to equate nature or a creature with its creator": this was the error of Arius.[17] "But know," warned Gilbert of Poitiers in his *Summa theologica* written about the same time, "that divine things infinitely exceed natural things, and reasons drawn from nature can have no consonance with divine truths. The natural philosopher argues thus: Socrates is a man, Plato is a man, Cicero is a man. Therefore Socrates, Plato, Cicero

[14b] *Ibid.*
[15] *Ibid.*, 82–3.
[16] *Ibid.*, 84.
[17] *Ibid.*, 85.

are men. The theologian, however, argues thus: the Father is God, the Son is God, the Holy Spirit is God. We therefore seek not natural but theological reasons about divine truths . . ." [18]

This desire for a disjunction between natural knowledge and revelation was embodied in the statute of the Dominican order regulating the order's studies, passed under its general Jordan of Saxony in 1228. After decreeing that the brothers fitted for training shall be sent "to study in a place where there is a university", it went on to declare:

"They shall not study in the books of the Gentiles and the philosophers, although they may inspect them briefly. They shall not learn secular sciences nor even the arts which are called liberal, unless sometimes in certain cases the Master of the Order or the general chapter shall wish to make a dispensation; but they shall read only theological works whether they be youths or others." [19]

By one of the great ironies, it was precisely from the study of the philosophers within the Dominican order that first Albert the Great and then St. Thomas refashioned the official teaching of the order and ultimately of the Catholic church. This did not, however, entail overturning the relationship between the sacred and the profane. Thomas was as unyielding over the primacy of revelation and its immunity from all the doubt and questionings of natural reason as any of the theologians within or outside his order. The difference was that Thomas did not see them as antithetical but as complementary. Since reason could not arrive at three Persons but only one God, in the example of Gilbert of Poitiers, he did not go on to deny reason any role in elucidating faith. In his own words: "The philosophers have admitted the study of literature for secular doctrines; but for the theologians the study of letters pertains principally to doctrine." [20] Ultimately, then, the change wrought by St. Thomas was the acceptance of Aristotle's natural philosophy for the natural order in

---

[8] *Ibid.*

[9] *Chart.,* I, No. 57; Thorndike, *University Records,* whose translation I have followed.

[20] *Summa theologiae,* II, questio 188, art. 5, *ad* 3m.

the way that all medieval thinkers accepted his logic to classify natural experience. In upholding Aristotle's metaphysics Thomas was being the more consistent to the priorities held in common by all theologians of the epoch. Unfortunately, for him, the repercussions went beyond redressing the balance between revelation and natural experience, which until the coming of Siger of Brabant had always been held decisively on the side of revelation, even in the arts faculty.

In the 1220's, however, this balance was showing signs of shifting, as we have seen from the statements of the theologians of the time. Their fears received papal support in Gregory IX's letter of 1228. This was in the form of a general reaffirmation of theological first principles; it named no names and renewed no bans. Nor can it be said to have been directed specifically at the arts faculty; it was more a warning shot fired in the air against the misapplication of Aristotelian natural philosophy. Its tenor was very much that of the theologians quoted above. Addressed to the regent masters in theology [21] it recalled them to the belief in theology as the "celestial doctrine." "The theological understanding which a man has presides over every other faculty as the spirit rules the flesh and directs it in the way of righteousness that it may not deviate"; It must not be mixed with the adulterine words of the philosophers. Unfortunately, said the pope, it had lately come to his ears that certain among them had in a spirit of vanity departed from the teachings of the fathers and occupied themselves instead with the "profane novelties" of treating their words and scripture in terms that inclined towards natural philosophy, a course that was not only ill-considered but profane. They must expound theology "according to the approved traditions of the saints and not by corporeal means." The handmaids must be the servants of the queen; nature must do tribute to grace. Faith understood what it was impious for natural understanding to seek.

If the allusions to "the followers of the natural books" were indirect, there could be no mistaking their import. For all the anathemas of 1210 and 1215, Aristotle's natural philosophy had not only continued to be propagated; it had begun to penetrate

[21] *Chart.*, I, No. 59.

the faculty of theology. The attacks on the adherents of the *libri naturalium* were no longer in the general terms that had been used in the first decade or of the thirteenth century; they had now come to focus on their encroachment into theology. This was the difference between 1215 and 1228. Aristotelianism was now aspiring to explain what hitherto had been reserved for dogma. What the authors of the earlier bans had feared seems to have been in the process of realization. To what degree cannot accurately be said. It is always hazardous to take the opinions of an age about its own state too strictly. But there is enough to show that the growth of Aristotelian philosophy was coming to be regarded as a serious threat by the time Gregory IX wrote his letter in 1228.

Once again, however, we are presented with the striking fact that these fears and threats were confined to Paris. Of Oxford we shall speak in the next chapter. But within a year of the pope's letter to the masters in theology at Paris, his new foundation of Toulouse university was sending out a letter that, among other things, informed the universities of Christendom that "those who wish to scrutinize the bosom of nature to the inmost can hear the books of Aristotle which were forbidden at Paris." [22] Two possible explanations present themselves: Gregory IX was acting in response to the fears of the theologians at Paris when he wrote his letter, and he regarded Paris as a special case; or he had a change of heart about the dangers of Aristotle. Neither alternative excludes the other; indeed it seems that most probably Gregory in fact came, perhaps through the arguments of the papal legate in France—Cardinal Romano, who was also grand protector to the new university of Toulouse—to recognize the merits of Aristotelian philosophy in helping to strengthen the faith. At a time of growing heresy arguments were necessary to convince those who, like the Albigensians, refused to accept a simple invocation of the articles of faith. Whatever the cause, within two years Gregory also reconsidered his attitude toward the teaching of Aristotle's natural philosophy at Paris. He did not do so by an open revocation of previous decrees. The change came with *Parens scientiarum*, in which, after enjoining the

[22] *Ibid.*, No. 72; Thorndike, *op. cit.*, No. 18.

masters to give one ordinary course of lectures on Priscian he went on, "and those books on nature which were prohibited in provincial council, for certain causes, they shall not use at Paris until these shall have been examined and purged from all suspicion of errors." This was far from being a *carte blanche* for the natural philosophy; the pope also added that the masters and scholars of theology should "not show themselves philosophers but endeavour to know God" and "dispute in the schools concerning those questions only which can be settled by theological works and the treatises of the holy fathers." [23] Nevertheless the break with past policy had come. Aristotle's natural philosophy was now admitted in principle. The pope did not stop there. On April 23, ten days after *Parens scientiarum,* he gave effect to his earlier decree by appointing William of Auxerre, then archdeacon of Beauvais, who had been a master of theology at Paris, and two other ecclesiastics to examine the banned "books on nature," and exclude from them what was "erroneous or likely to give scandal or offence to readers." In this letter the pope made the striking statement that "we have learned that the books on nature which were prohibited at Paris provincial council are said to contain both useful and useless matter." [24] Somewhere there had been a conversion.

The examining commission seems never to have completed its work. Why is not clear. Perhaps because of the death in 1231 of William of Auxerre, one of the outstanding theologians of his day. More important, however, would seem to be the new translations of Averroes's commentaries on Aristotle, rendering any final examination impossible at that time.

From this time onward Aristotle and his Arabian commentators came increasingly to be studied. They had been read privately before, even among orthodox pillars of the theological faculty and university, like Philip the Chancellor (from 1218 to 1236). His *Summa de bono,* written not before 1230, shows the much fuller use that was being made of Aristotle's works at the time of Gregory IX's interventions. There are references to the *Metaphysics,* the *Physics,* the old and new *Ethics, De genera*

---

[23] Translation from Thorndike, *op. cit.,* No. 19.
[24] *Ibid.,* No. 20.

tione, De caelo, De animalibus, comprising 177 citations in all,[25] as well as to Averroes especially on problems of psychology. Philip influenced Albert the Great, as well as the early Franciscan school of Alexander of Hales and John of La Rochelle, in the use he made of Aristotelian notions of being and knowledge within an essentially Neoplatonic and Augustinian framework. Together with William of Auvergne he helped to mark the transition to the new theological thinking that becomes apparent in the second phase.

1230–1260. There was no question, as we mentioned earlier, of any sudden influx of Aristotelian doctrines into the works of Christian thinkers after 1231. The anonymous guide to the arts faculty, written probably in the decade after 1230, shows that. The same can be said of the theological faculty. The difference was longer-term and did not come to be felt until the 1240's. Although before then men like William of Auvergne, Roland of Cremona, Philip the Chancellor, John La Rochelle, and Alexander of Hales had all utilized Aristotelian concepts, they had not attempted to recast St. Augustine's framework, in which they continued to work. That is to say there was a sharp division between the intelligible realm of the mind, or soul, and the world of the senses. Being was regarded in transcendental terms; awareness of all truth could only be gained from an inner illumination that ultimately, whatever the precise mode, derived from God. The material world of *generabilia* and *corruptibilia,* on the other hand, dealt with only the fleeting and the contingent, and could lead to no higher awareness of eternal truths. Like the stick, which in water appears bent, the senses could only give false awareness. Such an attitude led to a distrust of sensory knowledge and the laws that governed it, as we saw earlier, among the traditionalists. They rejected Aristotle's metaphysics and physics just because they derived from the world of created being; from an Augustinian standpoint they had no bearing on true being; this was inseparable from the intelligible concepts or essences—humanity equinity, number—which were the source of individual beings. Reality was the property of the universal, not the particular things in which it inhered.

[5] Grabmann, *I divieti,* 111.

In one sense only among the heteredox Aristotelians—the so-called Latin Averroists—and the Ockhamists—the so-called Nominalists of the later Middle Ages—was this outlook entirely rejected. For the majority of Christian thinkers—all who in fact sought some connection between the created and the divine—the belief in a transcendental order of reality was indispensable. Without it there was no means of proceding from the flux and multiplicity of individual beings to being itself; and without the concept of being over and above its created manifestations there could be no concept of a supreme being as the fount of all other being, that is to say, a metaphysical conception of a creator. It was precisely this that was lacking from the traditional theology. There had been few attempts to establish the existence of God or to relate the notion of uncreated being to created beings. The outstanding exception, St. Anselm's so-called ontological proof, had followed St. Augustine's Neoplatonic path of an order of intelligible reality from which God's existence could be deduced. It was independent of any metaphysical presuppositions other than the assumption that true being was essence and was therefore to be known in the mind by reference to its concepts—humanity, goodness, truth—and not to the individuals existing outside it in the material world.

The growing use of logic did not alter this basis; to analyze the meaning of terms and their correspondence with things, as Abelard and his successors did, could provide epistemological and psychological explanations of the process of knowing but not a metaphysical account of the constituents of being. For this there had to be awareness of the different modes of existence in the way described by Aristotle and adapted by his Arabian commentators. Accordingly until this began to be done there was no fundamental shift in approach either among the philosophers of the arts faculty or the theologians at Paris. In the case of the former, most of their activities until the 1240's were in logic.[26] John Pagus was one of the most prominent of those engaged in it. He was mentioned by Gregory IX in a letter of recommendation to the French king in 1230, probably on his return to Paris after having been to the papal curia over the suspension

---

[26] van Steenberghen, *Aristotle in the West* 100 ff.

of lectures. He was probably a master in the arts faculty until about 1231, when he entered the faculty of theology, becoming a master after 1242. Three of his works on logic have survived. William of Shyreswood was another logician, and one of the most outstanding of the thirteenth century, who probably taught at Paris before 1245; he was at Siena in 1246. His principal work was a *Summulae logicales,* a manual of formal logic. He also wrote the *Syncategoremata,* and the *Insolubilia;* both of the last-named were concerned with apparently insoluble problems raised in the debates (*sophismata*) in the schools and became a favorite genre of logical writing in the thirteenth and fourteenth centuries. The most famous of all the Paris logicians at this period was William's pupil, Peter of Spain, who later as Pope John XXI (from 1276 to 1277) started the inquiries at Paris that led to the 1277 condemnations. He was a master at Paris until about 1246. He also wrote a *Summulae logicales,* which, in this case, became the textbook for teaching logic during the rest of the Middle Ages. He was later rector of a faculty of medicine—probably at an Italian university, where he composed one of the earliest expositions of Aristotle's psychology, the *Liber de anima.* Others who taught in the arts faculty in the 1240's and 1250's and wrote on logic were William of St. Amour, whom we shall encounter again in the disputes on poverty; Lambert of Auxerre, again the author of a *Summulae logicales,* with close affinities to Peter of Spain's work of the same title; and Nicholas of Paris, a prolific writer of commentaries on the logical works of Porphyry, Aristotle, Gilbert of Porrée, and Boethius, as well as logical glosses on the books of Donatus and Priscian: he also concerned himself with speculative grammar.

Until the middle of the thirteenth century logic remained the central activity of the arts faculty; much of the surviving literature—most of which is unpublished—derives from the logical disputations (*sophismata*), which were, as we mentioned in Chapter Three, designed to teach proficiency in argument. These activities were far from sterile; logic was the universal art that lay at the base of all subsequent philosophical and theological activity.

There was also an interest in ethics among the masters of the arts faculty. Robert de Courçon in his statutes had, as we saw, permitted its teaching, and several commentaries on the *Nicho-machaean Ethics* are known that date before Robert Grosset-este's translation of the work between 1240 and 1243. Two of them are on the so-called *Old Ethics* (*Ethica vetus*), making up books two and three; one is a commentary on the first book known as the *New Ethics* (*Ethica nova*). The second and third commentaries both quote Averroes and so probably date from between 1230 and 1240; they also raise questions on the text after having first commented it literally. They are all noteworthy for treating the problems they bring forward—on the soul, the intellect, free will, natural and theological virtues, good and evil —in Christian terms; although inspired by Aristotle and Avicenna their solution was by reference to St. Augustine's teaching and dogma. Thus Avicenna's notion of a separated active intellect was rejected as abhorrent to the Christian belief in an individual immortal soul. Philosophy had not yet sought an autonomous terrain where it made its judgements independently of theological truth. On the other hand, the very need to distinguish theological truth from philosophical method, which all these commentaries recognized, contained the germs of this very divergence. As van Steenberghen has said, "It only needs some master of theology to press too strongly the philosophical viewpoint on some matter" to cause a conflict between philosophy and theology.[27] This was to happen with Siger of Brabant and his confrères less than two decades later. But it was a danger inherent from the first in the pursuit of philosophy as an independent activity, or, more accurately, within a separate faculty—of arts—where the criteria were precisely those of the logical arts taught there. This separation of arts from theology certainly accentuated the divergence between natural philosophy and Christian belief that came to a head in the 1270's. But it would be unreal to see the conflicts between them as merely the reproduction of the divisions within the university at Paris or elsewhere. Certain historians of the intellectual history of the period tend toward this view; but such an explanation ignores the vital fact that it was only during the 1260's and 1270's that the faculty of arts set the pace over Aristotle's philosophy. The great

---

[27] *Ibid.*, 107.

innovations had come either from secular masters of theology like Alexander of Hales or from the friars, Albert the Great, Bonaventure, St. Thomas, just as it was the theologians, Henry of Ghent, Matthew of Aquasparta, Duns Scotus, and a host of others, who after 1277 evolved a new relationship between faith and reason, and who later still with William of Ockham and his followers made an even more radical break with the past. That many of these—the seculars—had been masters of arts first does not alter the fact. Indeed, in retrospect, the developments within the arts faculty during those two decades were the nearest that it ever came to attaining doctrinal autonomy in the Middle Ages. The year 1277 was not so much the defeat of the arts faculty by the theologians as the reaffirmation of the supremacy of theology as the queen of sciences. If it effectively meant the end of the independent efforts of the philosophers to fashion their own outlook, it also ensured that the main doctrinal and intellectual developments in speculative matters remained the prerogative of the theologians.

Looked at from that standpoint, the growth of a movement of natural philosophy in the faculty of arts in the 1260's and 1270's was an aberration. It reversed the gradual assimilation of Aristotelianism into theological discourse. The achievements of the theologians stand as the lasting monuments to the intellectual life of thirteenth-century Paris; theirs are the systems that are remembered rather than those of the philosophers or logicians. This must not, however, diminish the significance of events in the arts faculty during the 1260's and 1270's. Their importance lay as much as anything in the failure of the movement of Siger of Brabant and his confrères: not only did it show the impossibility of a self-regulating natural philosophy, following its own criteria, at this time; it also provided the catalyst for the subsequent evolution of speculative thought. After 1277 nothing was, intellectually, ever the same again; neither theologian nor mathematician nor scientist—often the same individual—could neglect the lesson of where following natural criteria too far could lead. However much he might continue to turn to the pagan philosophy of Greece or of the infidels of Arabia for his concepts and natural explanations, they were never again allowed to extend to theological truths. If the world in the fourteenth century became progressively more knowable, God and revelation were correspondingly made to stand outside such knowledge; discourse about them was reserved to the articles of faith.

Accordingly when we come to consider the main philosophical developments between 1230 and 1260 they are to be found not in the logical preoccupations of the arts faculty but among the theologians who were making increasing use of the thought of Aristotle and Avicenna in particular. During this period there were no further attempts to ban their works at Paris.[28] At Paris, on the other hand, from the 1240's the works of natural philosophy were being commented though their study was not so advanced as at Oxford. Roger Bacon, coming to Paris in about 1245 from Oxford, where they had long been openly taught, lectured on Aristotle's *Physics* and *Metaphysics* in the arts faculty as well on the pseudo-Aristotelian *De plantis* and *De causis,* in the form of questions; unlike either the paraphrases of Albert the Great and Avicenna or the literal commentaries of Averroes and later St. Thomas Aquinas, Bacon treated the problems arising from the text according to the *pro* and *contra* (*sic et non*) method of scholasticism. In doing so he shows the degree to which he had assimilated the new philosophy. But this did not make him an Aristotelian. Not only did he severely criticize Averroes in particular, making him responsible for the attribution to Aristotle of the doctrine of the eternity of the world; he also, in the Oxford tradition, adhered to the non-Aristotelian tenets of a universal combination of form and matter (hylomorphism) as the stuff of all being, spiritual as well as material. This, among other notions, came to be associated with the so-called Augustinian school, but Bacon relied for many of his ideas on Arabian thinkers, Avicenna, Algazel, and Averroes, as well as being, like his master Grosseteste, strongly influenced by the Neoplatonic notions of the older outlook. This mingling of streams, widespread in the 1240's, was akin to a Neoplatonic Aristotelianism.[29] At this stage there was no attempt to synthesize the old and the new, the Neoplatonic and the Aristotelian, perhaps

[28] It is true that Innocent IV, in conferring the privileges of *Parens scientiarum* on Toulouse university in 1245 (*Chart.,* I, No. 149), was also repeating Gregory IX's prohibition on the *libri naturales,* but this hardly constitutes a deliberate renewal of the ban.

[29] van Steenberghen's term, *op. cit.,* 113.

because the *Liber de causis* was still ascribed to Aristotle so that there was no awareness of their divergence. Bacon in this period belonged to the arts faculty; but, as we have already said, one of the characteristics in the years before Siger of Brabant and the Latin Averroists was the artists' acceptance of theological criteria for their excursions into philosophy. Indeed, in the case of Bacon and Robert Kilwardby, who later as archbishop of Canterbury presided over his own condemnations at Oxford in 1277, they were always theologians even when they were members of the arts faculty.

Within the theological faculty itself we have remarked on the strong opposition to the new philosophy until 1230. Nevertheless by then three theologians had already emerged as examples of a new trend: William of Auxerre, William of Auvergne, and Philip the Chancellor. Of these William of Auvergne, who was bishop of Paris at the time of the great dispersion in 1229 and remained there until his death in 1249, went further toward combining the new developments into a distinctive outlook. Perhaps the most striking aspect of his attitude was his acceptance of Aristotle in what concerned the natural world: he should be supported in "all his statements in which he is found to be right." [30] William was also prepared to adapt Avicenna's notion of a separated active intellect as the active principle of the human intellect—which William opposed as it stood—by identifying the active intellect with God. He was thereby able to incorporate it into St. Augustine's doctrine of intelligible knowledge as the result of an inner illumination from God. God, for William, was the active intelligence who illuminated the human mind and so enabled it to have an intuition of what is necessarily true. He also accepted Alfarabi's and Avicenna's distinction between divine and created being. In this he was accompanied by Alexander of Hales who was a celebrated secular master in theology before he entered the Franciscan order in 1238 and became the first holder of the Franciscan chair in theology until his death in 1241. He and his pupil John of La Rochelle (died 1245), who wrote most of a *Summa universae theologiae*, completed in about 1256, which used to be ascribed to Alexander, betray the same combination of Aristotelian, Arabic, Jewish, and Neoplatonic influ-

[30] Grabmann, *I divieti*, 90.

ences. Like William of Auvergne they were concerned to establish a distinction between God and creatures in terms of different kinds of being. God was by definition both essence and existence in that his nature as creator entailed that he must exist necessarily and eternally; his creatures, on the other hand, were only *possible* beings in that of themselves they need not be; to become actual they required a creator. Accordingly, whereas God as a necessary being existed *ipso facto,* possible being did not. This distinction was a refinement on Aristotle's distinction between potential and actual being: only that which actually existed, was. Until the individual man, Socrates, took on an independent existence, his humanity—his nature as a man—was merely possible being; the essence *man* did not of itself entail the actual existence of the individual Socrates. Aristotle saw this transformation from potentiality into actuality as taking place through the agency of the form by which a being came to be what it was: the humanity of Socrates was the form by which he existed as a man. Its presence ensured his actuality as man; without it he would be merely formless matter which, by Aristotle's definition, was of itself indeterminate. Thus for Aristotle all being was actual existence, the realization of what was potentially being into actual being. For the Christian thinkers, as for Muhammadans like Alfarabi and Avicenna, this distinction between the essence or nature or form of a being and its actual existence served to emphasize the radical difference between God's being and all other being. God alone was infinite, necessary, eternal, self-caused, and fully realized (aseity); everything else was a composition of essence with existence superadded to it. This was tantamount to making existence accidental to essence, a position that both Averroes and later St. Thomas criticized.

The refinements do not concern us here. What is important to notice is the application of Aristotelian and Arabian metaphysics to theology at Paris by the later 1230's and the 1240's. There is no question that any of these theologians created new systems that integrated the tenets of faith into a comprehensive outlook. That was not to come until St. Bonaventure and St. Thomas. Nevertheless they went beyond previous developments by attempting to treat certain fundamental questions, especially God's existence, philosophically; that is, with reasons drawn from philosophy and the evidence of the created world. The fact that no theologian before St. Thomas was prepared to go the whole way in this approach and seek the source of human knowledge in natural experience gained through the senses must not be taken as a sign of philosophical immaturity which was due to the absence of a yet full-fledged Aristotelianism. The fierceness of the reaction to St. Thomas is the best illustration of the tendency among theologians of the Middle Ages toward a Neoplatonic explanation of reality. They turned away from the senses towards the intelligible world of essences and pure concepts in the mind. They treated them as two different realms corresponding to man's two different natures, the spiritual and the material. Far from the intelligible being nurtured by the senses, the senses were given understanding by the mind: it illuminated them. The intellect enabled a man to become aware of what he was experiencing through his senses.

This was perhaps the point at which St. Augustine's influence was greatest in the theology of the thirteenth century. His insistence on an inner illumination—he did not specify its mode with any philosophical precision—as the source of all understanding and higher awareness was the constant element in all non-Thomist theological thought. To call it Neoplatonist is merely to bandy terms. It is rather that those who adhered to this position were *ipso facto* dualists; they had to posit two different orders of reality, not just between the divine and the created, but at the created level. They could never therefore wholly take the laws that could be deduced from the natural world as the total frame of reference for a natural theology or Christian philosophy. Ultimately the barrier between the inner world and the world of the senses was the barrier between Augustinianism and Thomism; they were different as outlooks rather than as particular sets of philosophical concepts. Both drew on the same resources of Aristotle's logic and metaphysics together with the Neoplatonic concepts of his Arabian commentators. The different proportions in which they were used— in, say, Bonaventure and St. Thomas Aquinas—were secondary to the way in which they were used. There were no pure Aristotelians outside the philosophers in the arts faculty; but there were different attitudes toward the role that natural criteria could play in theological discourse.

It is only with Albert the Great that a change toward a more explicit recognition of the role of philosophy becomes apparent. It did not emerge until after he left Paris, where he was in the theological faculty from 1240 to 1248. This period shows a new interest in Aristotle among the theologians. William of Auvergne, Alexander of Hales, and John of La Rochelle were already active there, and in the arts faculty Roger Bacon was soon to lecture on the *Physics* and *Metaphysics*. One of the main pockets of conservatism was among Albert's own Dominican confrères at Paris. The early masters after Roland of Cremona—John of St. Giles, Hugh of St. Cher, Guerric of St. Quentin—doubtless partly under the influence of the Dominican constitutions of 1228, showed little interest in the new learning. Albert had later to overcome considerable hostility among the order in pursuing his intention to make Aristotle's works intelligible to the Christian world. During his eight years at Paris, however, his works were primarily theological, the product of his years in the faculty of theology, which he had entered as a bachelor in 1240. His previous training had also been largely theological. Albert had never, according to Bacon, studied arts in the schools. After a brief period at Bologna and Padua he had joined the Dominicans in 1223 and was sent to study at their house in Cologne. From 1228 to 1240 he taught theology in different convents in Germany before being sent to Paris. He spent his first two years there lecturing on the *Sentences*, from which his commentary, one of his most important theological works, originated. From 1242 until 1248 Albert occupied one of the two Dominican chairs in the theological faculty as regent master. During this period he produced his *Summa de creaturis*, another of his major theological treatises. It displays the vast erudition for which he was famed among his contemporaries, especially in Aristotle's works. Much of this is already apparent in his earlier work, *De natura boni*, written about 1236 or 1237; it testifies to the growing knowledge of Greco-Arabian philosophy in the West and particularly to Albert's determination to acquire it, even though he was a member of a religious order that had banned the study of the arts for other than theological ends. The need for such knowledge was

Albert's justification for pursuing an increasingly philosophical course in the years after he left Paris. It is doubly paradoxical that Albert, a Dominican, should not only have been the greatest influence in making Aristotle intelligible, but that his own progression was from theology to philosophy, culminating in his program of presenting all Aristotle's works to the Christian world. He did not begin this vast enterprise until after his return to Cologne to found the new Dominican *studium generale* there; he spent the greater part of his remaining life, which lasted until 1280, in Germany. But his influence extended far beyond. With the sympathetic cooperation of Humbert of the Romans, general of the Dominicans from 1254 to 1263, he succeeded in overcoming the hostility within the order to the study of Aristotle. To achieve his aim of making "all parts of the physics, metaphysics, and mathematics intelligible to the Latin world [*Latinis*]" he followed Avicenna's method of paraphrasing the works of Aristotle rather than commenting them in the manner of Averroes and later St. Thomas; although his commentaries were not equal to St. Thomas', Albert brought to bear his great store of knowledge and personal observation to amplify the texts he was elucidating. It was his preparedness to build further upon the natural knowledge and philosophy of the Greco-Arabian world and to take it, at the natural level, entirely on its own terms that constitutes Albert the Great's importance in the history of medieval thought. He was the first Christian thinker of the Middle Ages to accept natural philosophy as a self-sufficient discipline, relying for its validity entirely on natural and philosophical criteria. In doing so Albert was the first to recognize the corollary, that philosophy and theology were two distinct activities. They had different premises and different objects. The one was governed by reason and demonstration; the other by the articles of faith. The one treated natural evidence and logical proof as decisive; the other at best subordinated them to revelation and at worst rejected them should they conflict with it. With Albert they became demarcated, and each thereby gained a defined place: if reason could not demonstrate the more inaccessible truths of revelation, dogma was no substitute for observation and experience in what concerned the natural world. This was his greatest legacy, which was taken up above all by his pupil Thomas.

It did not, however, make Albert as a thinker markedly different from his contemporaries and predecessors. Like them his outlook was an amalgam of Aristotelian and Neoplatonic ideas that were never systematized. Indeed, one of Albert's main distinctions is that not only was the progenitor of a Christian Aristotelianism realized by Aquinas, but he also helped to inspire the Neoplatonic, speculative mysticism of Dietrich of Freiburg that culminated in Meister Eckhart and the Rhineland mystics; indeed, for all his reverence for Aristotle, Albert was hardly less strongly influenced by Proclus, the pseudo-Dionysius, Avicenna, and Avicebron, with their strongly Neoplatonist learnings. After leaving Paris and before turning to his program of glossing Aristotle's writings, he wrote commentaries on those of the pseudo-Dionysius. In one sense, then, Albert epitomized in his own work the division between theology and philosophy: he was at once theologian, philosopher, scientist, in which capacity he made his most original contributions, and mystic. What he lacked was the means of integrating such diverse proclivities, but that was perhaps the price of possessing them. The total effect was not a new revolutionary outlook, but rather the creation of a series of openings that were to lead others along new ways. For Albert, theology was still the queen to which all other knowledge must defer; Aristotle, he said, was not God; he could err whereas faith could not. In cases of conflicting judgements between reason and faith, reason must cede; St. Augustine was to be followed where faith was concerned. In all this Albert was no different from his predecessors or his followers, above all St. Thomas, who were ultimately theologians above all. Yet it was at this very point that such counsel was open to question in a way that had not arisen previously. The final arbitrament of faith need not follow from accepting the sovereignty of reason and natural experience in philosophy. Their separation for Albert, like Thomas, made them complementary, but not equal; when they could not agree philosophy had to submit. For them as for all theologians this was axiomatic. But what of those—in the arts faculty for instance—for whom it was not? As believers, certainly, they could not accept what contradicted the tenets of faith; but as philosophers they were under no obligation to reconcile what could be deduced by reason with what they held as Christians. As we shall see this was precisely what occurred in the arts faculty during the 1260's and 1270's. No less than St. Thomas's system, and the new investigations in natural science, the contradiction was inherent in giving philosophy its head.

These developments cannot, however, be laid at Albert's door. His work on Aristotle was not done at Paris; had it been, his presence there might have had a moderating influence. The legacy of Albert's teaching is to be seen in Thomas' synthesis between a philosophy predominantly drawn from Aristotelian concepts and a Christian theology. Even here, however, we must not exaggerate either Albert's or Thomas' influence at this time or during the thirteenth century. During Thomas's first sojourn of seven years at Paris, from 1252 to 1259, Bonaventure was regent master and holder of the Franciscan chair in the same faculty of theology from 1253 to 1257. The relation—or rather opposition—of their outlooks has been a matter of controversy, especially between Gilson and the Belgian school, Mandonnet and van Steenberghen. Bonaventure's main theological work, his Commentary on the *Sentences,* was written during this period; in 1257 he was appointed general of the Franciscan order. Thenceforth he was lost to full-time study and never wrote a systematic theological work of maturity comparable to St. Thomas's *Summa theologiae,* despite his numerous other treatises on the questions of theology, religious life, and mysticism. Bonaventure did not ignore Aristotle; far from it. He treated the problems raised by him and his Arabian commentators on the nature of the soul, the eternity of the world versus creation in time, God's relation to his creatures, and the metaphysical question of the role of forms in being. On a number of points he was prepared to accept Aristotelian concepts for the natural world; for example, the doctrine that knowledge of the created world comes through disengaging or abstracting the essences of things from the individuals encountered in the senses; or that man knows under the influence of an active intellect—which, contrary to the Arabian thinkers, Bonaventure located within the individual soul. But, even so, Bonaventure's acceptance of Aristotelianism applied only to sensory experience. Like St. Augustine and those who sought to renew his teaching in the face of Aristotelianism—for example, William of Auvergne, Alexander of Hales,

John of La Rochelle—Bonaventure saw true reality as the property of the intelligible and ideal; it was to be glimpsed by turning away from the world and by means of an inner illumination that came from God. Once again we cannot discuss the particulars here. But higher truth belonged to the realm of grace, not nature. Natural knowledge on its own was sterile and idle curiosity. The soul as spiritual being owed nothing to the senses. Love of Christ was at the center of man's life.

The part that Aristotle played in Bonaventure's outlook was a predominantly negative one; it led him to marshall the theological truths handed down by St. Augustine, which had gradually been furbished with philosophical notions, mainly Neoplatonist: inner illumination with special emphasis on the divine quality of light as the universal element of being; individual being as composed of a plurality of forms, including a distinctive form for matter; the soul as an independent spiritual being; seminal reasons or tendencies inherent within matter to receive certain forms (a notion taken over by St. Augustine from the Stoics). Within these divisions Bonaventure utilized Aristotle's distinction between potentiality and actuality to distinguish God's being from that of his creatures. But the context was non-Aristotelian; it was theological, with St. Augustine as the main authority for what was essentially a Christian spirituality. There are plenty of instances in St. Bonaventure's writing to show that he did not claim any special insight into Aristotle's philosophy.[31] Was this wholly due to the lack of a full knowledge of his works at this stage, a knowledge Thomas was to gain from his master Albert and to pursue by his own studies of Aristotle's works? Or was it from a different orientation? We can admit the first without seeing it as determining the second. Everything that we can tell of Bonaventure's outlook during his time as a Paris master and throughout his subsequent life points to a fundamentally different outlook from the Aristotelianism of Aquinas. Bonaventure's Augustinianism was not just a *faut de mieux* in the absence of a comprehensive natural philosophy; it belonged to a tradition that put inner experience before all external knowledge, that made the soul the center of awareness, and that sought illumination by

---

[31] For examples see van Steenberghen, *Aristotle in the West*, 150–1.

seeking God and following Christ. Bonaventure was a theologian, a mystic, and a Franciscan; to him, as to his spiritual master, philosophy and knowledge of the world were distractions from Christ's life and word. He had a deep distrust of the natural power of reason unaided by divine grace; this colored his attitude toward the pagan philosophers. Although he drew from them he did not lean on them; he always distinguished between them and the Christian authorities (*sancti*), and gave them no independent standing.[32] On the contrary, the most remarkable feature of Bonaventure's outlook was its thoroughgoing theological character; philosophy was not merely the auxillary of faith; it was governed by it. Bonaventure was so imbued with an awareness of God's presence that he sought to demonstrate it by arguments that went beyond the limits of demonstrable reason, such as his attempts to prove the creation of the world in time. This was the other extreme from the advocates of philosophy; far from recognizing it as an independent pursuit, he made no distinction between what was valid for natural experience and what was germane to faith. Or, more accurately, his concern for reason was merely as the adjunct of faith—to the point where it lost an independent standing. Bonaventure was neither antirational nor anti-Aristotelian. He knew enough of Aristotle to adopt what served him in the making of a theological synthesis. But it was the response of a theologian who put Christ and St. Augustine first. In this he was to be followed by a whole generation for whom—in the light of Aristotle's effects on the arts faculty—natural experience and rational demonstration could not be guides in seeking God.

From that point of view Bonaventure's outlook could be said to be antithetical to that of Thomas Aquinas. Whereas Bonaventure looked to Christ's word and example for wisdom, and would do with nothing less, Aquinas was prepared to turn to philosophy and the voice of reason when it could be heard in *rerum natura*. If he did not credit natural experience or man's human powers with any greater capacity than Bonaventure to elucidate the divine mysteries, he was also prepared to accept for them a less transcendent role: because man in his present state

---

[32] E.g., *Collationes in Hexaemeron*, F. Delorme, ed., (Quaracchi, 1934), 215 ff.

was bound to the physical world and gained his experience through the senses, these had to be the starting point in all his knowledge; such higher awareness as he could attain to in this state must be the outcome of the knowledge that he derived from it. Thus, whereas Bonaventure had posited a dualism between the intelligible and the sensory, and sought the former by turning away from the latter, Thomas turned to the lower to seek the higher; rather, he insisted that man must work from sensory knowledge to intelligible awareness, from the particulars given to him in the senses to the universal, which the mind could disengage from them. The higher knowledge that could thus be gained was not theological. It had no demonstrative bearing on God's nature, the Incarnation, creation in time, or the other articles of belief, which could only be held on faith. But it could offer an analogy between the created and divine, and, from the laws of cause and effect deducible from this world, point to a higher order of causality between God as first cause and his creatures. To do so Thomas turned to Aristotle, taking his distinctions between potentiality and act, matter and form, and his fourfold order of causality to establish the distinction and relation between God and the world; he thereby achieved a natural theology based on reason and natural knowledge that had been envisaged but not accomplished by Albert the Great. Thomas succeeded because he was the first to act on a thoroughgoing distinction between faith and reason, not to separate them, as the Latin Averroists did, but to buttress one by the other; reason was followed as far as it would lead, not along its own path but in the service of faith. Thomas employed Aristotle's four causes not simply for themselves but in order to prove God's necessary existence from their existence; he took the distinction between form and matter, actual and potential being, to point to the difference between God's necessary being and the potential being of his creatures. At the same time Thomas did not confine himself to Aristotle's metaphysics and natural philosophy. Not only did he give them an entirely new Christocentric and theological import, entirely lacking in Aristotle's naturalism; he also shared much of the same Neoplatonist inspiration as his contemporaries. Without a similar belief in such fundamental principles as divine ideas, containing the archetypes of all created beings, and man's soul as last in the hierarchy of spiritual beings, linked

to those above, there could have been no sense of God's participation in the world. Only thus was Aristotle's first cause and unmoved mover, devoid of all attributes other than its own eternal
actuality, transformed into the living God of Christian belief.
Participation was as indispensable an element in Thomas's system as causality and analogy. It was his achievement to fuse
them into a Christian philosophy. This very fact, that his system
was both Christian and philosophical, marked it off from both
the pure Aristotelians, who were to emerge from the arts faculty,
and the Augustinians, who continued to dominate the theological
faculty before, during, and after Thomas's time there.

The greater part of his writing on Aristotle was done away
from Paris, while teaching in the Dominican *studia* at Naples
from 1259 to 1268. Unlike Albert the Great, however, he returned there for a further three years from 1269 to 1272, and
was directly involved in the doctrinal conflicts that culminated in
the condemnations of 1270 and after his death in 1277.

Thomas had first come to Paris in 1245 to study under Albert,
with whom he went to Cologne in 1248. Four years later, in
1252, he entered the theological faculty at Paris as a bachelor;
after reading the Bible for one year he spent the two years from
1253 to 1255 on the *Sentences,* becoming in 1256 master and
holder of one of the two Dominican chairs until 1259. During
this period he wrote his first major theological' work, the Commentary on the *Sentences* together with a treatise *On Being and
Essence,* disputed questions *On Truth,* wrote commentaries on
two of Boethius's works, wrote a number of *quodlibeta,* and
began his *Summa contra Gentiles.* He owed his initial grounding
in philosophy to his years in the arts faculty at Naples, from
1239 to 1244, consolidated by seven years under Albert the
Great. Thus by the time he came to the theological faculty he
had had twelve years of philosophical training and knowledge of
Aristotle already assimilated to a remarkable degree. It enabled
him, as we have said, to be the first to attempt a synthesis of philosophy and theology, founding their harmony on the explicit
recognition of their distinctiveness. It worked for Thomas because of both his genius and his profound Christian conviction,
which made faith the final arbiter. To faith Aristotle no less than
any other pagan philosopher had to bow.

It was during the crucial decade when Thomas was in Naples

that the study of Aristotle at Paris broke through the safeguards to faith that he had erected. Whether his presence at Paris then could have prevented or mitigated this development, his absence, as well as Albert the Great's, meant that there was no middle way between those in the arts faculty who put Aristotle first and those among the theologians who adhered to St. Augustine and the Fathers in all matters of faith. By the time Thomas returned to Paris in 1269 the rift between the philosophers and theologians had become too absolute for him to do other than enter the struggle that culminated in 1277, three years after his death.

1260–1277. The beginning of the movement toward this impasse between philosophy and theology cannot be given any firm date; it becomes apparent by the later 1260's, mainly in the writings of St. Bonaventure, Albert the Great, and St. Thomas. Nor can the conflict to which it led be said to have any specific cause, even though it is principally associated with Siger of Brabant. The tendency inherent in the study of philosophy was to follow natural reason beyond the limits set by faith, and was to be found in the arts faculty, among those who taught and thought as philosophers. The dangers in such an approach arose precisely from the pursuit of nontheological knowledge within a theological context, as the questions raised by Aristotle's *Ethics* in the 1230's have already shown.[33] As time went on, however, what had been little more than a series of random exercises in philosophical argument became an anti-Christian cosmogony, largely inspired by Averroes's interpretation of Aristotle. It led to propositions asserting that, from the point of view of natural reason, the world could only be considered eternal, that there was but one intellect for all men (monopsychism), that men had no individual, immortal souls, that God acted merely as an indirect mover, and that in place of his providence were the celestial spheres working directly on all creatures. The consequence was both implicitly and explicitly the devaluation of theology as demonstrable truth and its relegation to matters of belief.

The inspiration of Averroes was central to this outlook in two vital respects. The first was his association with the doctrine of

[33] See p. 142.

monopsychism, by which Averroes alone of Aristotle's Arabian commentators interpreted the notion of a separated active intellect as leaving man with nothing but a material and corruptible soul. The intelligible knowledge that was gained under the influence of the active intellect and formed his understanding—the possible intellect—left him on death. For Christian theologians this was to deny man any independent spiritual property that survived the destruction of his body.

Averroes's other legacy came from his attempt as a Muslim as well as an Aristotelian to solve the antinomy between faith and reason. The very fact that the criteria of philosophy were derived from natural experience and reason meant that its pursuit was liable to lead to conclusions that conflicted with belief. In this Averroes, like Albert and Thomas, was attempting to delimit the two spheres; but whereas the two Christian thinkers insisted on the subordination of philosophy to theology, in the last resort, Averroes refused to try to reconcile the irreconcilable. The very differences between reason and faith arose from dealing with different levels of truth; to pretend that these did not exist was to injure both philosophy and theology. What was philosophically true was not necessarily true theologically, and when it was not the distinction should be stated, not artificially suppressed. At the height of the crisis the artists were accused, by Thomas among others, of affirming by reason what was contrary to faith. This is not apparent from the surviving works of the leading so-called Latin Averroist, Siger of Brabant, although after the first condemnation involving him, in 1270, he tended increasingly to stress that propositions held philosophically could be wrong when judged theologically. That, however, was not the same as "the double truth," because it did not posit two different truths, but, on the contrary, acknowledged that a philosophical proposition might be false according to faith. It is impossible to know whether Siger was sincere when he introduced this saving clause. Even if he was not, it was a valid position for a believer to take when he wished at once to pursue philosophical enquiry and safeguard his faith. He was not the first or the last to do so.

We have seen that the works of Averroes began to be known at Paris after 1230, mainly through Michael Scot's translations. There are signs that his doctrine of monopsychism was already causing concern in high circles by the mid-1250's. In 1256 Albert the Great, on a visit to Rome to defend the mendicants before the pope, was commissioned by Alexander IV to write a treatise against Averroes's errors. He did so in his *De unitate intellectus contra Averroem.* This is the first indication that Averroes was associated with the doctrine of monopsychism; a few years earlier both Roger Bacon and Adam of Buckfield, at Oxford, had interpreted Averroes as opposing the notion of a single active intellect for all mankind. At this stage Albert's arguments were directed against the Arabian thinkers as a whole, not as a broadside against a school of Averroist disciples within the heart of Christendom; Albert's attack centered on the question of personal immortality, which he treated as a theoretical matter rather than as a source of subversion. Nor must all the responsibility for the growth of Aristotelianism in the arts faculty be laid at Averroes's door; the statutes of 1252 and 1255, by extending the curriculum to Aristotle's works, were undoubtedly major factors. A curious sidelight in this connection was the reaffirmation by Urban IV in January 1263 of *Parens scientiarum;* [34] this included Gregory IX's prohibition of the reading of Aristotle's books of natural philosophy. The pope stated that he was renewing the bull, which had originally been issued to restore order after the enormous disturbances worked by the devil. We may grant that the pope now acting, *inter alia,* to restore tranquillity after the dissensions of Alexander IV's pontificate; but since this had ended two years previously there may well have been doctrinal reasons for including the ban on Aristotle's natural philosophy. On the other hand, too much must not be made of what may well have been a merely mechanical reissue of an earlier document in its original form. Thomas, writing against the Latin Averroists in the arts faculty in his *De unitate intellectus* in 1270, suggests that it had been growing "now for some little time." Certainly it was only from about 1267 that opposition to these heterodox tendencies mounted. It began with a series of Lenten lectures (*Collationes*) delivered by Bonaventure in that year and the following year at the Franciscan convent at Paris. In them Bonaventure attacked directly the errors of the pagan philoso-

[34] *Chart.,* I, No. 384.

phers that Siger and his followers were propagating: namely, that the world was eternal; that there was only one intellect in all men so that personal immortality was impossible; that God could not create out of nothing (*ex nihilo*); that a separate intelligence—that is, a spiritual being beyond the sublunar world —could create another spiritual being; and that everything was determined inevitably. These were more than Averroistic. They applied in greater or lesser degree to most of the teaching of Aristotle and his Arabian commentators; Bonaventure saw their source in following philosophy for itself. The only specifically Averroistic tenet was the oneness of the intellect, but it was central to much of the controversy. The argument that one intelligence could create another appears to have been a piece of ridicule on the part of the artists in inflicting on Christians the worst of both worlds: denying that God could create but allowing a mere intelligence the power of doing so. Bonaventure has been regarded as the instigator of the campaign that led to the condemnation of the teachings of Siger and his confrères. It may well be; but such a step would have been bound to come within a short time. Clearly such ideas as Bonaventure attacked could not have long remained unobserved in the very center of Christian thought.

The exact date at which Siger of Brabant started on his collision course is not known. He probably entered the arts faculty between 1255 and 1260,[35] becoming a master between about 1260 and 1265. He is mentioned in August 1266 in Simon of Brion's decree on the mode of electing a rector by the four nations.[36] He appears to have been involved in the capture of William, a canon of Tulle, and had to purge himself on pain of expulsion from the Picard nation. His writings have been the subject of a number of studies.[37] Many of his writings remain unpublished and the authenticity of some is disputed. This is not

---

[35] For details see van Steenberghen, *Aristotle in the West,* 209 ff.

[36] *Chart.,* I, No. 409, pp. 450, 456.

[37] In addition to van Steenberghen *Siger de Brabant, I,* see J. J. Duin, *Le Doctrine de la providence dans les écrits de Siger de Brabant* (Louvain, 1954), and P. Mandonnet, *Siger de Brabant et l'Averroïsme latin au XIIIe siècle* (Louvain, 1908–11). For a corrective to van Steenberghen see E. Gilson, *History,* 389–99.

the place to analyze his outlook, beyond trying to characterize it. Essentially it was the work of a philosopher, not a theologian; that did not prevent him from attempting to prove the existence of God or the relation between the first cause and the intelligences, but he was treating them from a philosophical standpoint. This was fundamentally Aristotelian, but there were also important elements of Proclus in his belief in the hierarchy of causes. Much of his writing is concerned with enumerating the opinions of the philosophers on the important questions rather than with expounding his own. It is therefore often difficult to discern his personal standpoint. On the whole he seems to have followed Averroes's interpretation of Aristotle rather than Avicenna's: this is true of his teaching on the doctrine of a single intellect, in which he supported Averroes in detaching both the active and possible intellects from man and locating them in the same separated intelligence. Yet even so, he did not adopt this position with the explicit intention of flouting Christian teaching; on the contrary, his position was hesitant and qualified, and he seems to have relinquished it and returned to a Christian view after Thomas' treatise on *The Unity of the Intellect,* written in 1270. Although monopsychism was undoubtedly one of the catalysts in the attack on Siger and his confrères, it should not be stressed to the exclusion of the other aspects of pagan philosophy or indeed even given preponderance, as the *Collationes* of Bonaventure show. The Aristotelianism under attack was a complex of doctrines that was anti-Christian primarily because it had been reached by philosophical enquiry. It came from following the pagans in their arguments. Inevitably, therefore, the issue increasingly turned upon the place of paganism in faith—certainly so far as Bonaventure was concerned. In 1273, the year before his death, he made the fiercest onslaught of his life on the artists, in a final series of lectures on the six days of creation (*Collationes in Hexaemeron*). Here he revealed clearly the gulf between the theologians and the philosophers. The latter—certainly in the pure form professed by Siger and his followers—were taking their texts as they found them and glossing them in the manner of the schools we discussed in Chapter Three. They were trained as exegetes to expound and dispute on the questions their exposition raised. As these were philosophical, so was their treatment. In one sense, then, the problem of Latin Averroism was the outcome of Aristotle's dominance of the arts-faculty curriculum from the 1250's onward. The study of his works inevitably became more than just an exercise in dialectical skills. Consciously or not, men who spend their time lecturing and commenting on texts can come to make them their own, at least methodologically. That this occurred during the 1260's and 1270's is strongly suggested not only by what Bonaventure and others like Giles of Rome and Giles of Lessines said of the artists, but by the diversity of opinions condemned in 1277. Many of them were probably compiled from hearsay and can hardly be taken very seriously as contributions to an intellectual debate. But they also suggest a climate of irreverence for ecclesiastical authority and the tendency to see problems in philosophical terms. It was this, more than anything Siger wrote, that threatened danger. The position was expressed by Bonaventure in his *Collationes in Hexaemeron.*

"It is more prudent to say that Aristotle did not think that the world was eternal, whether he himself thought so or not, for he was so great that all would follow him and affirm that he said so. All the light spread by that which has gone before would be extinguished. Let us follow him in the truth that he spoke, not in those matters where he was obscure, or which' he did not know or concealed." [38]

Bonaventure as a theologian was putting theological truth first, even to the exclusion—or, more accurately, suppression—of philosophical notions that in conflicting with it were *ipso facto* falsehoods. This was the attitude that was ultimately to prevail in the condemnation of 1277.

Thomas's attitude was entirely otherwise. Although he wrote against the errors of Averroism—on monopsychism—because he was a Christian, he argued as a philosopher. His *Tractatus de unitate intellectus,* written in 1270, used reason to expose Averroes's errors philosophically. He seems to have had some success with Siger, but not enough to turn the tide against philosophy.

[38] F. Delorme, ed. *Collationes,* 92. I owe this reference to Gilson, *History,* 726–7. The remark shows, incidentally, that Bonaventure had not become blindly hostile to Aristotle.

How could he have done so? He was himself implicated in the very movement of which the Latin Averroists were an extreme offshoot. Not altogether surprisingly, Thomas himself became an object of opprobrium that was to culminate in the inclusion of some of his own propositions among those condemned at both Paris and Oxford in 1277, three years after his death. By 1270, however, he had already come under attack. At about that time a disputation took place between him and John Pecham, Franciscan regent in theology at Paris and future archbishop of Canterbury, who was to add his own fuel to the flames of orthodoxy by renewing in 1284 the 1277 Oxford condemnation of mainly Thomist theses. According to the English Franciscan Roger Marston, "in the presence of brother Thomas Aquinas, of brother John of Pecham, and of about twenty-four other doctors" the Thomist doctrine of the oneness of form "was solemnly excommunicated as contrary to the teaching of the Saints, particularly of Augustine and Anselm." [39]

Both Siger and Thomas were, to the conservative theologians, tarred with the same Aristotelian brush. The words of Bonaventure quoted above represent the way the struggle had gone from an attack on Averroistic mono-psychism and the doctrine of the eternity of the world to a revulsion against the encroachment of pagan philosophy on theology. The first condemnation of 1270 was the prelude to an intensified campaign against Aristotelianism. In addition to Bonaventure's *Collationes in Hexaemeron* in 1273, Giles of Rome joined in with two treatises. The first, *The Errors of the Philosophers*,[40] written between 1270 and 1274, dealt with the doctrines of Aristotle, Averroes, Avicenna, Algazel, Alkindi, and Maimonides where they contradicted faith. Giles's treatise was directed equally at those Christians who followed them. He also wrote *De plurificatione intellectus possibilis*, refuting monopsychism along the lines of Thomas. Perhaps a measure of the desperation felt by those who saw the whole standing of philosophy threatened by the activities of Siger and his supporters was the action of Giles of Lessines. A Flemish

[39] A. Callebaut, "Jean Pecham O.F.M. et l'Augustinisme" *Archivum Franciscanum Historicum* (*AFH*), **18** (1925), 448.
[40] Text in Mandonnet, *Siger de Brabant*, II, 1–25; translated in H. Shapiro, *Medieval Philosophy* (New York, 1964).

Dominican and an adherent of Thomas on the burning question of the plurality of forms, he sent Albert the Great, some time between about 1272 and 1276, fifteen questions extracted from the teachings of "the masters in the school of Paris who are reputed the most important in philosophy." [41] They were the now standard ones in the unity of the human intellect, the eternity of the world, the immortality of the soul, God's relation to his creatures, and the existence of providence and free will. Albert's reply is revealing; he was by then seventy or more years of age and he was clearly out of touch with events at Paris: for him the root of the problem seemed to be bad philosophizing: "not philosophy but sophisms" made either in ignorance or malice against faith. He does not seem to have related the list of errors to the role of philosophy in faith; his own attempt to rectify matters was in recapitulating a largely Avicennan cosmology as, for example, the place of the active intellect.

In most conflicts the moderates are usually the losers. The struggle over Aristotelianism was no exception. Despite the efforts of Thomas, Giles of Rome, Giles of Lessines, and, in a less directed, way Albert, all upholders of Aristotelian doctrines in some degree, it was the conservatives who in the end won. The 1277 condemnations were a victory as much over Thomism as over so-called Latin Averroism. They cannot be regarded simply as the revenge of the faculty of theology over the faculty of arts. The whole climate of the preceding decade was increasingly antiphilosophical. Albert and Thomas were in a minority. The majority of theologians, of their own order and certainly outside it, were at the least chary of Aristotelian philosophy. Even had there been no Siger of Brabant there is nothing to show that Thomism would have quietly gained the day. Rather the radicalism of the artists precipitated the outbreak of the hostility of theologians at Paris and Oxford to paganism as a whole; this can be seen in the disputes that formed the aftermath to 1277.

The tone was set by the condemnations of 1270. The thirteen propositions censured in that year became 219 by 1277. The difference was more than one of mere number. In December 1270 Bishop Stephen Tempier, himself a former master in the

[41] Mandonnet, *op. cit.*, 29–52.

faculty of theology, seems to have acted in a strictly local capacity: there is no evidence of prior consultation with the papal curia; nor did his list contain any mention of those at whom his ban was directed.[42] A simple declaration of one sentence stated merely that "these errors are condemned and excommunicated together with all who should knowingly teach or affirm them." The errors were (a) that the intellect of all men is one and the same; (b) that it is false to say that man understands; (c) that man's will acts from necessity; (d) that all that happens in the world below is subject to the necessity of the heavenly bodies; (e) that the world is eternal; (f) that there was never a first man (that is, that there was no act of creation); (g) that man's soul, which is his form, dies with him; (h) that after a man's death the separated soul (that belonging to the separated intellect as a distinct spiritual being) cannot suffer from corporeal fire; (i) that free will is passive, not active; (j) that God does not know individuals; (k) that God knows only himself; (l) that there is no divine providence regulating human actions; (m) that God cannot make immortal and incorruptible what is mortal and corruptible.

These propositions officially formulated the main errors of the pagan philosophers. It is important to notice that only two of these articles—(g) and (h) on the soul—were exclusively Averroist; the remainder all derived from Aristotle's own doctrine and had been taken up by the majority of Arabian thinkers. What is specific to them is that they were, among the members of the arts faculty, framed in terms directly antithetical to Christian faith; that is, Aristotle's conception of the first cause and unmoved mover as self-contemplating being, oblivious to all that lay outside him, had become contraposed to the Christian view of God as creator. Similarly, the determinism of the heavenly bodies was set against God's providence. A hierarchy of intelligences perpetually acting on the world below was thus substituted for the direct relationship between God and his creatures. Such notions are not to be found among the surviving writings of Siger or of any other Latin thinker of the period. They are more likely to have been the kind of opinion put forward in

[42] *Chart.*, I, No. 432.

debates and disputations; it is possible that reports of them, as expressed by these propositions, may have been exaggerated. But there can be no doubt from all the other evidence, both before and above all in 1277, that such opinions had become sufficiently current to be a threat to the foundations of Christian belief.

The failure of Tempier's decree to silence the artists in 1270 ensured that any further official action would come with redoubled force. In retrospect what is surprising is the length of time before it was taken; perhaps Siger's own modified tone had something to do with it. Any delay was more than offset by the sweeping nature of the bishop's second proscription. It ran, as we have said, to 219 articles and extended from Aristotle to courtly love. On this occasion Pope John XXI (Peter of Spain, who had taught logic in the arts faculty at Paris in the 1240's), set the process in motion, although he had no part in the list that Tempier drew up and published on March 7. On January 18 John had written to Tempier, expressing concern at the reports of certain errors circulating at Paris "where the living source of the wisdom of faith wells up abundantly sending forth its limpid streams which carry the Catholic faith to the ends of the world." [43] He ordered the bishop to make immediate inquiry into where and among whom such errors were being propagated and to let him know without fail. Tempier must have set to work at once. Within a few weeks he had gathered together everything that sounded anti-Christian. It is likely that these were compiled by a number of hands, each bringing his own separate collection; for in his haste the bishop made no attempt to set them into any coherent order. The same propositions recur repeatedly.

Whether Tempier went beyond his brief in also pronouncing his ban on them is hardly a matter of any great importance. It is more than probable that, had he sent them to the papal curia, the pope would have done the same, including those articles that were Thomist; the pope, far from expressing disapproval at Tempier's action, ordered Siger of Brabant and Boethius of Dacia to appear before him. [44] Siger died at the papal court in

---

[43] *Ibid.*, No. 471.
[44] Callebaut *op. cit.*, 460.

Orvieto, between 1281 and 1284, where he had been in some sort of confinement. Moreover, Tempier's condemnation was not an isolated event; ten days later Robert Kilwardby, archbishop of Canterbury, made his own condemnation at Oxford, which was largely directed against Thomism.

The 219 theses themselves make repetitious reading.[45] They fall into the same main groups of error as those of 1270 and as found in many of the polemics of the preceding decade. This time, however, nothing was left out. The preamble states specifically that they are the opinions of "some studying in the arts at Paris and exceeding the limits of their faculty." Their authors, it goes on, defend them by saying "that they are true according to philosophy but not according to Catholic faith, as if there were two contrary truths, and as though to contradict the truth of scripture with the sayings of the pagans is the truth." [46] To prevent the faithful from being led into error by such imprudent talk, the appended 219 errors were prohibited and those who taught them or heard them were to be excommunicated unless they declared themselves within seven days ready to receive condign punishment. Tempier was not acting alone; the wise men and doctors of theology on whose advice he was acting included sixteen theologians, among them Henry of Ghent, one of the prime movers towards a new theological system in the ensuing years. The condemnation was the work of theologians in defense of theological truth against paganism. In its intentions and its content it was wider than an attack merely on one aspect—that of Averroism. Although it was at the same time directed against the complete dissociation of philosophy from theology that Averroes had advocated, the wish to follow reason and yet remain true to one's faith was equally inherent in any attempt by believers to be philosophers. To the theologians who advised Tempier the outcome was no less pernicious, whatever the motives. Hence their almost indiscriminate inclusion of any non-Christian sentiment. Among them was the *Liber de amore* or the *De deo amoris*, a treatise on courtly love by Andrew Capellanus, and works on necromancy and magic. The 219 propositions invite

---

[45] *Chart.*, I, No. 473, pp. 543–55.
[46] *Ibid.*, p. 543.

almost unlimited permutations and combinations; there are echoes of all the teachings of all the main Arabian thinkers besides, of course, Aristotle; a number were Thomist, of which the most important were on individuation, the intellect, and its relation to the will. Mandonnet has rearranged them all under twenty different heads, divided between philosophy and theology.[46] Useful as this is, it also makes for artificiality. It is doubtful whether the compilers saw them in this way. Essentially they bore on the main themes of the nature and power of God, the separated intelligences, man, and the natural world. Their treatment once again entailed conclusions similar to those condemned in 1270. At the same time there were now also propositions that directly challenged fundamental Christian tenets: God could not be a Trinity because tri-unity was not compatible with the absolute simplicity of God's nature (article 1); God could not generate a likeness to himself because it would be a sign of imperfection (i.e., incompleteness) in him (2). On the other hand, there were the familiar propositions that denied God his divine attributes as creator: he did not know anything other than himself (4); all separate spiritual bodies were coeternal with the first principle (5) (thereby making what exists the result of a necessary and eternal emanation on God's part, rather than a voluntary act of creation); as in 1270 he was denied the power to make the generated and corruptible eternal and perpetual (25); but he was now credited with infinite power only "in duration not in action," because he was not an infinite body, which, if it existed, could alone act infinitely (29). His power of creation was taken over by the superior intelligences (i.e., those above the heavenly spheres): it was they who created rational souls; the inferior or heavenly spheres created the vegetative and sensitive souls (30); God could only create primal matter by means of the celestial bodies (38). As first cause he did not know free future actions (future contingents) because they were particulars and God did not know particulars (42), a further example of the extension of one of the positions of 1270 into theological reaches. God was circumscribed into becoming merely an indirect mover. As propositions 43 and 44 expressed it: "the first

<hr>

[46] Mandonnet, *Siger de Brabant,* II, 175 ff.

principle cannot be the cause of diverse acts here below except by means of other causes . . ." and "from one first mover there cannot be a multiplicity of effects." It was just because God was treated philosophically as first mover, or first principle, that his relation with secondary causes was seen as indirect. Such a conception was common to all the Arab philosophers as it was to Neoplatonists and Aristotle; the difference was that for the Neoplatonists the One participated in all spiritual being as its ultimate source. This, however, was as the result of a necessary and eternal emanation, not from a free act of creation out of nothing and in time. There is no evidence of this sense of participation among the condemned propositions; God is conceived almost exclusively in causal relation to what came after him. As such he could only be directly responsible for what he had immediately caused.

This had two main consequences that recur throughout these articles. The first was that God acted necessarily, and transmitted this necessity to everything else through a chain reaction. The second was that the world was directly subject to the intelligences and heavens and only indirectly to God. In the first case God, it was held, could not cause or produce anything new (48) or change the mode in which things are moved (49); he moved eternally and necessarily (51, 53) so that things acted either always or never (52); the first principle could not produce anything other than itself (55); and that which it did produce— namely the first intelligence—was necessarily of the same duration (58). The interposition of the separated intelligences and heavenly bodies between God and this world is the most striking feature of these condemned propositions; for the believer it meant the usurpation of God's providence, the denial of his role as creator, the eternity of the world, and the subjection of man's will and understanding to astral forces. The intelligences effectively became the causes of the sublunar world: God as indirect cause could only act necessarily by means of such intermediaries (60) just as he could not know contingents except through proximate causes (56); as first unmoved mover he only moved others through intermediaries (67). The separated intelligences were eternal and unchanging because they were without matter and without any potentiality of lack (71, 72, 78); they in turn acted as creators through their own intelligences, influencing the rational soul in man (but not as part of him) as the celestial bodies influenced his human soul (73, 74); as spiritual being they were also infinite (86). Since neither they nor God could undergo change, the world itself, which issued from them, must also be eternal; its species, time, movement, matter, and action had always existed in the superior causes from which they derived (87, 92, 94, 95, 98, 99), although newly disposed (107). This was one of the points at which the propositions emphasized the divergence, indeed conflict, between natural reason and revelation: "natural philosophy must deny absolutely the newness of the world because it is based upon natural causes and natural reasons. The believer, however, can deny the eternity of the world because his faith is founded upon supernatural causes" (90). Consequently, "philosophical reason demonstrating that the movement of the heavens is eternal, is not sophistical; and it is surprising that men of understanding do not see this" (92).

This in turn led to man's subjection to the heavenly powers; it was not confined to astral necessitarianism but also manifested itself in the denial of an independent human will. From this time onward Aristotelianism became increasingly identified with a triple determinism: astral, intellectual, and psychological. These different aspects are all to be found abundantly among these propositions. Thus the movement of the heavens was on account of an intelligence; whereas movement could only be through the medium of a body (110), the latter was not, however, united to the intelligence that moved it (111); the superior intelligences impressed themselves on the inferior; and man's rational or intellectual soul knew through the active intellect to which his knowledge belonged (115). From this followed monopsychism and the lack of personal immortality (116–122, 125–7), for man possessed no spiritual powers or intelligible images on his own account. This dependence of the human intellect on the active intellect in turn subjected man's will to his understanding. The primacy of the intellect over will was a notion upheld also by Thomas; it became one of the great issues of the next three decades. Article 129, which held that right willing followed right reason ("if the intellect is right the will is right"), was attacked for contradicting St. Augustine. Article 159 put the preponderating power of the intellect more strongly, in asserting that "man's will is necessitated by his knowledge as the brutes are by their appetites." The identification of the primacy of the intellect with the absence of free will was one of the lasting legacies of the condemnation. As article 160 stated, "there is no freedom of action, but it is determined": by the stars and the celestial bodies (133, 161–2), by what is presented to it by reason (129, 163) and by its own appetites (134, 164). "The soul only wills when it is moved by something else; hence it is false to say that the soul wills of itself" (194). This belief had two further implications. First, that the world was governed by fate: God as first cause was also the most remote cause (190); accordingly, "fate, which is the disposition of the universe, does not come directly from divine providence, but by means of the movement of the higher, celestial bodies" (195). As a result the created world in proportion to the autonomy it enjoyed from God was immediately subject to the heavens and the stars (197, 198, 199): they could produce sins and monsters (196); they acted as the instruments of the first intelligence imprinting its forms in matter (187); the tendencies in a star could be reproduced in an offspring by parents who showed the same dispositions (188). There is a number of such notions. Their importance lies in showing the power with which their authors endowed the celestial intelligences at the expense of God's omnipotence.

The second corollary of this attitude was that it led to a doctrine bordering on amorality. That is not to say that the same people who stressed the role of the heavens also believed that men, in acting under their influence, were not responsible for their sins, but the two tendencies went together. For example it was stated that sin was from the passions, not the will, because the superior powers could not sin (165), and it was by them that the actions of the will were determined. Much more important, however, was the attitude displayed toward theological precepts. This was something different from the mere separation of philosophical from theological truth; it was tantamount to a rejection of theological values in what concerned man's moral virtues. Thus continence was not necessarily a virtue (168); and perfect abstinence from carnal acts destroyed virtue and the species (169). Chastity was not a greater good than perfect abstinence

(187); enjoyment of lovemaking did not impede the use of the intellect (171). Humility, which consisted only in self-humili-ation and reviling oneself, was not a virtue (171). The Christian law, like any other, contained tales and falsehoods. (174); it also impeded additional knowledge (175). Happiness belonged to this life, not to another one (176). Only innate and acquired virtues (that is, attained naturally as opposed to being super-naturally infused) were possible (177). Allowing for the ele-ment of deliberate distortion, which was doubtless responsible for some of the more extreme statements here and elsewhere among these propositions, the fact remains that they expressed a naturalistic ethic. As philosophers, those who upheld them were applying purely natural criteria to judge what was good or bet-ter or worse. They refused revealed truth the right to dictate to reason. All the good, they held, of which man is capable consists in the intellectual virtues (144); there was no question open to reason that the philosopher could not determine (145); he did so by taking everything into consideration. Consequently, he could decide what was possible and impossible (146). This was tan-tamount to reversing the order between the philosopher and the theologian: only the philosophers were wise so far as knowing the world went (154); moreover a man rightly orientated through the philosophical virtues was sufficiently disposed to gain eternal bliss (157). Conversely, no man should be content · with certainty gained from the decrees of authority (150).

We thus return to where we began: the 1277 articles, for all the probable garbling they underwent, show unmistakably that they were the outcome of taking Aristotle and his commentators in their own terms. Apart from a few of the more blatantly anti-ecclesiastical sentiments they were less an attack on the founda-tions of faith than the assertion of independently formed philo-sophical opinions. Therein lay the danger. They introduced not merely an antithetical body of ideas but another standard of truth. To call it the double truth is largely playing with words. It is enough that its validity was accepted for natural reason and natural experience. To have allowed it to remain would have meant dethroning theology; rather than that, philosophy had to withdraw. After 1277 it did—away from revelation and into the natural world where reason could have full play. 1277 was not the beginning of modern science or anything else modern. But it was the beginning of the end of scholasticism as the harmonizing of faith and natural reason. Within less than fifty years the age of the great systems was past.

The Aftermath. The last two decades of the thirteenth century were a period of reaction. Thomism was nipped by the same frost that blighted heterodox Aristotelianism. All Thomas's polemics against the Latin Averroists had not saved some of his own propositions from inclusion, and he shared in the subsequent discredit into which pagan philosophy fell. In particular, Thomism came under attack at four main points. The first was the principle of individuation, which Thomas, following Aristotle, had seen in the conjunction of form and matter: each individual embodied a form; its material existence in space and time separated it physically from the other members of the species to which it belonged. Its individuation therefore was because of matter. Together with this went the other distinctive Thomist thesis that each being had but one substantial form by which it was what it was—for example, the humanity by which Socrates was a man. Thomas thereby opposed himself to a fundamental Augustinian tenet, taken over from Neoplatonism, that each being was a plurality of forms, including one for matter (its form of corporeity by which it was material). For Augustinianism forms determined the individual as much as the species. Matter had no distinctive part in individuation. Second, as consequence, the Thomist and Augustinian notions of the human soul clashed. For Thomas the soul as the substantial form of a man was united with his body; he was a man by virtue of being an individual composed of a body and rational soul. For the Augustinians, again from a Neoplatonic inspiration, the soul was a spiritual being in its own right and with its own independent form. To treat it as the means of individual existence—in Thomist terminology the act of the material body, which alone would have remained merely potential—was to unite it with the generable and corruptible. In the context of the Averroist denial of individual immortality, this was seen as a threat to the soul's spirituality.

Third, there was the Thomist distinction between essence and existence, following Aristotle and Averroes, which referred not to different kinds of being but to the constituents of being. In contrast to the Augustinians, being for Thomas represented actual existence. Essence alone was not being; it needed God's creative intervention to become so. This was the difference between God's uncreated being, which by definition existed, and all other being (whether of spiritual or material), which structurally was a composition of essence and existence; namely, a nature and its realization into actual being. The degree of misunderstanding over Thomas's teaching here was great; even defenders such as Giles of Rome and Giles of Lessine interpreted it differently from its author. To those who opposed it, like William de la Mare, it became too easily confused with the notion that matter was entailed in all existence—something Thomas had never held for spiritual beings like angels. It also involved different conceptions of divine ideas.

Fourth, there was the relation of the intellect to the will; this was again closely bound up with the subordination of willing and doing to knowing which we have already remarked in the 1277 condemned articles. With the Thomist conception of the intellect itself suspect, to make the will dependent on the intellect was to seem to introduce determinism by intermediaries, whether astral or psychological, in place of the direct relation between God's will and human free will. It was also to reverse the traditional order from right willing to right knowing, which, for all actions worthy of God's reward, needed his grace. Here too, then, the issues were ultimately theological. They were made sharper by the Franciscan order's adoption in 1282 of the critique by William de la Mare of Thomas's teaching on these questions. The form in which he had made it—the "Corrective" (*Correctorium*)—helped to engender this opposition; it consisted in adding corrections to Thomas's own text and circulating them. William de la Mare's Corrective had in turn been answered by either Richard Clapwell or Thomas of Sutton who corrected la Mare's Corrective. These disputes concerned only certain aspects of Thomas's work, such as those we have just enumerated. This did not mean that thenceforth the Dominicans were Thomist and the Franciscans anti-Thomas or Augustinian. Although Thomas's teaching was officially adopted by the Dominican order in 1309, it was never throughout the fourteenth century adhered to by many of its members—for example, Durandus of St. Pourçain or Robert Holcot, to mention only two. Moreover, the disputes were not confined to the Dominicans and Franciscans even in the immediate aftermath: two of the most important thinkers of the later thirteenth century were Henry of Ghent—a secular—and Giles of Rome—an Augustinian—who lived into the first eighteen years of the fourteenth century. By then the concentration of outstanding thinkers in the two main mendicant orders was waning; an increasing proportion of seculars or members of other orders becomes apparent among the next generation: Bradwardine, Buridan, John of Mirecourt, Nicholas of Autrecourt, Gregory of Rimini, Albert of Saxony, Nicholas of Oresme, William of Heytesbury, John of Dumbleton, and Thomas Buckingham, to name only a few.

Nothing, in fact, could be more mistaken than to see the later thirteenth and the fourteenth centuries as dominated by Thomism, Albertism or Augustinianism as they had evolved by the 1270's. The year 1277 was a catalyst. Like all upheavals, it cleared neither the air nor men's minds. Instead of a new era of a now clearly defined body of admissable theological and philosophical doctrines there was flux. Controversy and considerable confusion were the aftermath; only gradually did they clear and the focus change. It began above all with Henry of Ghent. With Duns Scotus (d. 1308), a new point was reached; from it William of Ockham was to initiate the outlook that dominated the greater part of the intellectual life of Paris during the fourteenth century.

II OCKHAMISM

The history of both Ockhamism and of scholastic thought in the fourteenth century has yet to be written. This is not the place to attempt it. What was common to the century or so from about 1290 was the progressive disengagement of theology from natural knowledge and philosophy. This had always been one tendency among traditional theologians, who, as we saw earlier, resented the encroachment of pagan notions into the tenets of belief. The 1277 condemnation by Tempier enshrined this attitude. Philosophical notions that sought to treat God or creation in other than accepted Christian terms were anathematized. This impulsion were carried into the later thirteenth and the fourteenth centuries, above all at Paris and Oxford, which had been the centers of this crisis. The mere negative act of proscription was not, however, enough; nor were the criticisms and corrections of Thomas or the mere resuscitation of the older Augustinianism that underlay the greater part of them. A redefinition of the relation of philosophy and theology was needed. Thomas, following Albert's lead, had been the first to base a theological system on a conscious differentiation of the roles of philosophy and theology. It was this—together of course with the profound intellectual insight and power that went to its making—that was to guarantee the survival of Thomism. By the same token, it was the lack of provision for a disjunction between faith and reason that made the older Augustiniamism of Bonaventure unsuited to the problems of post-1277. For a time there were attempts to adapt or reaffirm different aspects of it, such as the doctrine of illumination, by theologians like Matthew of Aquasparta, Bonaventure's successor as general of the Franciscans from 1282 to 1288. But it needed more than piecemeal defense of the older positions to make them viable. They had to be given a speculative foundation in which both the relation of faith to reason was redefined, and the role of reason—metaphysically, physically, and logically—was not permitted to outrun the truths it was there to sustain: in other words, to restore dominance to theology with philosophy as the ancillary.

Such a need meant at once rethinking the relevance of philosophy to theology and reaffirming the essentials of revelation. Henry of Ghent was the first to attempt the task in a coherent way. Much that he did provided the basis of subsequent efforts. He was particularly well placed, as he had been one of the theologians who had advised Tempier over the condemned propositions; he was also steeped in a knowledge of Aristotelian and Arabian philosophy; and he remained at Paris almost until his death in 1293. His contribution lay in two main directions. The first was to reaffirm God's sovereignty not simply as supreme being but as the supremely free and omnipotent creator; Henry replied to the limitations imposed by Greco-Arabian necessitarianism by stressing the inherent contingency of everything other than God: far from his being unable to act, save through inter-mediaries, he could do anything, and whatever he did was through the free working of his will. Second, Henry of Ghent sought an alternative metaphysical basis for discussing God's being. He found it in Avicenna's concept of being as the most universal notion of all and the first object of knowledge—coming before any other category such as essence, existence, necessary or possible being, genera, species, or individuals. In this way the idea of God could reside in an abstract notion, independent of sensory things. Henry employed both these different facets of God to restate the basic Augustinian position; but they were now related to a concept of God as infinite being who was by that fact also infinitely powerful. Many of Henry's *quodlibeta* were occupied by his disputes on this question with Giles of Rome.

It was Duns Scotus who took over these positions to create a new system, which, although it owed much to Henry of Ghent and their common inspirer, Avicenna, went beyond them. In making the same radical distinction between God and creation as Henry had made, Duns Scotus dispensed with the greater part of the Augustinian impedimenta of illumination and the traditional interpretation of divine ideas. He also radically re-duced the area of knowable divine truths, including the immor-tality of the soul. Nothing certain could be posited of the actions of God's will. This was not voluntarism in the sense that God was governed by the caprices of his will; it meant rather that so far as creation was concerned God's actions were determined by nothing but his infinitely free willing: the pagan hierarchy of intermediaries between him and this world was cut away and the direct action of God's will put there instead. At the same time Duns carried Henry of Ghent's view of being to its logical conclusion by refusing to conceive of God save in the most abstract of all abstractions—as infinite being. It was this that metaphysically distinguished him from all other beings; as in-finite, God was necessary and self-caused, whereas everything else was by definition finite and only possible, as liable not to be as to be and dependent for its existence on God as creator. There could be no analogy between two such incommensurable levels, which had nothing in common beyond the most universal fact of being as opposed to not being. Nor could there be any defined causal relation between them, save that all that was not God enjoyed being by virtue of divine will: this offered no other explanation of his willing than having willed. For that reason man knew only what he encountered through the senses as the effects of God's willing. Duns rejected inner illumination; the knowledge man gained was knowledge of the contingent, not the necessary. In consequence, beyond positing God as infinite being, philosophy and metaphysics could go no further. The effect of Duns's system was thus to reduce the common philosophical ground between God and creation to the most general notion of being. To speak of God beyond saying that he was omnipotent was to enter the realm of faith and to be guided by its tenets.

With William of Ockham (d. 1349) we reach the final separation of faith and natural reason. This had nothing in common with the heterodox Aristotelianism of the 1260's and 1270's. Indeed, both Duns Scotus and, even more, Ockham were products of Oxford as much as Paris; although their influence is apparent at Oxford, their greatest impact was at Paris, where the 1277 upheavals had been greatest and where its international character had left no room for the kind of school that had grown up at Oxford. From the later 1330's Ockhamism was in the ascendant at Paris. It continued until the fifteenth century.

There can be no direct comparison between Aristotelianism and Ockhamism. The former, as we have abundantly seen, was a complex of non-Christian doctrines that ultimately came to challenge the foundations of Christian belief; in their pure philosophical form they could only clash with revelation. Yet for all that it was under their impact that the greatest systems of the Middle Ages were fashioned: between about 1240 and 1275 the intellectual tendency at Paris was toward harmonizing philosophy and theology. Ockhamism grew up as a reaction to the failure to achieve harmony between them; it was a reaction from Christian theologians intent on disentangling what belonged respectively to revelation and reason. Ockham and many of his followers were actuated by an impulse similar to that of Henry of Ghent and Duns Scotus. They shared the same almost obsessive awareness of the contingent, finite nature of creation to which they contraposed the infinite freedom of God; like Duns, they rejected any attempt to try to adduce proofs for God's existence from the laws of natural experience, either by analogy or causality; and they reduced the elements of knowledge to what could be derived from a direct intuitive awareness of the individuals given to the senses, rejecting internal illumination or any direct correspondence between divine ideas in God and intelligible ideas in the mind. Ockham, however, went further. He took two decisive steps that, despite these common traits, transformed his outlook out of recognition from that of Duns. He made all knowledge individual; only that which existed outside the mind was real, and only that which corresponded to it was true. With the individual as the sole reality, all nonrepresentational images and general concepts were mere figments of the mind: not illusions or hallucinations, but the mind's response to the data of the senses. Thus from the individuals Socrates and Plato encountered the mind formed the concept *man*. But this was not an existent being and had no independent standing. It represented nothing but was rather the mind's shorthand for a diversity of individuals.

Ockhamism meant the rejection of all universals and general categories as the constituents of being: natures, essences, genera, species lost their independent status. Being was reduced to individual existence; metaphysics was displaced by physics and mechanics and measurement. Categories like movement, time, and place became the attributes of objects extended in space and no longer independent principles. Demonstration had to be founded on verifiable experience; there was no self-evident reason for affirming the relation of one thing to another that could not ultimately be verified in experience. In this purge all that remained of the vast conceptual apparatus of a century of metaphysical speculation was the knowing subject and the object known—in both cases individuals. Duns's last remaining bridge of univocal being, between the finite and the infinite, was swept away with the rest. There was no more place for such a concept in a world of individuals than there was for the Thomist notions of essence and existence or for their different kinds of distinction.

Duns's categories formed Ockham's target in his prologue to his Commentary on the *Sentences;* but that must not deceive us

into making intellectual life at Paris in the first half of the fourteenth century center around their differences, or into seeing in
them the renewal of the earlier conflicts between Nominalism
and Realism. For all their very real metaphysical divergences,
both thinkers were inspired by a similar desire to reassert God's
freedom and the freedom of the human will and to cut each
loose from all traces of neccessitarianism. Moreover, though they
reached diametrically opposite conclusions on the significance of
universals, Ockham owed his own epistemological division between intuitive and abstractive knowledge—differently as he interpreted it—to Duns. But nowhere was Duns's influence more
apparent than in Ockham's use of the concept of God's omnipotence. It was founded on the distinction between God's ordained power, which was his law for this world, and his absolute
power, which referred to his own unlimited omnipotence bound
to no set dispensation. Duns had given it a new currency to
stress God's power to do directly what he normally did through
secondary causes, or not to do it at all. It was invoked to show
that God could, as in a miracle, supersede the ordinary laws of
creation, thereby underlining the contingency of the created order. It was a direct riposte to the determinism condemned in
1277, when among other propositions, it had been held that God
could not make accidents stand without a subject (articles
138–41). Although used sparingly by Duns, the concept of
God's two different powers became one of the hallmarks of Ockhamism; [47] initially a theological device to set God free from the
inexorability of an order in which he was only a remote cause, it
ended by acting as the solvent of a natural order. It thereby
became as much of a threat to authority as the Lating Averroists
had been, but in an entirely different way. Latin Averroism had
challenged authority in the name of determinism; Ockhamism
did so by indeterminacy. Moreover, whereas the effect of heterodox Aristotelianism on God was to deny him as a creator, Ockhamism exalted him in this role to the point at which creation
became almost an arbitrary exercise in divine power. The main
beneficiary was free will and the main victim was moral theol-

[47] What follows is based on my "The Changing Pattern of Thought in the
Earlier Fourteenth Century," *Bulletin of the John Ryland Library*, 43
(1961), 354–72.

ogy; grace and the supernatural virtues lost their intrinsic effica-
ciousness: like other secondary causes God could dispense with
them and reward free will, whatever the nature of its actions.
God was so free that he could love the sinner and damn the man
in grace; he was rewarding the act, not the moral state. Ockham
was the first to give sustained application to this conception of
ethical neutrality, or rather to vest its judgement in God. The
wheel had come full circle. Human will, from being the prisoner
of fate, the stars, the intellect, and the appetites, had now become so free that it might do anything and be rewarded. God
alone would decide and in his own way.

It was largely for calling into question the theological virtues
and the doctrine of grace and original sin that Ockhamism—
especially among such followers of Ockham as Adam of Woodham, Thomas Buckingham, Robert Holcot, John of Mirecourt,
Nicholas of Autrecourt—was so disruptive of the traditional
teaching. Together with its denial of any valid means of establishing proof for God's existence or any of the basic articles of
faith, it spelled the end of the attempt to harness natural reason
and knowledge to theology. What it called into question it did in
the name of God's unknowability, not the wisdom of the philosophers. Reason could not extend beyond individual being to universal being, let alone infinite being. In this context the invocation of God's absolute power was a warning against trying to
discuss God except according to revelation. From the point of
view of reason he could, by definition, be regarded only as omnipotence; it enabled man to recognize God's supreme freedom
as creator and the contingency of everything he had created.
This was not to deny God the accepted attributes of wisdom,
goodness, justice, or mercy; but merely to acknowledge that man
as a finite and contingent being had no certain knowledge of
such terms. The way in which man saw them offered no guarantee that they meant the same for God or that God could not
supersede them. Ultimately it was man's ignorance of how God
operated that must make the believer trust implicitly at once in
God's law and his power to override it.

Ockhamism was, however, far from being wholly negative or
destructive. If it destroyed the harmony of the moral order, it
also opened up the physical and natural world. Its laws, no less

than those concerning grace and the theological virtues, were equally liable to interruption. To begin with, man's natural knowledge was as contingent as the world he knew; God could make it illusory, so inducing man to know what did not exist. In the same way he could suspend the normal workings of the laws of physics or mechanics: two bodies could occupy the same space at the same time; a form could be made infinitely intense; the world could be finite or eternal; there could be several infinite worlds; something could exist as two separate instances in time. Here, however, Aristotle, not the church, was the sufferer. His own conception of a fixed and eternally unvarying order was disturbed. If he was followed microcosmically, in the workings of physics and the other natural sciences, macrocosmically the possibilities of an infinite universe and the mathematical speculations that accompanied them led to new thinking. Moreover, the cutting away of unnecessary concepts, in which Ockham been the spearhead, led to new and fruitful explanations for physical phenomena. Thus John Buridan's theory of impulse (*impetus*) [48] to account for violent—as opposed to natural—movement was an elaboration of Ockham's revolutionary simple explanation that it moved because it was in movement. Aristotle had sought to account for it by presupposing a separate mover, which, in natural movement, inhered within what was moving: that is to say, an essence or form of movement. Buridan changed the concept of this cause from an inner virtue to some external agent that imparted the initial impulses—as when a stone is thrown —which continued to propel it, until it was gradually overcome by the resistance of air and weight. Thus movement as a disembodied principle came to be displaced by movement as an attribute of an individual moving in space.

It was by such a change of attitude that Ockhamism released the human mind from a mesh of abstractions that had caught up individual experience in it. Moreover, that a thinker like Buridan could be associated with such tendencies while opposing the more outrageous opinions of some of Ockham's followers points to another fundamental difference between Ockhamism and Aristotelianism. Ockhamism answered some universal need at

[48] See Shapiro, *op. cit.*, 529–36, for a translation of Buridan's theory taken from his commentary on Aristotle's *Physics*.

Paris and indeed throughout northern Europe during the fourteenth century. Whereas Aristotelianism had never been more
than a minority movement, even in the arts faculty at Paris,
Ockhamism became the dominant school of thought in the
majority of universities north of the Alps. It gave a new outlet to
intellectual doubt while engendering fideism. In that sense it was
in harmony with the atmosphere of the schools, expressing the
deep-rooted antinomy between doubting by reason what was
held on faith. In that sense, too, it can be regarded as the logical
and historical outcome of the tradition of the schools.

We can distinguish two principal phases in the development of
Ockhamism. The first was from about 1320 to 1350, when its icono-
clasm was threatening the established Christian values in the
ways we have mentioned. This period saw a series of condemnations against some of its more egregious exponents, beginning
with Ockham himself at the papal court at Avignon in 1326, and
culminating in three separate actions at Paris during the 1340's.
During this time it also stirred up the hostility of more traditional
thinkers, especially Gregory of Rimini (d. 1358) at Paris and
Thomas Bradwardine at Oxford. It would be artificial to attempt
to separate events at Paris too sharply, because a number of the
most prominent Ockhamists were English scholars, like Adam of
Woodham, Robert Holcot, and Thomas Buckingham, for whom
Oxford was not their center. Nevertheless, during these thirty
years the predominant effect of Ockhamism at Paris, as elsewhere, was disruptive. It largely transformed the questions under discussion and the mode of discussion. After Ockham the
Commentary on the *Sentences* shrank drastically. How far this
resulted from the reduction in the time devoted to reading them
from two years to one is not certain. Clearly halving the time
must have had a considerable effect. But this cannot alone explain the growing concentration on a few central problems:
these were now mainly in the form of a prologue and a number
of questions, often not so many as a dozen, and not always even
taken from all four books, from the total of about five hundred
in the Lombard's *Sentences*. They concerned certain logical, epistemological, and physical problems: the relation of the three
persons of the Trinity, of knowing to willing, of man's will to
God's will as it affected grace, merit, and God's knowledge of

free future actions, and the problem of intensifying and remitting forms, usually discussed in the context of the elements of the eucharist. Equally striking was the omission of so much of the metaphysics of the earlier commentaries: essence and existence, a plurality of forms, as well as the psychological questions of the soul. Richard FitzRalph was one of the exceptions; he treated it very much in later thirteenth century terms of the active and possible intellects; but he wrote in the early 1330's when there was still some continuity with the previous epoch. Many of his contemporaries, however, like Holcot, Buckingham, and Bradwardine, virtually or entirely ignored the problem.

Another feature of the period after 1320 was the disappearance of the *quodlibet* as a vehicle for discussing the great issues of the day. As we have said earlier, many of the disputes, such as those over essence and existence and a plurality of forms, had been carried on quodlibetically between Thomas Aquinas, John Pecham, Gerard of Abbeville, Henry of Ghent, Giles of Rome, and Godfrey of Fontaines. After Ockham's very important series of free questions they rapidly lost their importance. This may well be related to another factor, more apparent among English than Paris thinkers: that much of their work was being done elsewhere. In itself this was not new. We have seen that both Albert the Great and St. Thomas had carried out some of their greatest enterprises away from the schools in the *studia* of their own order. But there was, from the third decade of the fourteenth century, a perceptible shift away from Paris. It was owing in no small degree to extraneous causes: Ockham, the dominant speculative thinker of the epoch from 1320 to 1350, fled from Avignon in 1326 with Michael of Cesena, general of the Franciscans, and spent the remainder of his life at the court of Ludwig of Bavaria, German emperor. With him there were Marsilius of Padua and John of Jandun, as well as a number of Franciscan dissidents. They were lost to the life of the schools, to which, in their preoccupation with political issues, they did not even contribute from afar with new writings. There was also the Hundred Years' War, which impeded free interchange between Paris and Oxford, and in Germany and other parts of Europe new universities sprang up during the fourteenth century, drawing away scholars from Paris.

The position of Paris university had always been closely bound up with the papacy and the mendicant orders. After the humiliation of Boniface VIII by Philip the Fair at Anagni in 1303 and the eventual establishment of the papal curia at Avignon in 1309 under Clement V, the pope never enjoyed the same unquestioned authority in the affairs of other kingdoms. Nor did the mendicant orders sustain their vitality into the fourteenth century. The Franciscans were riven by internal conflict of which Ockham's defection to the emperor was one of the consequences; the Dominicans failed to harness St. Thomas's teaching to a coherent school of thought during the fourteenth century. Lack of focus was indeed the dominant trait of the intellectual life of the period, reflected equally in the loss of hegemony by Paris and the prevailing intellectual eclecticism and individualism. Ockhamism ministered to the spirit with its twin emphases on the sovereignty of individual experience for the natural order and of faith for the supernatural. The two aspects cannot be separated: Ockhamism meant fideism as much as positivism, belief as much as rational doubt, theology as much as philosophy. It was not alone in this. The Rhineland mysticism of Meister Eckhart and his disciples was an equally powerful influence and probably far more pervasive in its effects on simple believers. It represented a comparable withdrawal of faith from natural experience, and reason, and a conviction that God's ineffability was beyond ratiocination.

Perhaps for these reasons the emergence of Ockhamism did not have the cataclysmic effects of heterodox Aristotelianism. Its impact on the traditional outlooks was no less devastating; but, however much it was opposed, it was ultimately the response of theologians rather than philosophers. However pronounced the purely captious element, there was also a genuine seriousness of purpose, namely, to rethink the scope and limits of rational enquiry, not merely in matters of belief but in the accepted metaphysical assumptions. For that reason Ockhamism presented a challenge to both theology and metaphysics. These were the grounds on which first Ockham's teaching and then the more extreme theses of some of his followers were attacked both in the official condemnations at Avignon and Paris and among opponents like Bradwardine and Gregory of Rimini.

The first official reaction came in 1324 when Ockham was

summoned to appear at Avignon to answer fifty-one articles that had been extracted from his writings, especially his Commentary on the *Sentences*. The censure seems to have originated with John Lutterell, chancellor of Oxford university, who attacked Ockham's doctrines in a tractate. They were formally condemned by a papal commission in 1326.[49] They show clearly the new indeterminacy his teaching had introduced. The main theses singled out for attack were that God could accept an act of free will alone as meritorious, without the need for a prevenient gift of grace (articles 1–3); that sin could be remitted without grace (4); that God could be rightly hated (5–6); that the will in a state of grace could refuse blessedness (6, 46); that grace and sin did not contradict each other (7–8); that sin could be engendered without the act of sin (9); that the vision of something could continue after its object had been destroyed (10); that, naturally, man could only know the proposition that God was the highest good without knowing that he was a Trinity (13) or anything about his essence (14–18); that God's attributes and his ideas could not be formally distinguished (25–30, 41–45); that the principle of something could be believed but the conclusion known (34); that Christ, as a man without grace, could have sinned (36); that the same body could be in several different places at the same time (47) and several bodies in the same place at the same time (48). As can be seen God, man, and nature each lost many degrees of certainty; God's goodness was affirmed without attempting to correlate his actions with a preconceived notion of it; he could be rightly hated and his grace did not necessarily mean the deletion of sin or the desire for blessedness. Man's knowledge, as we said earlier, could be illusory and the laws of nature disturbed.

These conclusions contain the germs of Ockhamism as it developed especially at Paris in the 1340's. Presented in this form, they suffer from the distortion that all such arbitrarily selected extracts produce; they do not do justice to the complexity and validity of Ockham's critique of accepted positions, or to his own seriousness of intent without which no thinker can succeed in

---

[40] Published by A. Pelzer, "Les 51 articles de Guillaume d'Ockham censurés en Avignon en 1326." *Revue d'histoire ecclésiastique*, **18** (1922), 240–70.

achieving new insights. But at the same time the articles distil those elements in Ockham's outlook that were to preponderate in the writings of his followers. Pursued along these lines they were bound to clash with theological orthodoxy. There is evidence of this in 1330's in the reactions from thinkers like Bradwardine, Walter Burley, and, in a more oblique way, Richard FitzRalph. They did not, however, come to a head at Paris until 1340. In that year the rector of the university, John Buridan, himself as we have seen influenced by Ockham though not an Ockhamist, issued a general admonition to the arts faculty.[50] He criticized some within it for doubting the respected authorities of the church and for denying the correspondence between words and things which led to such conclusions as "Socrates and Plato, God and creatures were nothing." Here, then, at the epistemological and philosophical level, the effect of Ockhamism was the direct opposite of Aristotelianism: instead of an alternative naturalism, there was a strict empiricism that refused to go beyond what could be verified in natural experience. The dangers to theology lay in this neutralism, as the rector's letter recognized.

Ockhamism, however, was more than a system of individual knowledge; it also had direct theological implications in its view of God's omnipotence. This again was evident well before the next series of condemnations at Paris in 1346 and 1347. Those two years marked the climax of official action there—or anywhere else—against these new doctrines. On May 19, 1346 sixty articles taken from the writings of Nicholas of Autrecourt were condemned. They were followed the next day by a letter from Pope Clement VI to the masters and scholars of the university as a whole.[51] It was concerned with the recent tendency in both theology and philosophy to embrace "new and strange sophistical doctrines, which are said to be taught in certain other places of study": they led to futile and fruitless opinions, and to disregard of the Bible and the sacred authorities, the very foundations of faith, for philosophical questions and suspect opinions.

To judge from those of Nicholas of Autrecourt, a bachelor in theology, whose propositions were condemned to be burned to-

---

[50] *Chart.*, II, No. 1042.
[51] *Ibid.*, No. 1125.

gether with his other writings, the pope's complaints were not groundless.[52] Taken together they amounted to a denial of natural certainty, the very attitude of which Buridan had complained in 1340 and against which he wrote. According to Nicholas, knowledge of the existence or nonexistence of one thing did not entail knowledge of the existence or nonexistence of another (1–8); there was no certainty of the existence of natural substances or causality (9–19); or that one thing was more noble than another (20–1); or that God was the most noble being of all (22); or that the expressions "God" and "creature" signified anything real (32, 54–5). Thus at the level of natural experience, from the point of view of God, God could command a rational creature to hate him (58), and, if this creature's will were dependent on God's will, he could not sin or err (59).

The following year fifty propositions of John of Mirecourt, a Cistercian, were also condemned.[53] Their tenor was not markedly dissimilar from Nicholas of Autrecourt's; the main difference was that in Mirecourt's articles the emphasis was on the moral aspects of God's omnipotence touched on in articles 58 and 59 of Nicholas's list. John of Mirecourt was particularly concerned with God's role in an act of sin; God, he held, in moving free will to perform a sinful action, was its cause as he was the cause of all its actions (10–14, 16–18, 32–9). He also believed—in common with the majority of Ockhamists—that God could make the soul hate him (31–2); and that Christ could mislead his disciples, himself be misled by God and hate him (1–6)—conclusions bound up with the problem of God's knowledge of free future actions, which if they were to be truly free and contingent, could not be foreknown by God with certainty; hence his prophecies, in referring to the future, could be falsified by events as Christ's could: therefore both God and Christ could mislead and Christ be misled. Mirecourt was also censured for saying, somewhat inconsistently, that God predestined men on account of their future good works and a proper use of their free will (47–50). Finally, like Nicholas of Autrecourt, Mirecourt asserted that a being higher than God could be envisaged (46).

[52] *Ibid.,* No. 1124.
[53] *Ibid.,* No. 1147.

The emphases of the two thinkers were complementary. Nicholas of Autrecourt expressed an attitude of philosophical doubt as to the certainty of all inferential—let alone metaphysical and theological—knowledge, which enabled nothing certain to be posited of God; on the assumption that he was omnipotent, God could command a creature to hate him. John of Mirecourt, on the other hand, in these propositions showed concern only with the moral conclusions that could be drawn from God's omnipotence. The consistency with which they were pursued in an antitheological direction shows the extent to which Ockhamism had become a device in the hands of even a member of a religious order. Nicholas of Autrecourt was compelled to retract.[54] How seriously Mirecourt meant his conclusions is not certain, even though he did defend them subsequently.[55] Whatever his intentions, and those of so many of his contemporaries, the idea of God's omnipotence allied to the limitations of natural knowledge had effectively destroyed the means of a natural theology. Theological truths had to be taken on faith and believed, or they became a mere object of speculation, intrinsically no more certain than any other nondemonstrable propositions. God's omnipotence only increased the uncertainty.

Such an atmosphere of fideism and doubt was not one in which great systems could thrive. After Duns Scotus, with the possible exception of Nicholas of Cusa (d. 1464), there was none. That is not to say that there were no great thinkers except for Ockham. Gregory of Rimini, John Buridan, John Gerson, Thomas Bradwardine, and Nicholas of Oresme were all in different ways, outstanding minds; but they were no longer building on an accepted foundation. Nor did they attempt the same harmonization of nature and supernature. Buridan, Bradwardine, and Oresme were scientists as much as, or more than, theologians or speculators. They made little attempt to integrate their different activities, even when, like Bradwardine or Gregory of Rimini, they introduced mathematical proofs into their philosophical or theological discussions. There was a growing recognition that theology was the preserve of the believer

[54] *Ibid.*, No. 1124.
[55] F. Stegmüller, "Die zwei Apologien des Jean de Mirecourt," in *Recherches de théologie ancienne et médiévale*, 5 (1933), 40–78, 192–204.

bounded by the articles of faith. It ceased to have the standing of knowledge (*scientia*), which for a time in the heyday of the thirteenth century it had seemed to enjoy. Its practical rather than its speculative nature was stressed; its purpose was to elucidate scriptural truth and fortify belief. It therefore dealt with what was inaccessible to human reason.

The hardening of the division between faith and reason was the legacy of Ockhamism. After 1347 there were no more such explosions at Paris. The intellectual atmosphere became more quiescent. The reasons were not wholly doctrinal. The Black Death from 1348 to 1350 was a watershed; it carried off many of the previous generation, or they disappeared from the scene at this time. Little is yet known about the years which followed. Certain thinkers like Buridan, Gregory of Rimini, Richard Fitz-Ralph, Thomas Buckingham, and Adam of Woodham lived into the 1350's or beyond, but most of them not at Paris. The foundation of new universities in Germany drew away foreign thinkers like Albert of Saxony, Henry of Langenstein, and Marsilius of Inghen. Equally important was the growing preoccupation of the leading theologians, Langenstein, Gerson, and d'Ailly, with the problems of the church precipitated by the Great Schism in 1378. Between the demands of ecclesiology, on the one hand, and the pursuit of natural science, on the other, the older, speculative theology, already undermined by Ockhamism, became increasingly academic and formal. When the intellectual history of this later epoch comes to be written it may well be found that scholasticism went out with neither a bang nor a whimper; like a chrysalis it gradually—under the pressure of events and its own tendencies—changed into something new; or more accurately split into its components of theology, ecclesiology, and natural knowledge. By the fifteenth century their development no longer took place within a predominantly scholastic framework or principally at Paris.

III POVERTY

The doctrine of poverty lies outside⁻ the strictly academic limits of Paris's intellectual history; but it was of the first impor-

tance in the outlook of the high and later Middle Ages and nowhere more so than in the disputes between the seculars and the
mendicants at Paris.

We have earlier discussed the circumstances that led to the
strife lasting for well over a decade, from 1254 to around 1270.
The veneration of poverty was common to most medieval movements of religious reform; it had inspired heretical groups, like
the Arnoldists and Waldensians, as well as those recognized by
the church. In the thirteenth century its foremost exponents were
the mendicant orders: both St. Dominic and St. Francis had
made poverty and living on alms part of the very foundation of
their rule. But whereas for the Dominicans poverty had from the
first been subordinated to their main aim of conversion, for
which theological training and some degree of learning were
essential, the Franciscans had sought to remain true to the ideals
of their founder, for whom poverty was foremost among the virtues to be practiced in this world. This had put an increasing
strain on the need to reconcile theory with practice; to the Franciscans no less than the Dominicans had soon come involvements,
to meet which St. Francis's primitive rule of wandering poverty
was unsuited. Beginning with Gregory IX's decree *Quo elongati*
in 1229, a series of papally sponsored dispensations from the literal interpretation of the rule had by the middle of the thirteenth century given the Franciscans identical privileges and
possessions to the Dominicans while theoretically preserving
their rule of poverty.

The intricacies of the disputes that arose in the Franciscan
order as a result cannot be considered here.[56] They were between the official wing of the order—the Conventuals or the
Community—and the Zealots or Spirituals, a minority who held
firm to the literal interpretation of St. Francis's teaching and rule,
above all the sanctity of poverty. Its progressive relaxation under
papal auspices led them increasingly to oppose the authority of
St. Francis to that of the pope; they came to see the struggle
over poverty in terms of a crusade between righteousness and
evil until by 1254 poverty was no longer merely a way of life but
the doctrine of spiritual regeneration and its observance was the

[56] For a recent account see my *"Heresy in the Later Middle Ages,"* I,
Chapter 1.

badge of Christ's true disciples. In forming this outlook a powerful influence had been the teachings of the Calabrian abbot, Joachim of Fiore (d. 1202),[57] who had divided the world's history
into three great states or eras; the first two were in turn sub-
divided into the seven epochs, which corresponded to different
phases in the history of the Old Testament (for the first state)
and the New Testament (for the second state). The age of the
Old Testament he had called the age of the Father; the second
age was the age of the Son; the third age would be of the Holy
Spirit, and would be distinguished not by a new testament as
such but a new spiritual understanding of the Bible as a whole.
The present phase of the world (that is, in the thirteenth century), according to Joachim, marked the transition from the pen-
ultimate sixth to the seventh and final epoch of the second age of
the Son: with the coming of the seventh epoch the end of the
present dispensation would be at hand, ushering in the third age
of the Holy Spirit, which would bring a thousand years of sab-
batical peace; its ending would mark the end of the world and
the coming of the last judgement.

Now the power of Joachim's prophecy lay above all in its direct bearing on the thirteenth century and especially on the
hopes and aspirations of the Franciscan Spirituals and other
persecuted groups. According to Joachim's elaborate concor-
dances and computations, the sixth epoch would run from 1200 to
about 1260. With its ending a period of tribulation and suffer-
ings would inaugurate the seventh epoch of peace, leading to the
third age. Joachim's very lack of precision and his elaborate symbolism only heightened the sense of expectancy. Moreover, his
message seemed directly to apply to the Franciscans; for he saw
the sixth epoch as heralding the renewal of Christ's teaching,
symbolized by the sixth angel of the Apocalypse bearing the
book that contained the knowledge of Christ's teaching. It would
finally triumph through the coming of a new order of spiritual
monks, with whom for a time both the Dominicans and Franciscans identified themselves; before they triumphed they would
have to struggle against the forces of Antichrist, which, symbol-

[57] *Ibid.*, and especially E. Jordan's article in the *Dictionnaire de théologie
catholique* Vol. VII, cols. 1425–58; and M. E. Reeves "The *Liber figurarum* of Joachim of Fiore," *Mediaeval and Renaissance Studies*, II (1950),
57–81.

ized by the seven-headed dragon of the Apocalypse, would use every resource of deception and cruelty to crush them. Many Franciscans—not only the Spirituals—took the angel of the sixth seal for St. Francis and his rule as the renewal of Christ's teaching. For the Spirituals it only increased their sense of the sacrosanctity of poverty and of themselves as the harbingers of a new era, for which they must suffer.

How deep this conviction had become was suddenly revealed in 1254 by the so-called affair of the Eternal Gospel at Paris.[58] A young Franciscan, Gerard of Borgo San Donnino, at the Franciscan house in Paris published an *Introduction to the Eternal Gospel,* in which he explicitly identified the eternal gospel of the third age with Joachim of Fiore's three major writings on the Apocalypse, the Concordance of the Old and the New Testaments, and the Psalter of the Ten Chords. They had, according to Gerard, replaced the books of the Bible in 1200 when the spirit of life had departed from the two Testaments and entered Joachim's three books.[59] Joachim as the author of the new spiritual revelation became the angel of the Apocalypse, who after the sounding of the sixth trumpet appeared from heaven clothed with a cloud and a rainbow on his head.[60] From there Gerard went on to apply Joachim's prophecies concerning the sixth and seventh epochs to the Franciscan order: they were the new spiritual monks of which Joachim had spoken as the renewers of Christ's teaching; and their founder St. Francis was the angel of the sixth seal who "had the seal of the living God" upon him (*Rev.* 7:2). The year 1260 would see the coming of the first Antichrist—the second and great Antichrist, Gog, would appear at the world's end leading to the last judgement—against whom St. Francis's disciples, the barefooted monks, would finally prevail.

The scandal that ensued from the appearance of Gerard's *Introduction* reverberated through the Franciscan order and provided their opponents among the seculars, above all William of St. Amour, with further ammunition. John of Parma, Franciscan

---

[58] The relevant surviving documents have been edited by H. Denifle, "Das Evangelium aeternum and die Commission zu Anagni," *Archiv für Literatur und Kirchengeschichte des Mittelalters,* I (1885), 49–142.
[59] *Ibid.,* 99–100.
[60] *Revelation* 10:1, 2.

general, resigned, to be succeeded by Bonaventure in 1257. Gerard's work was condemned by a papal commission at Anagni and he was imprisoned, dying in captivity. Joachim's writings themselves were not condemned generally then or afterward; but the effect of Gerard's work was to associate them increasingly with insurgency, above all among the Franciscan Spirituals. In treating Joachim's symbolism literally and historically Gerard had set the example of applying it to actual events and persons; it was only a short step from making St. Francis the angel of the sixth seal to seeing the opponents of his rule, and insistence on poverty, as members of Antichrist. To think in terms of a third era in addition to those of the Old and New Testaments, which would be an age of gold on earth, was to invite apocalyptic expectations in those who believed that the truth lay with them. Joachim's antitheses between the present era and the new one to come, between literal and spiritual understanding of the Bible, between the carnal and the spiritual church, became translated into real terms until by the fourteenth century Joachism had come to be an historicism justifying poverty and opposition to authority.

These developments had not arisen in 1254; nor did they form any part of the disputes between the mendicants and seculars. But the association of the Franciscan ideal of poverty with such apocalyptic beliefs—even though held only by a minority— heightened the tension between mendicants and seculars.

As we have seen, initially the issue was over the mendicants' privileges: the right to beg without performing manual labor, to exercise pastoral care without being subject to diocesan authority, to teach in the university without submitting to its corporate demands. There were two phases in the disputes that these anomalies had engendered. The first lasted until about 1260. It was more in the nature of a prologue to what followed ten years later. The two main works around which it centered were William of St. Amour's *De periculis novissimorum temporum* and the anonymous reply to it—very probably by Thomas of York, a Franciscan—the *Manus que contra omnipotentem tenditur*. The two works were wider in scope than most of the works of the second phase, and by the same token less concerned with the technicalities of what was in the second period to be the dominant question: the mendicants' *raison d'être,* and especially their claim to perfection. The second phase reached a climax between the years 1267 and 1271, in a series of polemical writings and disputations between Gerard of Abbeville, Nicholas of Lisieux, and William of St. Amour, for the seculars, and Bonaventure, John Pecham, and Thomas Aquinas, on the part of the mendicants. The seculars, William of St. Amour in particular, received the corrosive support of Rutebeuf and Jean de Meung, the authors of the *Roman de la Rose.*[61]

William of St. Amour, already the mendicants' main antagonist among the secular masters at Paris, was the first to turn the affair of the *Introduction* of Gerard of Borgo San Donnino against the friars. In 1255 he published his polemic on the perils of the most recent times (*Tractatus de periculis novissimorum temporum*).[62] In an apocalyptic tone, not dissimilar from that of Gerard, he declared that the writings of scripture revealed the approaching end of the world, with all its attendant dangers. As they came nearer all Christians must take heed; to cause them to do so was William's purpose in writing his treatise. He then proceeded to show how the mendicants were the forerunners of Antichrist and how they utilized their pastoral privileges, such as hearing confession, to enter the houses of the faithful and seduce them from their true priests. In the same way the friars by their preaching were the pseudoprophets against whom the faithful had been warned in the Gospel of Matthew. As St. Paul had said (*Romans* 10:15) only those who had been sent could preach; but this could only be if they were first elected. The friars were not, and therefore were usurping the office of the truly ordained priests. William recognized that, in taking up this position, he was opposing himself to the pope and bishops who had author-

[61] See especially Rutebeuf, *Poèmes concernant l'Université de Paris,* H. H. Lucas, ed. (Manchester, Manchester University Press, 1952). Rutebeuf's support for William of St. Amour went to the point of condemning St. Louis for banishing him at the pope's behest. Both poets pilloried the pretensions of the mendicants to be following a life of perfection, especially their living from alms instead of their own labor. Like the secular masters, they made the begging of the friars the center of their attack.

[62] Partially edited by M. Bierbaum, *Bettelorden und Weltgeistlichkeit an der Universität Paris* (*Franziskanische Studien,* Münster. i.W., 1920), 1–36.

ized the friars to preach; in order to overcome this difficulty he put forward a doctrine of extreme diocesan autonomy that effectively gave the clergy the power of deciding who could engage in pastoral activities in their dioceses—by invitation.[63] William also divided the ecclesiastical hierarchy into two classes: the upper, consisting of seculars—bishops, priests, and deacons; and the lower, composed of faithful laymen and catechumens (including the regulars). As ordained by God, none of the lower class could act among the upper class. Hence for the mendicants to preach was to go against God, and to be branded pseudo-prophets and deceivers having only the appearance of piety. It was this that enabled them to mislead the faithful, pretending to be the friends of simple believers and taking their secrets from them in confessions.

But the real impact of William's attack came in his direct confrontation with the Joachism of Gerard of Borgo San Donnino; he did not mention Gerard by name but he paraphrased the ideas of the *Introduction,* excerpts from which he was responsible for having sent to the pope for condemnation.[64] Of special interest is the way in which William roundly rejected the Joachist conception of a seventh epoch to be followed by a new era on earth, even while accepting that they were living in the last age of the world. The end was near, but it would be the end of the world, not an epoch: "the eighth age will be that of the resurrection." The present represented the world's eleventh hour. He gave eight signs for its imminent ending, all of which were taken from the affair of the Eternal Gospel in the previous year. The first sign was to be seen in the attempt to change the meaning of the gospel—a direct allusion to Gerard's identification of it with the writings of Joachim of Fiore. This William took as evidence that Antichrist was at hand. Second was the appearance of the *Introduction* in 1254, which showed that dénouement could not be long in coming; and so on. All eight signs treated Gerard of Borgo's writing as the key to subsequent events and the warning of the perils and tribulations to come. It exposed the pretensions of the friars to be true upholders of Christ's

[63] *Ibid.,* 11–12.
[64] *Chart.,* I, No. 243. What follows is contained in Chapter 8 of *De periculis* (Bierbaum, *op. cit.* 19–25).

teaching when in fact they were prepared to desert his gospel for the so-called "Eternal Evangel." Theirs was a false sanctity, and a further sign of the dangers of the times.

The remedy was to inhibit the friars from any pastoral work, preaching, or teaching; [65] in fact, to deny them any religious or scholastic privileges at all. William saw the source of their falsity in their idleness and their worldliness. These disqualified them from any claim to be living an apostolic life or having apostolic powers. He particularly attacked their mendicancy: those who lived from alms "became adulators, detractors, liars and robbers, falling away from righteousness." [65a] To give all for Christ and follow him was to emulate him in doing good, not begging, which St. Paul had prohibited. Perfect living, having given away all one's possessions, was by one's hands in manual labor or by entering a monastery. Christ's apostles had not begged but had legitimately gained their bread through their apostolic life. Indeed, William flatly denied that Christ had begged at all; he had been sent by God as his son; to accuse him of having begged was not merely to be heretical but an heresiarch in questioning the very foundations of Christian faith. Christ could not be compared with the friars. In rejecting the claims, of the Franciscans at least, to be emulating him, William of St. Amour cut at the very root of the claim that mendicancy was the path of perfection in this world. For William, as for so many other seculars, it was mere hypocrisy. He could draw on plenty of scriptural support, as well as pointing to the invidiousness of one "sect," as he called the mendicants, claiming superiority over others on the grounds of not having possessions. In no way did lack of goods make those without them more perfect.

We have dwelt at some length on *De periculis* because it contained all the main elements of the seculars' case against the mendicants. It showed the resentment at their privileges not only of being able to live on alms but of taking them as a sign of a more perfect religious life.

The friars' first response to William's attack was to retaliate by appealing to the pope to have *De periculis* condemned, which

---

[65] *Ibid.*, Chapter 12, pp. 27–36.
[65a] *Ibid.*, 31.

he did on October 5, 1256.[66] There was also a reply, the *Manus que contra omnipotentem tenditur,* written probably by the Franciscan Thomas of York; [67] but because of the condemnation of *De periculis* this reply was not published until a number of years later, when it elicited a rebuttal from Gerard of Abbeville, *Contra adversarium perfectionis.*[68] *Manus que* defended the mendicants' renunciation of the world as true to Christ's teaching; to live on alms was to follow Christ's example of contempt for the world not simply as an interior attitude but in exterior actions, of which living in poverty was the highest expression. Far from being a sign of duplicity and false sanctity with all the attendant vices that William of St. Amour attributed to its adherents, to own nothing in private or in common was the most perfect contempt for possessions taught by Christ. Those who renounced worldly goods should therefore be commended, not reviled; they were following a state more perfect than any other; the source of sin was appetite and they were denying it. Thomas of York also sought to counter William of St. Amour's examples taken from scripture of Christ having had possessions, above all the case of the apostles' purse that Judas carried; in reply, he drew upon the argument of condescension to infirmity: Christ had dispensed money not for his own needs but from compassion for those to whose needs he was ministering; it provided the same justification for the church's use of money.[69]

After this work little more was heard of the issue again until the later 1260's.[70] A number of events helped to revive it. Leaving aside the endemic hostility of the seculars to the mendicants, which had been in no way assuaged by the events of the previous decade and which was always liable to erupt, the mendicants had shown little indication of wishing to forgive or forget. They had in 1259 refused to join in an appeal to the pope

---

[66] *Chart.,* I, Nos. 288, 289, 291.

[67] Bierbaum, *op. cit.,* 37–168.

[68] Published by S. Clasen in AFH, **31** (1938) 276–329 and **32** (1939) 89–200.

[69] Bierbaum, *op. cit.,* 60.

[70] For this second phase see P. Glorieux, "Les Polémiques contra Geraldinos," *Recherches de théologie ancienne et médiévale,* **6** (1934), 5–41, **7** (1935), 129–55.

for the recall of William of St. Amour, an action that had in-flamed ill-feelings. Then in 1267 Clement IV renewed Alexander IV's grant of pastoral rights without the need for prior diocesan assent; his legate, Simon of Brion, in the following year annulled the restrictions imposed by the synod of Compiègne on the friars' pastoral activities. These measures seem to have led di-rectly to a renewal of conflict in the university. It was inaugu-rated by Gerard of Abbeville, archdeacon of Ponthieu, an estab-lished master of theology, supported by Nicholas of Lisieux, also a master in the theological faculty and treasurer of Lisieux ca-thedral; they were aided by William of St. Amour from his exile in Burgundy; he had never given up the struggle and had con-tinued writing against the friars. To attempt to follow all the exchanges, in which nearly thirty writings have been recorded, would be otiose. Many of them were in the form of quodlibetal disputations, which rapidly followed each other from 1269 to 1271 and provided a further example of the immediacy of this kind of exercise. Gerard of Abbeville's opening short sermon, de-livered at the Franciscan church on New Year's day 1269, set the tone.[71] It accused the mendicants, in having renounced posses-sions, of attacking the position of the church; its endowments had been sanctioned both in scripture and by the Donation of Constantine. To demand their abdication was to undermine the church's authority and so fall into heresy. The church's care of souls depended on its being able to minister to those in need. It was upheld in this by the example of Christ's purse; why should he have had it if not because it was his intention also to bear it? Moreover, ecclesiastical possessions were not held privately but in common by the church as a whole. From this, Gerard, fol-lowing William of St. Amour, drew the conclusion that bishops, as the apostles' successors, enjoyed a state of higher perfection than the mendicants and other religious who had renounced all worldy goods, and did not reserve anything for tomorrow; they did not therefore seek to provide for the needy and the infirm as Christ had done. "Oh, brothers," he declared, "open your eyes." The perfection they claimed from denying the senses was not to be derived from the status of a particular religious order but was

[71] Published in Bierbaum, *op. cit.*, 208–19.

a personal matter. The highest degree of ecclesiastical perfection lay in pastoral office; temporal goods, far from diminishing its excellence, enhanced it.

Reply and counter-reply followed in quick succession. The arguments of the seculars were countered as we have said, by Bonaventure, Pecham, and Thomas Aquinas, who directly replied to Gerard when they met in the Lenten *quodlibet* at the beginning of March 1269. Later in the year Gerard wrote his reply to *Manus que* and published it anonymously. He did not merely re-affirm his previous defense of ecclesiastical possessions but went on to raise the two main arguments against Franciscan poverty that recurred again and again: that the legal distinction between papal possession and Franciscan use of the order's belongings was a mere fiction, and in the case of goods consumed, directly untrue; for how could the pope be the owner of the food that the Minors ate or of the clothes and other items expended by them? As for books and buildings, they possessed these in a no less certain way than the other orders. Gerard's treatise called forth the *Apologia pauperum* [72] from Bonaventure, perhaps the finest memorial to the dispute. Its perfect symmetry and deep awareness of all the issues, spiritual and ecclesiastical, however, still could not make the case for the perfection of a mendicant life entirely convincing, especially in the face of their undeniable affluence. His defense of Franciscan poverty recognized that it was not the highest virtue, but the best means of making imper-fection in this world less imperfect. He demonstrated fully that poverty came far down in the scale of goodness, compared with charity, which was a supernatural gift and the source of all per-fection. He was therefore for the first time facing the problem St. Francis had never envisaged: the need to define the place of poverty in the whole spectrum of values while remaining true to it as a way of life. Bonaventure did this by insisting on the need to follow poverty as the only means of overcoming cupidity, the root of all sin, as charity was of perfection. Poverty was thereby the counterpart to charity: it was the means in this world of fol-lowing Christ's human example without aspiring to be compared with him as God's son. It was the best that man could attain in

[72] Bonaventure, *Opera omnia*, VIII (Quaracchi, 1898), 233–330.

this world. Only by renouncing material possessions could man hope to escape the affiction of the spirit that they engendered. Bonaventure thus reaffirmed St. Francis's teaching of poverty as a way of life; it was to be practiced in emulation of Christ's life. Bonaventure's insistence on effective austerity and the utmost simplicity helped to make him one of the architects of what was to be called the *usus pauper*—poor usage, or living—in the next generation; he never wavered in recalling the order to its observance.

The greater part of Bonaventure's treatise was taken up with defining the relation of Franciscan poverty to the church. He sought to balance the claim that absolute poverty was the highest perfection (in this world) with a recognition of the perfection of the monastic orders and the secular ecclesiastics who owned property in common. He did so by making them all share in the same perfection as disciples of Christ. It was not an easy task and it can hardly be said that Bonaventure would have succeeded in assuaging those who resented the mendicants' belief in their superiority as an order. Nevertheless, he sought to heal any rift between them, whereas Gerard of Abbeville and his confrères worked to open it. The reconciliation of the differing degrees of perfection was the more vital for the Franciscans in that their own claim to be in absolute poverty depended on the pope being the owner of what they used. Bonaventure therefore had to justify possessions and money in certain cases: he did so by the same argument used by Thomas that they were licit when used to minister to men's infirmities as Christ had done with the money carried in Judas' bag. Possession was then not for self-gratification but to serve others in charity. In the case of the Franciscans, papal ownership enabled them to follow Christ naked. From this position Bonaventure answered Gerard's charge that the Franciscan distinction between use and possession was a fraud; he sought also to establish that the goods the order consumed were those only of "simple use," the bare essentials necessary to preserve mortal life in this world. To have mere subsistence was not to own goods or to betray the vow of poverty. To Gerard's further point that the pope could not be the owner of that from which he gained nothing, Bonaventure replied that the gain was spiritual; he also cited the analogy of a son who consumed his father's goods without being their owner.

The importance of Bonaventure's doctrine of poverty in the subsequent history of the Franciscan order cannot concern us here, save to say that its impact—together with teaching of John Pecham, who followed Bonaventure closely in his treatise on poverty written a few months later [73]—was profound; it gave the Spirituals a new theoretical justification for strict poverty and their opponents new grounds for regarding poverty as merely an external.

Nothing could be more indicative of the difference between the Franciscan and Dominican outlooks on perfection than Thomas' treatise *Contra impugnantes cultum dei.*[74] Poverty itself was only one among a range of issues: one chapter of three folios among twenty-three chapters totaling thirty-three folios. There are plenty of other places where it was treated in connection with manual labor and mendicancy; but it had none of the central importance that it had in Bonaventure's *Apologia,* in which it was the spinal column of the work. Indeed, Thomas only reached the topic of poverty in the sixth chapter, as but one aspect of a religious order; even allowing for his archetypally impersonal tone, the absence of any reference to the ideal of his founder is in striking contrast to Bonaventure's invocation of St. Francis as the fount of Franciscan life.

Aquinas began his treatise with a discussion of the nature of religion and religious perfection; it consisted in worship of God and interior perfection. He then went on to discuss the credentials of a religious order to teach, belong to a university of secular masters, preach, hear confessions, and exercise the cure of souls; he replied affirmatively to mendicant participation in each. He then went on to argue that a religious was no more bound to do manual labor than a secular priest; it was neither a precept nor a' counsel; and, if it were, it would have applied universally to all. Hence there was no reason why a religious should work with his hands. On renunciation of all possessions, Thomas emphasized the obligation to live in poverty; it is instructive that he discussed the question as "whether it is permissible for a religious to relinquish all his goods. . ." There is no suggestion that it is either necessary for a religious order to do so or that he

---

[73] In C. L. Kingsford, A. G. Little and F. Tocco, eds., *Tractatus tres de paupertate* (Aberdeen, 1910).
[74] St. Thomas Aquinas, *Opera omnia,* Vol. XVII (Venice, 1593), 127–60.

himself was a member of an order—which by then the Dominicans were not—having had originally no possessions in common. He accepted that to follow Christ in selling all and giving it to the poor belonged to Christian perfection; but this meant really living in poverty, not just wanting to do so: an unmistakable allusion to his Franciscan counterparts who were caught up in precisely that contradiction. Thomas's defense of mendicancy was therefore against those who attacked it as a sin rather than as an evocation of its virtues in the manner of Bonaventure. He also accepted the fact that the use of money should be restricted to cases of necessity, although accepting that there was no precept against it: Christ had employed it in just such circumstances for helping the infirm. Thomas treated mendicancy, on the one hand, as the corollary of being possessionless. For those in that state it was permissable, provided they had given up all for Christ and had no other means of subsistence. Moreover, anyone could give alms out of Christian charity and they could be rightly accepted. But it was also justified for those who preached God's word, if authorized; indeed it was for preaching that alms should be given above all: "Among all ecclesiastical occupations the most noble is making known the word of God." [75] At the same time Thomas counterattacked the seculars for attacking mendicancy by pointing to the great number of them who neither had care of souls nor lived from manual labor. The religious were far more entitled to live without performing manual labor if they preached. In doing so they were, in fact, receiving a just return for their efforts. The third part of Thomas's treatise showed the way in which the mendicants had been defamed by their opponents over each of their main activities. Like all Thomas's work, the *Contra impugnantes* displayed breadth and balance; each of the main issues was considered and none was magnified at the expense of the others. It was an apologia not for poverty but for religious orders and nonsecular forms of life; poverty and mendicancy were but a part of these, of no greater importance than learning or teaching, and ultimately, as we have seen, subservient to preaching.

It would be unnecessary as well as tedious to prolong this ex-

[75] *Ibid.*, Chapter 7, 145 va.

amination. Enough has been said to show the character of the disputes over poverty, the issues raised, and the differences they revealed both between the mendicants and seculars and between the Franciscans and the Dominicans. In the end the friars were vindicated by the papacy as they had been over William of St. Amour's *De periculis*. Articles from Gerard's treatises attacking them were sent to the pope; Gerard retracted in a number of apologetic works.[76] He died in 1272, the same year as William of St. Amour.

The wider controversies did not end there. In 1274 hostility against the mendicants at the Second General Council of Lyons led to proposals—rejected—for their disbandment. Feelings continued to erupt from time to time. In 1281 Martin IV's bull *Ad fructus uberes* started, as we earlier mentioned, a chain reaction among the theological faculty in the quodlibets of the next few years. In the fourteenth century hostility gathered in a series of virulent attacks to be found at the end of the century in the writings of Wyclif and the Czech reformers, as well as Chaucer, and the issues of poverty and evangelical perfection dominated the Franciscan order and much of John XXII's pontificate. The disputes at Paris were a formative phase in these developments. The main repercussions, however, were elsewhere—in the Franciscan order, the popular religious movements, and the ecclesiology of the later Middle Ages. Although it varied according to the different contexts, the problem of poverty and the nature of evangelical perfection introduced a new element into the outlook of the later thirteenth and fourteenth centuries. Largely under the influence of Joachism and the call for a return to first apostolic principles, the present church came increasingly to be contrasted to the life of Christ and the apostles. There was a growing sense that the church had betrayed its primitive ideal; it is to be found not only among the Franciscan Spirituals, the Waldensians, and the Fraticelli, but in the political doctrines of thinkers like Dante, Marsilius of Padua, Ockham, Wyclif, Hus, to name only the most egregious. A return could be made only by the disendowment of the church, taking it away from wealth and privilege and worldliness and returning it to the poverty, humil-

[76] D. M. Douie, *Archbishop Pecham* (Oxford, 1952), 33–4.

ity, and simplicity preached and practiced by Christ and his disciples. The disputes of the schools went far beyond their walls.

The doctrinal and intellectual history, then, of Paris in the thirteenth and fourteenth centuries was on a universal scale. Its schools and the religious houses were the nerve center of all the main phases of thought and the focus of most of the crises and tensions. We have been able only to point to the tip of the iceberg; in addition to the famous names—only a fraction of them French until the fourteenth century—there was a host of others engaged in the same controversies. Although Paris continued to enjoy a dominant position for the first half of the fourteenth century, it became less ecumenical and more French. On the one hand, involvement in the affairs of the French kings grew, beginning with Philip the Fair's struggle against Boniface VIII at the turn of the century and then his suppression of the Templars in 1311–12, and culminating in the prolonged efforts to end the Great Schism, and the Council of Constance from 1414 to 1418. On the other hand, the intellectual center of gravity was shifting outward to the new foundations that some of Paris's own alumni helped to sponsor, while Oxford led in new scientific developments that were then taken up by Nicholas of Oresme and his contemporaries. If by then Paris was no longer *parens scientiarum*, it never lost the pre-eminence that derived from 150 years of intellectual ascendancy.

FIVE

Oxford: Doctrinal and Intellectual Developments during the Thirteenth and Fourteenth Centuries

The intellectual histories of Paris and Oxford are so closely interconnected that in one sense it is artificial to separate them. The phases, and problems, were common, from the coming of Aristotle to the emergence of Ockhamism; many of the personnel belonged to both universities: Edmund of Abingdon, John Blund, Roger Bacon, Richard Rufus of Cornwall, John Pecham, Roger Marston, Duns Scotus, and William of Ockham, to name the most prominent; their syllabuses and academic methods were, as we have seen, almost identical. Accordingly, much that has already been said about Paris applies to Oxford. At the same time there was a difference alluded to earlier. Oxford was insulated from the worst pressures at Paris; it was a native university in a way that Paris was not. In general the interchange was from Oxford to Paris and back rather than from Paris to Oxford. Far from this making Oxford an intellectual suburb of Paris, however, it testifies to the vitality of Oxford's life, and the succession of great thinkers associated with it. Moreover, Oxford had a continuity that Paris never enjoyed; this gave its thought a unity that can be traced from Grosseteste to Bradwardine, and entitles us to speak of an Oxford school in a way that we cannot of Paris. It consisted, however, in more than mere cohesiveness;

Oxford thought owed more to Grosseteste than either university owed to any other scholar; he gave it an impetus that carried it forward into new positive scientific studies and was able to out-run the more singular aberrations of the Ockhamist school. It was probably not an accident that neither Aristotelianism nor Ockhamism had the same disruptive effect as at Paris. Kil-wardby's condemnations of 1277 at Oxford were largely a reflex action of those ten days earlier at Paris, and Pecham's decree in 1284 resulted as much as anything from his own obsession, from his Paris days, with the Thomist doctrine of the unity of the sub-stantial form. There were no doctrinal disputes between seculars and mendicants over poverty and evangelical perfection. Ox-ford's intellectual history, like its institutional development, was spared the worst vicissitudes of Paris although retaining the es-sential attributes that made it second only to Paris.

I GROSSETESTE AND THE OXFORD SCHOOL IN THE THIRTEENTH CENTURY

We considered in Chapter Three the transmission of Aristo-telian and Arabian learning to England and Grosseteste's role as a translator. There were at Oxford no bans and no condemnation of Greco-Arabian philosophy either in the first years of the thir-teenth century or at the time of Gregory IX's action against the *libri naturales* from 1228 to 1231. By the 1240's they had become sufficiently established at Oxford for Roger Bacon to lecture on them in the middle years of that decade in the arts faculty at Paris with an accomplishment lacking among the majority of its members.

Among the Oxford scholars at the beginning of the thirteenth century who can be definitely said to have taught and studied there, besides Grosseteste, were Edmund of Abingdon, later archbishop of Canterbury, and John Blund, who was passed over in that office in favor of Edmund.[1] Both commented various works of Aristotle. As we have seen, they were not the first Eng-

[1] For what follows see particularly D. A. Callus, "The Introduction of Aris-totelian Learning to Oxford," *Proceedings of the British Academy,* 29 (1943), 229–81.

lish scholars to adopt the new learning. Alexander of Neckham and Alfred of Sareshel, in particular, writing at the turn of the thirteenth century, were two of the most prominent examples. Neckham was an "ardent Aristotelian," to use the late D. A. Callus's expression.[2] Alfred of Sareshel was among the first to comment the *libri naturales,* and his *De motu cordis* was taken into widespread use, becoming a textbook in the arts faculty at Paris. His definition of the soul was generally accepted, and was mentioned among others by Philip the Chancellor, John of La Rochelle, and Albert the Great. He was also an unacknowledged source for Bacon, which did not prevent him from inclusion among Bacon's wide circle of adversaries. Despite Alfred's influence on thinkers at both Oxford and Paris, there is no evidence that either he or Neckham taught in the schools.

Edmund of Abingdon, however, taught arts at Oxford from about 1202 to 1208 after having incepted in them at Paris. According to Bacon he was the first to lecture on Aristotle's *Sophistici elenchi,* one of the books of the New Logic.[3] Apart from that little is known of his scholastic career, and even less of the shadowy Hugh, a contemporary master, and John of London. John Blund is the one to emerge most clearly; he, too, taught at both Paris and Oxford, where he lectured in arts on the *libri naturales.*[4] He also was an enthusiastic supporter of Aristotle. He may have first studied at Paris. Like Edmund, his teaching career at Oxford was probably interrupted by the suspension of the university in 1209–10. Like Edmund, also, he probably migrated to Paris, where he seems to have remained until the dispersion of 1229. During that time he turned to the study of theology: on his return to Oxford he taught as a regent master in theology, later becoming chancellor of York after his failure to be appointed archbishop of Canterbury in 1232. He died in 1248. Blund is of special interest as being among the first thinkers in the West to attempt to employ the new ideas—above all those of Avicenna—in a coherent way, especially in his treatise on the soul. Unlike his forerunners, he was not content merely to cite Aristotle and the Arabian philosophers but at-

[2] *Ibid.,* 235.
[3] Quoted *ibid.,* 238–9 from Rashdall, ed., *Fratris Rogeri Bacon,* 34.
[4] Callus, "Aristotelian Learning," 241 ff.

tempted to develop their doctrines to a purpose. Despite the width of his references, which included Cicero, Boethius, and Plato's *Timaeus,* he came down firmly on the side of Aristotle; he was among the first to take issue with two of the notions that were to be the hallmark of the Augustinian outlook: the plurality of forms and the hylomorphic composition of all beings, spiritual as well as material. Although he did not embark on any sustained metaphysical speculation, Blund bears witness to the degree to which Avicennan Aristotelianism had penetrated Oxford before the middle of the thirteenth century.

It would, however, be artificial to the point of falsity to depict the intellectual history of Oxford in the thirteenth century in terms of the increasing assimilation of Aristotle. Aristotle, as we have said, together with his Arabian commentators, came to be as familiar there as at Paris; but Aristotelianism as an outlook never had the same hold. In 1277 Thomism was as much the object of reprobation as Aristotle or Averroes. The reason is Robert Grosseteste. This was not because Grosseteste was anti-Aristotelian; far from it. We have seen that he was responsible for translating Aristotle's *Ethics;* he also, when in the arts faculty in the first decade of the thirteenth century, commented the *Sophistici elenchi* and the *Prior* and the *Posterior Analytics.* Moreover, many of Grosseteste's treatises were concerned with metaphysics; he also wrote a commentary on the eight books of the *Physics* and translated the first two books of *De caelo.*[5] This activity extended over the qreater part of Grosseteste's career, which, so far as his writings are concerned, was in two phases: the first was from his becoming master in arts to his translation to the bishopric of Lincoln in 1235; during that period he composed his commentaries on Aristotle and the Bible and wrote his numerous scientific treatises. From 1235 until his death in 1253 he made his translations from the Greek; in addition to the works of Aristotle these included the Neoplatonist pseudo-Dionysius and Maximus the Confessor, the Epistles of St. Ignatius, and the writings of John Damascenus, as well as Aristotle's Greek commentator Simplicius and pseudo-Aristotelian works such as *De virtute.*[6] By his translations Grosseteste did more than any other

[5] For this, *ibid.,* 252 ff.; and especially Callus, "Grosseteste as Scholar," in D. Callus, ed., *Robert Grosseteste* (Oxford, 1955) 1–69, especially 12 ff.
[6] Callus, "Grosseteste as Scholar," 34.

man to bring Greek learning to England. That this took place during his time as one of the outstanding bishops of the thirteenth century makes his achievement all the more remarkable. According to Bacon he invited Greeks to England and procured Greek manuscripts and grammars.[7] He undoubtedly received help in this work, though not to the degree that Bacon stated. The most notable part of these translations was the rendering into Latin of the pseudo-Dionysian corpus, which Grosseteste accompanied by commentaries. These included the *Celestial Hierarchy*, the *Ecclesiastical Hierarchy*, the *Divine Names*, the *Mystical Theology*, and so-called *Scholia* of Maximus the Confessor. As in the case of his rendering of the *Logica, De haeresibus, De fide orthodoxia*, and other writings of John of Damascus, Grosseteste did not make a new translation, but revised and improved those already in being. He came in for criticism from contemporaries for prolixity, which his close adherence to the Greek original involved. His versions did not have any formative influence on Dionysian studies, for by then the translation of the pseudo-Dionysius had been completed at Paris. None of the Paris masters, Albert, Thomas, Henry of Ghent, John Pecham, or Gerard of Abbeville, made use of Grosseteste's work on the pseudo-Dionysus; that only happened toward the end of the thirteenth century and the earlier fourteenth century.[8] Grosseteste's version of the *Ethics*, however, was a striking and immediate success. He accompanied it, as in his other translations, with a commentary.

I have mentioned this aspect of Grosseteste's work first because, although belonging to the later part of his career, it was then that he also came nearest to theological speculation, through his glosses, or *notulae*, to the texts he was rendering. He was not a systematic thinker in the way that St. Thomas or Henry of Ghent of Duns Scotus was. The *Summa theologiae* that he probably intended to write on the four books of the Lombard's *Sentences* was never completed; he left a series of treatises that date from his mastership in theology. The most important and influential was that on free will (*De libero arbitrio*). These writings seem to have originated as disputed questions that were later

---

[7] *Ibid.*, 38, citing R. Bacon, *Opus maius*, III, H. Bridges, ed., I (London, 1900), 67.
[8] *Ibid.*, 60–1.

written up in the way we noted in Chapter Three.[9] They included ones on truth (*De veritate*), on divine knowledge (*De scientia dei*), and on the truth of propositions (*De veritate propositionis*), as well as a group of theological questions.

Of Grosseteste's biblical commentaries, that on the *Hexaemeron* is the most interesting [10]; he brought into play his knowledge of Greek to compare the opinions of the Greek and Latin Fathers, a new and promising development, which his departure from Oxford to Lincoln prevented from maturing. He made no attempt to reconcile the teachings of the pagan philosophers with Christian belief; Aristotle was not a Christian, and to attempt to treat him as one could only lead to heresy—a standpoint abundantly confirmed after Grosseteste's death in the 1270's. The *Hexaemeron* was the best known of Grosseteste's biblical commentaries. But as with the majority of these writings, it only became popular in the fourteenth and fifteenth centuries.[11] The cause lay principally in Grosseteste's old-fashioned approach; he belonged to the biblical outlook of the decades each side of 1200, in which theology and exegesis were kept very closely together. He never adopted the practice that became accepted at Paris by about 1230 of making the Commentary on Peter Lombard's *Sentences* the main—though not the exclusive —vehicle of theological speculation. It was probably because of his attitude that the Commentary on the *Sentences* came later to Oxford. For Grosseteste the study of the Bible entailed treating it in all its aspects, particularly the spiritual one. Like that earlier celebrated English scholar and ecclesiastic Stephen Langton, Grosseteste saw in the spiritual exposition of scripture a means toward the moral reformation of society: "Light comes when the carnal [i.e., literal] sense of scripture bursts forth into the spiritual sense." [12] Grosseteste also adhered to the older methods of continuous exposition rather than the new ones of division by chapter; he eschewed the application of dialectic to solve exegetical questions. He sought rather an historical context for the atti-

[9] *Ibid.*, 28–9.
[10] B. Smalley, "Grosseteste: the Biblical Scholar," in D. Callus, ed., *Robert Grosseteste*, 70–97, especially 78–9.
[11] For this, *ibid.*, 83 ff.
[12] *Ibid.*, 85.

tudes and actions under examination in a genuine attempt to find the correct answer, such as who was right in the controversy between Jerome and Augustine concerning the supersession of the precepts of the Old Law. He saw it as the result of mutual misunderstanding due to lost letters and the distance of the two fathers from one another.[13] This was an entirely personal response that had nothing to do with the new techniques of the schools or indeed with any other school. Grosseteste, in centering theology on the study of the Bible, set an example to Wyclif, who shared his same passionate belief in preaching as the means of moral reformation.[14]

It was for his mathematical physics and light metaphysics, however, that Grosseteste stands out above all as the founder of the distinctive outlook of the Oxford school. As Paris was to Aristotelian metaphysics, Oxford was to mathematics and optics. If the first made for the more comprehensive speculative systems, the latter made for a more thoroughgoing scientific attitude combined with a more refined conception of inductive and deductive truth. Ultimately the scientific revolution and the outlook associated with it was to owe more to Oxford's mathematical Platonism than the Aristotelian categories of physical science. That is not to say that Grosseteste rejected Aristotle; on the contrary, he did for Aristotelian scientific method what the theologians of the first part of the thirteenth century did for Aristotelian natural philosophy, in Neoplatonizing it. But with this difference: that Grosseteste brought to his work a mathematical insight and originality that all his contemporaries lacked in their speculative theology. He did not—as they did—take the categories, which were transmitted in the translated works of Aristotle and his Arabian commentators, and explain them and manipulate them in order to bring them into harmony with an accepted theological framework; nor did he attempt to substitute dialectical for metaphysical problems as so many of his contemporaries did. On the contrary, as in his biblical commentaries, he sought to bring his own experience and observation to the questions confronting him; but in the case of his scientific work it made him not just original

[13] *Ibid.*, 90–3.
[14] *Ibid.*, 95–6.

and out of vogue, but out of sight of the rest of the Christian world. He was speaking in a new idiom that—although it had its inspiration in a Neoplatonic proclivity for mathematics, light, and intelligible truth—bore directly on Aristotle's categories of demonstration and scientific method. Whereas his contemporaries accepted Aristotle's logic without fully being able to assimilate his metaphysics, Grosseteste gave a new import to the logic and created his own metaphysics. That was Grosseteste's distinction and the distinctiveness of the school that he initiated. Metaphysics for him was light and its understanding only possible by means of mathematics. The desire of the Augustinian theologians until the time of Duns Scotus to retain the independence and supremacy of intelligible truth while recognizing the indispensability of sensory knowledge was solved in an entirely new and oblique way by Grosseteste. In making scientific enquiry rather than mere speculation the basis of certain, demonstrable knowledge he was able to use mathematics to establish the priority of the intelligible over the sensible; he did so not just by asserting the primacy of one over the other in the formal dialectical manner of the majority of the masters in the schools, but by establishing an order of demonstration that depended on the superiority of mathematics over sensory or physical verification.

How was Grosseteste able to achieve this? [15] The starting point for it was his Commentary on the *Posterior Analytics.* It was almost certainly written before his treatises on optics and astronomy and other scientific problems such as the rainbow. In keeping with his a priori Neoplatonic approach he began with the methodology of investigating the natural world and then proceeded to apply it in his treatises on specific questions. It was based on Aristotle's principles of induction and demonstration. Aristotle had distinguished between knowledge of a fact (translated into medieval Latin as *quia*) and knowledge of the reason of the fact, its wherefore (*propter quid*) or cause. Grosseteste took this over; he would, he said, call "syllogism *quia* everything

---

[15] This account is based principally on the pioneering work of A. C. Crombie, *Robert Grosseteste and the Origins of Experimental Science* (Oxford, 1953), 1100–1700; and a resumé of his main conclusions in "Grosseteste's position in the History of Science," in D. Callus, ed., *Robert Grosseteste,* 98–120.

which shows through the effect and syllogism *propter quid* everything which shows through the cause." [16]

The object Grosseteste set himself was to establish a scientific method that would enable the *propter quid,* or reason, of the facts to be deduced from their empirical investigation. The very need to do so reflected man's inability to attain to certain knowledge in his natural state; this could come only through divine illumination. Physical light—which, as we shall mention shortly, he saw as the source of all created being—had its analogy in the spiritual light by which the mind received a knowledge of the unchanging principles that informed all being. These, like St. Augustine, Grosseteste regarded as the reflection in the mind of the divine ideas that were the eternal exemplars of all that was. They were therefore prior to and independent of all individuals and the means "through which particular things are what they are." [17] There was accordingly a hierarchy of truth: the more intelligible and universal and independent of individual images derived from the senses, the higher and more certain and closer to the divine light it was.

For this reason the science of separate incorporeal substances is more certain than the science of corporeal substances bound to a body . . . because we hold that divine things are more visible to a healthy sight of a mind not obscured by phantasmata just as the brightest bodies illuminated by the sun are seen better by a healthy bodily eye accustomed to the vision of bright things.

"But in man's fallen state weighed down by the weight of a corruptible body and with the appearance of corporeal things" men were better adapted to knowing through the senses.[18] Certain knowledge could come only through the irradiation of the intellect by God; this alone enabled the pure intelligible truth of each thing to be known in conformity with the divine word, whereas metaphysical knowledge could never be certain. In default of this, however, there were degrees of truth, which the

---

[16] Crombie, *Grosseteste and Experimental Science,* 53, quoting from Grosseteste's Commentary on the *Posterior Analytics,* I, 6.

[17] *Ibid.,* 128, citing text of Grosseteste's Commentary on the *Posterior Analytics,* I, 18.

[18] *Ibid.,* 129, quoting the Commentary on the *Posterior Analytics,* 1, 17.

mind could attain by abstracting the general principles that inhered in all individuals. As Grosseteste expressed it,

"The form is threefold. One is that which, in terms of being and for purposes of study, is in matter and is that which the natural philosopher studies. The second is that which the mathematician studies, which is abstracted from motion and matter, not in being but for the purposes of study. The third is that which the metaphysician studies, which is abstracted from matter and motion both in terms of being and for the purposes of study, of which kind are the intelligences and other separate substances, for example God and such like." [19]

Of these three types of knowledge only the mathematical was certain to man in his unaided human state: physics was uncertain because it dealt with the flux of changeable things; metaphysics could not provide, by purely natural means, knowledge of eternal and spiritual being.[20] Hence the importance of mathematics in demonstrative knowledge: its premises were both self-evident and immediately demonstrated; for example, the definition of a triangle as a figure bounded by three straight lines also contained the demonstration of what a triangle was; it needed no further verification in experience. It thereby at once gave knowledge of the premises and the conclusions.

The role of mathematics was directly related to Grosseteste's conception of the natural world. It had two aspects: one was the kind of knowledge that it could provide; the other was its metaphysical structure. So far as the first was concerned we have already seen that knowledge of a thing's existence was in itself incomplete because it did not contain knowledge of its causes or reason (*propter quid*). To attain it required first describing the thing observed by distinguishing its different attributes and then seeking to reconcile them in a theoretical statement about its nature. Grosseteste called this procedure resolution and composition. Like Aristotle, he began from the most general term—genus—and descended to the most particular—from the humanity of Socrates to the color of his eyes and hair (not an example employed by Grosseteste or Aristotle). In that way the elements

[19] *Ibid.*, 58.
[20] *Ibid.*, 59.

of the composite picture of Socrates as a man were broken down inductively. Having done this, the process was reversed: beginning with the most specific features and ascending to the most general (resolution), that is trying to deduce from the individual's attributes a general statement about his nature. In that way the theory deduced could be compared with the evidence derived from the initial inductive observation. As Grosseteste put it,

". . . the natural way for us to arrive at knowledge is to go from . . . whole objects which follow from the principles themselves . . . The way of knowledge is . . . from confusedly known whole complete objects . . . into the parts themselves by which it is possible to define the whole object itself, and from the definition to return to determinate knowledge of the whole object." [21]

The cause, that is to say, could only be reached from the effects and by verification of them. The properties isolated or resolved in the object investigated could be brought into causal relationship and so the nature or the quiddity that they composed demonstrated. Grosseteste's own example was to find the common nature of horned animals and the cause of the attribute of "having horns." For this he began with a survey of horned animals, which revealed that the connection between having horns went with having more than one stomach and the absence of teeth in the upper jaw. From this a descriptive definition could be arrived at. But the cause (*propter quid*) demanded a rearrangement of the observed phenomena in a causal definition which in this case ran: "The cause of having horns is not having teeth in both jaws, and not having teeth in both jaws is the cause of having several stomachs." [22] Thus a deductive statement was framed, based on prior inductive investigation. Now it was at this point, in the ability to generalize the empirically observed connection between having horns and not having teeth in both jaws, that the mind's own attributes entered; logically there was no immediate connection between stating a formal regu-

[21] *Ibid.*, 55.
[22] *Ibid.*, 68–9.

larity between two sets of evidence and deducing a causal relationship between them. It came about, said Grosseteste following Aristotle, by an act of intuition on the part of the mind, which on the basis of observing certain regularities was able to deduce from them a universal law. Grosseteste, however, did not stop there; and it was his refusal to do so that took him beyond the more facile acceptance of his contemporaries that the general abstracted from the particular was of itself true. On the contrary, he recognized that before such a deduction could be accepted it had to be tested by resolution—or induction—just because it was only a possible cause. The very absence of certainty from physical knowledge meant that, unlike mathematics, the premises were not given in the conclusion; accordingly, the cause deduced from the effect had to be verified by isolating it from all other factors: that is, by experiment. If the two repeatedly went together they could be accepted as cause and effect.

Thus ultimately Grosseteste's insistence on the need for verification came from an Augustinian recognition of the uncertainty of the knowledge derived from natural experience. It led him to take over Aristotle's principles of demonstration and investigation and apply them in a more rigorous procedure to natural knowledge. Grosseteste's originality raises him above designations such as Neoplatonist or Aristotelian; he drew from both sources, as he did from Boethius and other Latin writers, in his use of the categories of resolution and composition and the methods used in medicine.[23] But the total effect was a new methodology of scientific experimentation based on the need for verification and falsification as a means of testing conclusions, or more accurately, the hypotheses made about them. In this he drew also upon Aristotle's principle of the uniformity of nature: that the same cause in the same conditions produces the same effects; and the principle of economy (*lex parsimoniae*), that the fewer the premises the better. The influence of Grosseteste in all subsequent medieval scientific thought and activity cannot be overestimated.[24] He himself formulated the methodology rather

[23] *Ibid.*, 75–6.
[24] *Ibid.*, 84–5.

than carried out experiments. But he directly inspired others to do so, above all in optics: Roger Bacon, Witelo, and Theodoric of Freiburg.

It was in this sphere that Grosseteste's greatest importance and originality lay. As we can see from what has already been said, he was no mere empiricist. The attention he gave to natural knowledge flowed from his awareness of its inherent uncertainty; hence his desire to ensure its verification. Grosseteste held a strongly Neoplatonic conception of truth and the order of reality which was expressed in what is generally known as the light-metaphysic. Not only was spiritual understanding the result of the spiritual illumination that came from God, but the world itself was the result of physical light. In his treatise on light (*De luce seu de inchoatione formarum*),[25] Grosseteste described how light was the first corporeal form. From it all created being derived. The reason was that light had the power of propagating itself instantaneously and in every direction. It was at once the first form and the first matter, a point without dimensions that by self-diffusion led to extension in space and so to material dimensions. For Grosseteste this was the means by which the universe had been brought into being; light's infinite multiplication had engendered a finite world, the limits of which had been reached when light had exhausted its capacity for further generation. The farther it had gone the more extended it had become; accordingly, light was denser at the center of the world and more rarified at the extremities. Since light moved spherically it produced a sphere. This first sphere was called the firmament and was composed of nothing but the first matter and the first form; once in existence, it radiated light (*lumen*), which in turn produced a second sphere, and so on until all the nine celestial spheres and the four elementary spheres of the Aristotelian universe had been produced. Light, then, was the universal constituent of both the higher bodies and the lower bodies. By that Grosseteste did not simply mean light in a visible form but as constituent of being, the source of all magnitude and movement; visible light was only one among the natural phenomena. In con-

---

[25] Translated in H. Shapiro, *op. cit.*, 254–63.

sequence the natural world could only be understood by understanding the way in which light, as its active principle (*virtus*), operated.

It was this that gave mathematics its pre-eminence, not simply as the most certain form of human knowledge but in scientific investigation. On the one hand, the physical sciences were subordinate to it, in that they made particular statements about, say, the observed movement of the heavenly bodies in astronomy, which mathematics could deduce from geometrical theory. Mathematics studied abstract quantity; it could therefore provide knowledge of the reason for the fact derived from the lower physical sciences, "since quantitative dispositions are common to all mathematical sciences . . . and to natural sciences." [26] The latter were therefore dependent on the general principles that mathematics contained.

"Such sciences, of which one gives knowledge *propter quid* and the other knowledge *quia* about the same thing, are those which have such a relationship to one another that one is subordinating and the other subordinated. For example the science which is concerned with the study of radiant lines and figures falls under geometry, which is concerned simply with lines and figures; the science of constructing machines, as architecture and other mechanical arts, falls under the science of the figures of bodies; the science of harmony falls under arithmetic; and the science which sailors use to direct the course of ships by the appearance of the stars is subordinate to astronomy." [27]

On the other hand, because of the light-metaphysic, the fundamental study of created being was optics, which was governed by geometrical laws; hence subordinate to mathematics. Both in the order of knowledge and in knowledge of the natural world, then, mathematics was the key to understanding.

"The usefulness of considering lines, angles and figures is the greatest because it is impossible to understand natural philosophy without these. They are efficacious throughout the universe as a whole, and its parts, and in related properties as recti-

[26] *Ibid.*, 91.
[27] *Ibid.*, 91–2.

linear and circular motion. They are efficacious also in cause and effect, and this whether in matter or the senses . . . For all causes of natural effects have to be expressed by means of lines, angles and figures, for otherwise it would be impossible to have knowledge of the reason (*propter quid*) concerning them." [28]

Geometry was therefore the indispensable instrument:

". . . these rules and principles having been given by the power of geometry, the careful observer of natural things can give the causes of all natural things by this method. And it will be impossible otherwise, as is already clear in respect of the universal, since every natural action is varied in strength and weakness through variation of lines, angles and figures. But in respect of the particular this is even clearer, first in the natural action upon matter and later upon the senses, so that the truth of geometry is quite plain." [29]

This more than any other single element in his teaching was Grosseteste's most important legacy to Oxford and ultimately to experimental science. He took the first decisive step toward a mathematical physics, in which different physical powers could be explained quantitatively, in terms of geometrical structure. He himself set the direction in his own application of his methodology to the study of optics—mirrors, lenses, and the rainbow. His investigations were thereby different in kind from any previous medieval thinker. They took place within a framework that had light as its basis. This had the effect of at once distinguishing mathematics from the natural sciences and of subordinating the latter to it. Here, too, he carried further Aristotle's previous distinction: mathematics could not deal with the efficient or material causes because it was an abstraction from them; but it could help toward knowledge of the formal and final causes —the ultimate nature and *raison d'être* of the events taking place in space and time. It led ultimately to the displacement of physical for mathematical categories of being, evidence of which is apparent among fourteenth-century Oxford and Paris mathematicians. Categories of substance and attribute were then being

[28] *Ibid.*, 110.
[29] *Ibid.*

replaced by mathematical relations, as can be seen in Bradwardine's *Treatise on Proportions.*

This orientation toward optics and mathematics became the hallmark of the Oxford school; it did not mean the exclusion of the metaphysical speculation that dominated the Paris schools; but it set it in a different context. Oxford thought remained closer to the original Neoplatonic, Augustinian conception that had underlain Grosseteste's outlook. Not only did it inspire the study of mathematics and optics, which led to a new genre of writings like those on proportions as well as an insistence on the need for experiment; it also gave rise to a more direct attitude toward theology, with the emphasis on the Bible rather than a natural theology. That this remained one of the features of Oxford intellectual life can be seen in the succession of thinkers associated with it. The earliest was Adam March, Grosseteste's disciple and the first Franciscan to incept in theology at Oxford; he lectured from 1247 or 1248 until 1250 but has left no extant works save his letters. Bacon praised his great knowledge of science and languages, which was in the direct line of Grosseteste's teaching.

The most celebrated of Grosseteste's followers was Bacon himself; his acerbic comments on his forerunners and contemporaries form one of the sources of circumstantial evidence about thinkers at Oxford and Paris for over half a century. Bacon more than anyone can claim to be the true disciple of Grosseteste in his pursuit of mathematics, optics, and the study of languages and the Bible. He was also loyal to the memory of his master —whose lectures he probably never heard—even if he perhaps gave Grosseteste less than his due over his translations from the Greek.[30] He seems to have become a member of Grosseteste's circle in about 1249.

Bacon, like Grosseteste, began by commenting Aristotle's *Posterior Analytics;*[31] he emphasized the same questions of induction, experiment, and mathematics as the means of understanding universals and the natural world. Like Grosseteste, Bacon maintained that absolute certainty came only through internal

---

[30] Callus, "Robert Grosseteste as Scholar," 37 ff.

[31] For Bacon's scientific work see Crombie, *Robert Grosseteste,* 139–162.

illumination by the divine light.[32] For human knowledge attained naturally he made the same distinction between experience and reasoning:

"Reasoning draws a conclusion and makes us grant the conclusion, but it does not make the conclusion certain, nor does it remove doubt so that the mind may rest on the intuition of truth, unless the mind discovers it by way of experience . . . For if a man who has never seen a fire should prove by adequate reasoning that fire burns and injures things and destroys them, his mind would not be satisfied thereby, nor would he avoid fire until he placed his hand or some combustible substance in the fire so that he might prove by experience that which reasoning taught. But when he has actual experience of combustion his mind is made certain and rests in the full light of truth." [33]

Besides its exclusive prerogative of confirming the conclusions reached by deduction, Bacon also saw the role of experience as adding new knowledge to the existing sciences and creating new ones. The importance of mathematics was primary: it was "the door and key" of knowledge of this world, alone giving natural certainty. His reasons were again those of Grosseteste: "all categories depend on a knowledge of quantity, concerning which mathematics treats, and therefore the whole excellence of logic depends upon mathematics." [34] In an almost prophetic passage Bacon continues,

". . . the categories 'when' and 'where' are related to the quantity, for 'when' pertains to time and 'where' arises from place; the category of 'condition' (or habit) cannot be known without the category of 'where' . . . the greater part, moreover, of the category of 'quality' contains affections and properties of quantities . . . whatever, moreover, is noteworthy in the category of relation is the property of quantity, such as proportions and proportionalities, and geometrical, arithmetical and musical means and the kinds of greater and lesser inequality." [35]

[32] Bacon, *Opus maius,* V, II, 167–8.
[33] *Ibid.,* quoted from Crombie, *Robert Grosseteste,* 141.
[34] *Ibid.,* 143.
[35] *Ibid.,* 143, translated from Bacon, *Opus maius,* I, 103.

Thus, as for Grosseteste, mathematics was prior to the other sciences and gave the greatest certainty. "Wherefore it is evident that, if in the other sciences, we want to come to certitude without doubt and to truth without error, we must place the foundations of knowledge in mathematics." [36] Bacon made a similar attempt to apply these precepts to the study of optics; he, too, regarded light as the type of the multiplication of species and the universal form of all spiritual and material being; hence the importance in its study of lines, angles, and figures. Bacon's contribution to the science of vision was of lasting importance until the seventeenth century, especially his treatment of the working of the eye, for which he drew heavily upon Avicenna and Alhazen.[37]

The influence of the teachings of both Grosseteste and Bacon is to be seen in the anonymous *Summa philosophiae*, written between 1265 and 1275. As its title states, it was a philosophical, not a scientific, work. Its emphasis was on the generating power of light as the most universal form.[39] This was a doctrine also found in the writing of Richard Fishacre, the first Dominican to incept at Oxford and to comment the *Sentences*. John Pecham and Roger Marston were others in whom the same outlook can be seen. Pecham in particular shared Grosseteste's and Bacon's appreciation of experimental science; in common with them he regarded light, mathematically treated, as the means to knowledge of physical causes. On the continent the influence of Grosseteste is to be seen in Albert the Great, Witelo, and Dietrich of Freiburg, particularly in the study of the rainbow and other problems connected with optics. At this point we must pause before we consider the ramifications of Grosseteste's tradition on fourteenth-century thinkers; for, with Duns Scotus, Ockham, and Bradwardine in particular, all in their different ways innovators of the first magnitude, we move on to a different plane, where the methodology became separated from the philosophy of illumination and the light-metaphysic. None of these three thinkers was like each other or Grosseteste in outlook. Yet they all took

---

[36] *Ibid.*, 143; Bacon *Opus maius*, I, 106.
[37] *Ibid.*, 151.
[38] *Ibid.*, 162.

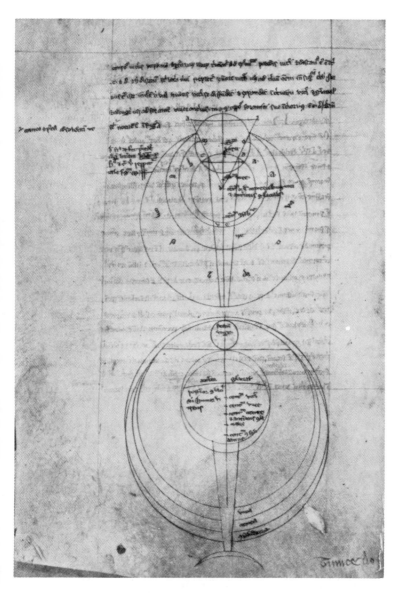

Diagram from Bacon's optics.

over different aspects of Grosseteste's experimental or mathematical approach, in Bradwardine's case with far-reaching scientific results.

As we remarked in the last chapter, Oxford also had its condemnation in 1277, which was repeated in 1284. It, too, was directed against Aristotelianism, but in a strongly Thomist form. Both this fact and the much more limited scale of the condemnation suggest that there was not the same widespread heterodoxy at Oxford; nor is there any other evidence that there was. On the contrary, the assimilation of Aristotelianism at Oxford seems to have been on much more traditional Augustinian Neoplatonizing lines right down to 1277 and beyond. Adam of Buckfield, a master of arts about 1243, commented all the old corpus of Aristotle's works with no doctrinally deleterious effects.[39] Even Thomism is not in evidence among Kilwardby's contemporaries. This must be attributed once again to the strong influence of Grosseteste both on the Franciscan school—such thinkers as Adam Marsh, Roger Bacon, John Pecham—and among Dominicans like Richard Fishacre. In this respect the Dominicans are not really distinguishable from the Franciscans; and it was one of Thomas's own confrères, Kilwardby, who pronounced the condemnation of 1277. He had studied arts at Paris. In 1245 he succeeded Richard Fishacre as Dominican regent at Oxford, in which position he remained until 1261. He was made archbishop of Canterbury in 1272, and died in 1279.

The divergence between Kilwardby and Aquinas, both of the same generation and both Dominicans, is instructive of the difference between Aristotelianism at Oxford and Paris. At Oxford Aristotle's metaphysics played less part in theological speculation, and the older, more Neoplatonic orientation of Avicenna was correspondingly more influential. Although the history of ideas cannot be written solely in terms of individuals, more perhaps, in this than in most domains individuals can have a decisive influence: at Paris Albert the Great gave a new orientation to the pursuit of Aristotle; at Oxford Grosseteste put an even greater imprint on the study of mathematics and optics, leaving the older theological framework largely unaltered. But whereas

[39] Callus, "Aristotelian Learning," 255–6.

Paris was heterogeneous and international, and the stimulus of Aristotle led to conflict with the traditionalists, Oxford was a more cohesive society and the pursuit of science was less disruptive of tradition. Hence Kilwardby was more concerned to censure—he did not declare them heretical—those teachings of Thomas that contraverted the Augustinian tenets: above all those of the plurality of forms and universal hylomorphism. Kilwardby's own outlook was framed entirely in these older terms, although he did not confine himself to theology. Besides commenting the *Sentences,* he has ascribed to him commentaries on Aristotle's logical works, the *De caelo, De anima* and *Metaphysics,* as well as a number of shorter scientific and theological treatises on time, forms, relation, conscience, theology, and the classification of the sciences. His condemnation of 1277 took place on March 18, ten days after that of Etienne Tempier's at Paris.[40] It can therefore be regarded principally as a response to events outside Oxford. Kilwardby acted in his capacity as archbishop of Canterbury; but he went beyond Tempier when he stated that he had done so with "the consent of all the masters, regent and nonregent at Oxford." Maybe he had; if so, it is further evidence that any threat to the faith hardly came from within the university. The censured articles numbered only thirty; they were also arranged thematically, in contrast to the jumble of the Paris propositions. Four concerned grammar; ten logic; and sixteen natural philosophy. Those in grammar all referred to the validity of statements that, doctrinally and metaphysically, can be passed over as neutral. Of the ten in logic, the fourth, "that every man is animal" suggests undue sensitivity to the discussions over the status of the soul, propositions concerning which came in the third section on natural philosophy. The sixth and the seventh were of greater substance, especially for the future debates between the Ockhamists and their opponents in the 1330's and 1340's. The sixth restricted the necessity of the truth to the constancy of its subject: that is, it did not exist independently of that to which it referred; the seventh in the same vein affirmed that there could be no demonstration without the existence of the objects of demonstration. Both of these thus denied

[40] *Chart.,* I, No. 474.

that there could be knowledge unrelated to objects. The reply to the second of these two propositions again foreshadows what the Ockhamists were later to say: that demonstrations about nonexistents were possible—an example of how conservatism and radicalism can come full circle. No less significant was the eighth article: that every true proposition about the future was necessary. Here again this was to be an issue of the first importance: whether and in what way there could be necessary knowledge (in God) of future actions without destroying the freedom of free will to perform them. It is noteworthy that this was a proposition debated particularly fiercely at Oxford by Bradwardine, who was to come down in favor of the censured proposition. The third part, on natural philosophy, was the most contentious, and led to criticism of Kilwardby by Peter of Conflans, Dominican archbishop of Corinth, to which Kilwardby in turn replied. It centered on three main issues. First that of seminal reasons—that is, the Augustinian conception of pre-existing tendencies in matter to receive certain forms before they are actually impressed on it—as opposed to the Thomist belief, taken from Aristotle, that matter was of itself purely potential and passive and only became being through the presence of a form (articles 1–5). The second issue was over the plurality of forms, which the Augustinians upheld as the foundation of all beings, matter included. Here Kilwardly especially singled out the soul, which Thomas had conceived at once as a single form and as man's whole form, of body as well as soul. Article 6 expressed this notion of the unity of the substantial form, affirming that "the vegetative, sensitive and intellective souls are all one in man and in the human embryo." Kilwardby's condemnation of this was to be remembered, among others, by Richard FitzRalph and Adam of Woodham in their debates in the early 1330's. Article 7 likewise was censured for the view that the introduction of an intellective form destroyed the vegetative and sensitive forms; article 12 said much the same as article 6. Article 14 held that matter did not have an independent essence by which it was distinguished. There was little in these articles that was strictly Aristotelian in the sense of many of the Paris articles. The nearest were article 16, which said that the intellective soul was united to the first matter so that it was destroyed with it, and article 10, which denied that Aristotle taught the continuance of the intellective soul after its separation from the sensitive soul; but these were far from taking up the position of Siger and his followers at Paris, that such statements were true philosophically.

All told, Kilwardby's censures, which did not go beyond the penalties of expulsion for bachelors and deposition for masters found holding these opinions, represented a small haul. Thomism, immediately the main victim, was ultimately the gainer; for Kilwardby's action rallied supporters to Thomas's side, so that seven years later Pecham, now archbishop of Canterbury, renewed Kilwardby's censures. He probably had more cause than his predecessor. In the intervening time there had grown up the war of the Corrections, mentioned in the last chapter. William de la Mare, the first to begin it, for the Franciscans, was answered probably by the Dominicans, Richard Clapwell and Robert Orford, from their Oxford friary; and Roger Marston, Pecham's old pupil, refurbished his master's teaching and used it as a rather clumsy missile against the Dominicans.[41] Pecham promulgated the decree on October 29; in the following year he excommunicated Clapwell for failing to appear before him, but he was soon absolved. That was effectively the end of the affair. It never reached dimensions approaching the condemnations at Paris; nor does it seem to have disturbed the arts faculty or the university in any noticeable way. There were no summonses to ringleaders by pope or archbishop; no recantations or apologies. What trouble there was came afterwards as the result of Kilwardby's activities.

There was nonetheless plenty of discussion on these matters at Oxford in the later thirteenth century as there was at Paris. There are numerous disputed questions extant over forms, the soul, the relation of the will to the intellect.[42] No less than at Paris the climate at Oxford was changing. Moreover, in a technical sense, the two foremost agents in the change, Duns Scotus and Ockham, can be said to have initiated it at Oxford. Indeed, it is not too much to say that each derived important elements from the Oxford tradition of Grosseteste. They both expressed

---

[41] For these events surrounding Pecham's renewal of the censures, see Douie, *Archbishop Pecham*, 273 ff.

[42] Little and Pelster, *Oxford Theology*, passim.

the central paradox of later medieval thinking, that its main motive-force came from the progressive driving of Aristotle from the universe with weapons fashioned by him. That is to say, the attack on Aristotle's cosmology in 1277 led to a twofold development: on the one hand, the reassertion of a divine omnipotence and with it cosmic indeterminacy at the macrocosmic level; and on the other, a more minute analysis of nature microcosmically. The first aspect meant the rehabilitation of an essentially Augustinian conception of God; the second led to re-examining and testing Aristotle's theories of physics, on movement, place, change, and so on, and their increasing subjection to a mathematical critique on the model inspired by Grosseteste and developed by Bacon. In this sense a non-Aristotelian cosmology had its counterpart in a non-Aristotelian quantification of Aristotle's qualitative categories of substance, form, matter, and so on.

II THE FOURTEENTH CENTURY

To see this development as coherent or consistent would be utterly mistaken. Rather it took its impetus precisely from the breakdown of the established categories that came with the new emphasis on God's infinite freedom of action. Whereas Aristotle had denied the possibility of atoms, void, or infinite or plural worlds, thinkers as diverse as Richard of Mediavilla (writing in the last decade of the thirteenth century), Scotus, Walter Burley, Ockham, Gregory of Rimini, and Nicholas of Autrecourt all affirmed the possibility in the name of God's omnipotence. This did make them anti-Aristotelians; at the natural level Aristotle's categories were indispensable for the discussion of physics and mechanics. Nor was there accord over the possible different interpretations of movement, change, and so on presented by Plato, the Atomists, Aristotle, and Arabian scientists like Avempace. It would therefore be unrealistic to see a series of universally held theories replacing those of Aristotle in the fourteenth century. Uniformity was no more the characteristic of the Middle Ages than of classical or modern times. What was general, however, was the new framework in which these problems were discussed. This made for a new precision, in virtue of the absence of more universal metaphysical laws that could be applied to creation as a whole; and it was here that the Oxford tradition of induction, experimentation, and mathematics was of the greatest importance. There can be no doubt that it contributed to the innovations of both Duns Scotus and Ockham, which between them transformed the intellectual climate of the fourteenth century. This is the more paradoxical when their outlooks as a whole are compared with Grosseteste's and with one another. They both denied knowledge by an inner illumination; for neither, did the light-metaphysic play any part, nor, strictly speaking, did metaphysics at all for Ockham; neither engaged in mathematics and optics, the pursuit of which had distinguished Grosseteste's Oxford disciples. Nevertheless they took over Grosseteste's methodology of induction and hypothesis; in particular, they both utilized Grosseteste's Commentary on the *Posterior Analytics* to develop the principles of uniformity and economy in nature on which Grosseteste had rested the testing of hypotheses. Ockham's so-called razor had been fashioned a century before he applied it to make verification by experience the criterion of truth and falsity; by this means he swept away the traditional metaphysics as well as those of Duns Scotus. Yet it was Duns who led the way in the developments to which his own notions were to fall victim; he did so by employing Grosseteste's principles of verification while rejecting his doctrine of illumination and the light-metaphysic. Since he also denied Thomas's doctrine of analogy between the created and the divine, he thereby took the momentous step of leaving man no certain knowledge other than that derived from experience and the operation of reason. This he distinguished into three kinds: knowledge of self-evident propositions, based on the law of contradiction, and necessary statements such as that the whole is greater than the parts; immediate intuitive experience of objects given to the senses; and inner awareness of the mind's own states.[43] Duns recognized that judgement could err over what the senses experienced, as when a stick in water appears bent; but he was prepared to

[43] Text given in Crombie, *Robert Grosseteste*, 168–9, from the Commentary on *Prior Analytics*, d. II, q. 8.

accept that the principle of uniformity in nature allowed the deduction of universal principles from regularly observed occurrences: "Induction is the progression from certain singulars, or from all those sufficiently enumerated, to a universal conclusion." [44] Complete experience of all singulars was impossible; hence a representative sample sufficed to lead to an empirical generalization that could be taken as universally binding, even if it was never certain: "although it is not possible to have experience always of all particulars, but only of a large number, one who knows by experience knows infallibly that things are thus, always thus, and thus in all." [45]

Duns thus displayed a confidence in reason to arrive at universal propositions, which contrasted with Ockham. It enabled him to arrive at the Avicennan notion of being as the most universal of all categories, which at its most abstract and general—as mere being as opposed to not being—could be applied to God and to creation. In the same way Duns held that the mind's recognition of universals corresponded to real qualities or essences. There thus remained the Neoplatonic Augustinian conception of being as essence to enable Duns to stay within the framework of the traditional metaphysics, and to adhere to a natural theology, tenuously based though it was on the notion of universal being. Ockham, however, cut this one remaining link in his radical application of Grosseteste's principles of verification. The fact that it led to a complete rejection of Augustinian metaphysics has caused some to see Ockham as desiring a return to Aristotle. But such a view neglects two fundamental things: the first is that Ockham took a strongly Augustinian attitude to God's freedom; the novelty here lay only in the sustained way in which he developed the paradoxes that could flow from divine omnipotence, as considered in the previous chapter. Ockham was a theologian in the same tradition as Duns Scotus. The second point is that Ockham largely rejected Aristotle's metaphysics: he denied that the universal had any independent standing outside the mind, and thereby with it the reality of all mental concepts. They belonged to the logical order; experience of actual entities was con-

[44] *Sentences,* I, d. III, q. 4; Crombie, *Robert Grosseteste,* 169.
[45] *Ibid.*

fined to individuals. This led him, as we mentioned earlier, to reject concepts of motion, time, and place, as without separate existence; they were words describing relations between real individuals, which alone were actual. In the case of motion this led Ockham to reject the Aristotelian theory that local motion was a realized potentiality, just as he had rejected the Aristotelian idea of substance as a composition of form and matter. Instead, for Ockham motion consisted in the successive existence of an object moving from place to place without rest. By that view movement had no reality apart from moving bodies, and could not be independently perceived. Thus, unlike the majority of his contemporaries, Ockham saw no need to posit a form of movement as a distinct quality or essence:

"Motion is not such a thing wholly distinct in itself from the permanent body, because it is futile to use more entities when it is possible to use fewer . . . For it is clear that local motion is to be conceived as follows: positing that the body is in one place and later in another place, thus proceeding without rest or any intermediate thing other than the body itself and the agent itself which moves, we have local motion truly. Therefore it is futile to postulate other such things." [46]

In this he was ahead of thinkers like Buridan, who in his celebrated theory of *impetus* could not go to the length of dispensing with the notion of movement as an unbroken flow (*forma fluens*).[47] Here, as in every other case to which he applied it, Ockham refused to look beyond the individual for the categories under which it could be subsumed. In one sense this was an extension of Bacon's manifesto that everything must be reduced to mathematics. But in Ockham's case this was a philosophical, rather than a scientific conception, which he applied logically, not mathematically; although it had fruitful scientific consequences in the highest degree,—Ockham's own theory of motion had affinities with the Newton's principle of inertia [48]—he

---

[46] Ockham, *Tractatus de successivis*, P. Boehner, ed., (New York, Franciscan Institute for St. Bonaventure, 1955), translated by A. C. Crombie, *Medieval and Early Modern Science*, II (New York, 1959), 64.
[47] Crombie, *Medieval and Early Modern Science*, II, 61–2.
[48] *Ibid.*, 64–5.

did not make it the starting point for scientific experiment in the manner of Grosseteste's disciples. In these philosophical and logical aspects Ockhamism was probably more influential at Paris than at Oxford. Not that English scholastics, like Holcot, Woodham, or Buckingham, were any less affected by its tenets than John of Mirecourt or Nicholas of Autrecourt, and their conclusions were only slightly less outrageous. It was rather that there was a more distinctly non- or anti-Ockhamist school at Oxford, which had as its leading representatives Walter Burley and Thomas Bradwardine, both eminent scientists in the tradition of Grosseteste and both members of Merton College, which was the great center of science from the 1320's to the 1360's. Our knowledge of the thinkers and ideas of the fourteenth century is still very far from complete. It may be that further investigation will reveal a comparable body of natural philosophers and mathematicians at Paris in the same period; there were certainly great individual scientists like Buridan, Nicholas of Oresme, and Albert of Saxony, who had enough affinities with one another to be regarded as a school in a similar sense. But they seem to have been *sui generis* rather than, as at Oxford, representative of a wider outlook.

If this is so, it does not detract from their achievements; in Nicholas of Oresme Paris had perhaps the greatest scientific mind of the century; his notion of fractional powers and his development of the latitude of forms—expressing changes in quality quantitatively—anticipated later mathematical developments in the seventeenth century and set him apart from his fellow Parisians Albert of Saxony and Marsilius of Inghen. Yet it was at Oxford that these new mathematical methods had been pioneered above all by Thomas Bradwardine. It has been said the scientifically "he stood in the same relationship to Oxford thought in the fourteenth century as Grosseteste did to that in the thirteenth century."[49] It could perhaps be added that Oxford stood to Paris in mathematical physics in the fourteenth century as Paris had stood to Oxford in theology in the thirteenth century. What Bradwardine began in his *Treatise on Proportions* was carried on by his Merton contemporaries and disciples Heytesbury, Swineshead, and Dumbleton. Before briefly

[49] Crombie, *Robert Grosseteste,* 178.

considering what this entailed, it is worth trying to clarify the doctrinal setting.

It is, as we have already said, a paradox that, although Grosseteste was inspired by a Neoplatonic notion of truth and being, the most outstanding of his successors in the fourteenth century were not. Duns and Ockham, however, at least held to an extreme Augustinian conception of God's freedom, even while denying both divine illumination and, in Ockham's case, any constant mode of divine operation. Bradwardine, on the other hand, was so strictly orthodox in his views on the regularity of God's ways and the certain manifestation of his attributes that he went to the opposite extreme, in combating Ockhamism, of virtually reducing all human and created actions to a mere extension of God's. In his *De causa Dei* he sought to establish God's omnicausality by a series of mathematically ordered proofs and corollaries, in which he employed the same "word algebra" of letters of the alphabet and words to describe variable quantities to be found in his *Treatise on Proportions*. His concepts, however, owed little to Grosseteste's Neoplatonist inspiration; his main arguments were all in terms of Aristotelian first and second causes, to which he reduced the problem of the relation of God's will to free will. Indeed, Bradwardine came closest among the thinkers of his epoch to employing Aristotle's terminology and metaphysics in a manner reminiscent of Thomas, but without the latter's subtlety and breadth of vision. Bradwardine, living post-1277, was so aware of the dangers of rivals to God's powers that he ended by making everything subject to divine determinism. For this purpose there was no better model to follow than Aristotle's fixed hierarchy of causes. *De causa Dei* stands as a monument to the challenge of indeterminacy—which itself had been the Christian response to the Aristotelian determinism condemned in 1277. It shared none of Grosseteste's notion of a universal form of matter, nor his atomistic tendencies of seeing the universe as the result of the infinite diffusion of points of light, nor any leanings toward a doctrine of seminal reasons. On the contrary, Bradwardine refuted the idea that continuous matter consisted of atoms or points continuously joined together.[50]

That Bradwardine was nevertheless the great exponent of

[50] Crombie, *Medieval and Early Modern Science*, II, 39.

mathematical physics shows two things: first, that the pursuit of mathematics had taken on its own momentum independently of the Neoplatonic light-metaphysic that had inspired Grosseteste and his disciples. As so often in the history of thought an outlook had outgrown its original impulse. It is accordingly important to recognize that the mathematical work of Bradwardine and his confrères did not represent a Neoplatonic challenge to Aristotle, just as other scientific developments were not made in explicitly Ockhamist terms; that is not to say that a thinker like Ockham, who followed his own ideas of induction and verification consistently, did not arrive at the most striking results. But it ultimately needed the scientific application to specific problems that Ockham did not bring to his theory of movement; this is what Bradwardine, Burley, Buridan, Oresme, and the others who obtained the results did, even if these were rarely correct as they stood. From that it can be said that successful investigation needed less a specific doctrine than a climate of enquiry, in which the ways had not been closed by authority—Aristotle's or any other.

It was along non-Aristotelian paths that medieval scientific enquiry reached its most notable developments in the thirteenth century, with the exception of Albert the Great's zoological investigations to which Aristotle's classificatory method was particularly suited. The belief of Grosseteste that light was the stuff of the universe had led him into a quite different direction from Aristotle; as the result of it mathematics and experiment became part of a new universal methodology. These tendencies received a vast reinforcement from the 1277 condemnations. So much has been ascribed to their effect that we must be wary of claiming too much for them. It is not to be seen in the condemnation of any specific proposition such as that which denied that a first cause could create several worlds (article 34)—taken by the eminent French historian of science Paul Duhem, at one point, as the date of the birth of modern science.[51] It rather belongs to the reaffirmation of God's omnipotence as the overriding consideration in all that concerned created beings. The novelty of this position lay not in what it proclaimed but in its context. It was

[51] Quoted by Gilson, *History*, 349.

now not only the ultimate criterion by which to judge God's actions, but directly opposed to an Aristotelian cosmology. Infinity, multiplicity, indeterminacy, were set against an eternal, finite, and invariable universe in which all its operations were inexorably regulated. This opening of the universe to almost unlimited possibilities affected the foundations of scientific knowledge. It invited a new appraisal of Aristotle's solutions to specific problems of dimension, place, gravitation, projectile motion, free fall, intension and remission of forms, which formed the basis of scholastic enquiry. The thinkers involved were not thereby anti-Aristotelian, but Christians working within another and now more consciously formulated context. This did not make for uniformity of approach, as we have seen: Nicholas of Autrecourt's probablism, which took Ockham's principle of verification to the limits of doubting whether knowledge of causes or substances was possible at all, was at the other extreme to Bradwardine's faith in the certainty of mathematical calculation. Yet both thinkers brought to problems of physics the fruits of a non-Aristotelian approach either to the universe or to nature. In Autrecourt's case it led to the questioning of Aristotle's assumptions, in Bradwardine's to a desire to confirm Aristotle's calculation in the face of criticisms of it, which in turn led to a radical departure from Aristotle. Uniformity in nature does not extend to the actions of free will as Duns Scotus recognized; we should be advised not to seek a single cause in the diverse approaches to scientific questions in the later thirteenth and the fourteenth centuries.

New assumptions bred both a new methodology and a reconsideration of existing questions. The freedom reclaimed for God was essentially a theological concept; thirteenth and fourteenth century thinkers investigated nature not so much as theologians but as Christians who sought explanations that theological speculation had prompted. It was here, in turning to nature, however, that other, scientific, criteria were called for. If 1277 restored the universe to God's own devices, it also allowed a greater autonomy for science just because it was no longer harnessed to a cosmic hierarchy of causes. The desire to shake God free from natural necessitarianism also liberated thinkers from the notion that efficient and material causes had invariably to be associated with formal and final causes. Duns had hoped to retain their connection, setting himself the ideal of a progression from intuitive experience of individuals to the formulation of necessary universal propositions; Ockham had explicitly rejected the possibility of doing so. Bradwardine, who theologically hankered after a more rigid causality than possibly any other Christian thinker, was nonetheless prepared to submit natural phenomena to the mathematical treatment—perhaps just because he had so little faith in the power of reason to derive any certainty from natural experience. Each in entirely different ways was thus accepting what in retrospect can be seen as the great new intellectual fact of the later Middle Ages: the divorce between faith and knowledge based on natural experience. Bradwardine's reaction was to put the same reliance on mathematics as his Oxford predecessors had done; he thereby set in motion a new wave of mathematical activity that reached its climax in Nicholas of Oresme in the middle and later decades of the fourteenth century. In the fifteenth century it was diverted into a backwater, with most other scientific investigation, by the revival of literary humanism, which was once believed to have rescued culture from the barbarism of the Middle Ages. Whatever else the Renaissance may have achieved, it also led to the decline of medieval science and speculation and a hiatus in scientific and philosophical thought until the seventeenth century.

Bradwardine's *Treatise on Proportions*[52] was important in two main respects. It employed a complex mathematical function to express a physical law; and, more technically, it pointed to the distinction between velocity and acceleration in relating time elapsed in movement to the distance traversed. Although Bradwardine was thus the first to apply geometry in physical theory, an approach taken up and extended by his successors—especially the Mertonian calculators—he had been prompted to solve a specific problem concerned with Aristotle's laws of motion: to restore Aristotle's conception of movement, as interpreted by Averroes, that the cause of the successive character of movement was a real resistance from the medium to what was moving. This explanation had been displaced by the widespread

[52] Edited and translated by H. L. Crosby, *Thomas Bradwardine, His Tractatus de proportionibus* (Madison, Wis., 1961). What follows is based mainly on the editor's introduction.

acceptance of the hypothesis of Avempace (Ibn Bagda, the twelfth-century Spanish Arabian thinker) that velocity was proportional only to power of movement; resistance only reduced it. In order to make Aristotle's somewhat imprecise formulation— which, as it stood, Bradwardine questioned—more precise, Bradwardine sought mathematically to relate change in velocity to power of movement and resistance. The defects of his treatment were principally those of medieval science in general—the failure to make specific measurements and experiments. Nevertheless he succeeded in formulating the problem in terms of an equation that foreshadowed the use of logarithmic functions. He was thereby the first to make the treatment of physics quantitative, in particular establishing his method among succeeding calculators, whenever a quantity was definable in terms of relation between two others. Like Ockham, Bradwardine had posed the question of how something occurred rather than why; in that sense they might both be said to have shared the same empirical approach to natural phenomena: Ockham sought his answer in logical demonstration, Bradwardine in mathematics. Bradwardine's method was the one ultimately to prevail with Galileo and the seventeenth-century physicists. He himself had only made a beginning; he lacked a mathematical symbolism, still using names for the different proportions; he remained too wedded to Aristotelian methods of classification rather than active measurement. These weaknesses are also apparent among Bradwardine's fellow Mertonians, known as the Calculators, a sobriquet expressly given to Richard Swineshead (or Suisset); the others were William of Heytesbury and John of Dumbleton. Of these Dumbleton (1331–49) [53] was closest to Grosseteste's tradition of science, especially his interest in light. His *Summa logicae et philosophiae naturalis* discussed many of the central problems of contemporary physics, upon which he brought to bear Bradwardine's geometrical method. The first part of the work treated the logical problems concerned with the signification of terms and definition, employing Grosseteste's method of resolution and composition, and the distinction between formal and material definitions. In the second part Dumbleton was concerned with

[53] For Dumbleton see Crombie, *Robert Grosseteste*, 181 ff., and *Medieval and Early Modern Science*, II, 91 ff.

the problem of changes in quality: the intension and remission of forms, or the latitude of forms. These were central topics among fourteenth century thinkers, to be found in the majority of commentaries on the *Sentences* as well in special treatises like Dumbleton's. They centered on how change in qualities, such as heat (or charity, the question with which the Lombard in his *Sentences* had initiated scholastic discussion), could be measured quantitatively. Aristotle had distinguished quantity and quality as absolutely different categories; in his view a change in quality, unlike that in say extension, did not entail the addition or subtraction of a like part, but the displacement of one species by another; it was this that led to the change.[54] Duns and Ockham had both opposed this distinction, arguing that a change in intensity could be measured by abstracting the quality (of, say, heat) in the same way as the magnitude of quantity. The Mertonians, and the Paris School of Buridan, Oresme, Albert of Saxony, and Marsilius of Inghen, developed methods for expressing the change graphically: the "latitude" of intensity was put on the vertical axis, and extension—sometime called "longitude"—on the horizontal axis.[55] This constituted the second method of expressing functional relationships in the fourteenth century—geometrically by graphs. Dumbleton was one of the first to employ it. He distinguished between quality "in reality and in name"; there was no real change in quality but rather in each degree of intensity, which could be regarded as of a different species. In that way, when a body acquired or lost, say, heat, it lost or acquired a real species of heat. It could thereby be said to have undergone the addition or subtraction of so many degrees of intensity. Dumbleton used the same method of latitudes in the fifth part of his book in connection with the varying intensity of light according to distance. He sought to express quantitatively the relation between the strength of a luminous body and the distance through which it acted at different intensities. It was Kepler who formulated this exactly, although Oresme made the greatest advances in the graphical method of the later Middle Ages.

[54] Crombie, *Medieval and Early Modern Science*, II, 85 ff., for the historical background.
[55] *Ibid.*, 90–1; Crombie, *Robert Grosseteste*, 182.

William of Heytesbury in his *Regulae solvendi sophismatae* defined uniform acceleration and uniform retardation, following Bradwardine's model; his kinematic descriptions of the different kinds of movement were to be of importance. Together with Dumbleton and Richard Swineshead he proved arithmetically the rule for mean speeds, which Oresme afterwards demonstrated geometrically. Heytesbury also applied the same methodology of proportions to problems of logic, as the title of his work implies. Swineshead gained fame in the later Middle Ages for his *Liber calculationum.* His work and that of his fellow Mertonians enjoyed widespread popularity at Paris and in Germany in the fourteenth century, in Italy, especially Padua, in the fifteenth century, and at Paris again in the sixteenth century. The writings of Swineshead and Heytesbury as well as the scientific treatises of Bradwardine, Buridan, and Albert of Saxony were all printed between 1480 and 1520 at Paris and Venice. That Dumbleton and Oresme were not included indicates the decline in the scientific movement; its greatest weakness was its exclusively theoretical nature. It could too easily degenerate into idle speculation on any arbitrarily chosen theme; unlike the work of Galileo it was not directed by empirical investigation; and it was increasingly used for purely imaginary sophismatic problems toward which medieval education was so strongly biased.

If we are to seek a decline in the schools of the later Middle Ages, it lay not in a loss of intellectual power but of seriousness of intent; this was facilitated, but not caused, by the greater elaborateness of techniques. Scholasticism in the fifteenth century was caught between two fires: on the one hand, the breakup of the medieval outlook as a whole; on the other, the rejection of the scholastic tradition by the humanists. The attention to problems, of method and verification, divorced from problems of metaphysics and science, could only lead to intellectual barrenness. By the fifteenth century, scholasticism as a method of enquiry had outlived its usefulness; its procedures were caught up in a web of formal refinements that impeded the processes of coherent thought.

This is to be seen in the reaction of John Wyclif (d. 1384) [56]

[56] For an account of Wyclif's doctrine see my *Heresy in the Late Middle Ages,* II, Chapter 7.

to the hold of Ockhamism or terminism at Oxford. Wyclif sought a return to Neoplatonic Augustinianism. Yet, despite his rejection of the prevailing outlook of the Oxford schools—where he spent his entire career, save for a brief period of public service with John of Gaunt, until he withdrew to Lutterworth three years before his death—he was steeped in the same logical formalism. He used its devices time and again to resolve problems in purely verbal terms; his realism was so uncompromising that he went to limits perhaps greater than any other medieval thinker in endowing all concepts with intelligible being in God. From this he concluded that all individual being was indestructible since its essence remained eternally in God; later the same position led him to deny that the sacramental bread and wine of the eucharist had been transubstantiated into Christ's body and blood. If this second consequence represented the main theological error by which Wyclif's disciples—the Lollards—came to be identified with and condemned for heresy, the first had palpably no bearing on experience; however being might be envisaged archetypally, in this world to deny the destructibility and transformation of at least material things was to strike at the whole edifice of science and scientific method that had been built up over the preceding century.

As metaphysics Wyclif's doctrine had little significance; its importance lay in its theological and ecclesiological repercussions. His realism certainly influenced Hus and his confrères at Prague in the last years of the fourteenth century and the first two decades of the fifteenth century. But this was as much as anything a counter to the official terminist doctrine of their predominantly German opponents in the university. The superficial nature of their realism can be seen from the *quodlibet* of 1410, on the existence of a first necessary cause; it was little more than a formal exercise in disputatory methods, at striking variance with the deep religious conviction of the majority of the participants as reformers. This gulf is indicative of the split between matters of belief and what can only be called academic expertise. It was not that Wyclif and Hus were insincere; on the contrary, their evangelical fervor was so all-embracing that it extended to attempting to demonstrate the articles of faith. In the context of an all-pervasive positivism in philosophy Wyclif, fol-

lowed by Hus and the Czech reformers, sought once again metaphysical formulation of theological truths. They came to nothing
because at Oxford Wyclif's teaching foundered on the eucharist
and was suppressed by the action of Courtenay, archbishop of
Canterbury in 1381 and 1382: at Prague they were always
subsidiary to practical matters of religious reform. The assault on
Wyclif's doctrines and followers at Oxford by Courtenay constituted the last important intellectual event of this period; Arundel's visitation in 1410 was, as we saw in Chapter Three, concerned principally with enforcing ecclesiastical authority. In May
1381 Wyclif's eucharistic doctrine was censured by a commission
of twelve Oxford theologians appointed by the chancellor, William Barton. Wyclif, after unsuccessfully appealling to Parliament, left Oxford in the summer of the same year. Between then
and the following May there occurred the Peasants' Revolt and
the resurgence of Wyclifite teaching at Oxford. Although not
connected, they seem to have prompted Courtenay, as archbishop of Canterbury, to take official action against Wyclifism.
At a synod held at Blackfriars on May 17, 1382, twenty-four
articles drawn from Wyclif's teaching were condemned as heretical, and fourteen as errors.[57] They dealt almost exclusively with
the eucharist and the other sacraments, and matters of ecclesiology, including Wyclif's attacks on the church hierarchy and the
religious orders. In order to make this decree effective Courtenay
then turned his attention to Oxford, where in May and June
Wyclif's followers had been publicly defending Wyclif's teachings on the eucharist. On June 8 he summoned Rigg, chancellor
of the university, to him in London for not having enforced the
Blackfriars decree at Oxford; Rigg was himself accused, before
the reconvened synod, of having given comfort to the Lollards,
as Wyclif's followers were called. Rigg submitted to Courtenay
and agreed to publish the banned articles from Wyclif's teaching, which he did a few days later. Wyclif's three leading Oxford
supporters, Hereford, Repingdon, and Aston, were in turn summoned before the archbishop at Blackfriars; Aston was imprisoned there and then; the two others were subsequently excommunicated. By November, when Courtenay held the Canterbury

---

[57] D. Wilkins, *Concilia Magnae Brittaniae*, III (London, 1737); 157–8.

convocation at Oxford, Lollardy at Oxford had been crushed. It never recurred there, becoming predominantly a movement of artisans and unbeneficed clerks.

It is sometimes suggested that the actions of Courtenay, and more particularly Arundel, in proscribing Wyclif's works and those of his closest followers, delivered a body blow also against philosophy and speculative thought.[58] This may be doubted. Wyclif's own career is evidence of the slowing down of the speculative arts at Oxford. Other universities, like Paris, Heidelberg, and Prague, without such condemnations, were not noticeably more original or intellectually vital in the earlier fifteenth century. Wyclifite metaphysics were a dead end; Wyclif's ecclesiology had no bearing on the main lines of intellectual investigation at Oxford or Paris either before or after his condemnation. He is significant less for his speculative thought than for the political consequences to which it led, above all among the Lollards, who after 1382 had no part in the life of Oxford.

III CONCLUSION

The intellectual history of Oxford then, in the thirteenth and fourteenth centuries is inseparable from that of Paris. From the first Oxford went its own way in its response to Aristotle's works, without suffering the disruptive effects that Paris underwent. If Oxford during the thirteenth century was secondary to Paris in theological speculation, it was, under the influence of Grosseteste, achieving a distinctive scientific and mathematical tradition, which was instrumental in the emergence of the outlooks of Duns Scotus and Ockham. From about 1330 until 1360 Oxford was at least the equal of Paris in speculative thought and, in Bradwardine, Burley, and the Mertonians, predominant in mathematics and physics. It is, as we have seen, only possible to appreciate the achievements of Oresme and most of the Paris school in relation to the work of the Mertonian school. During this flowering, from about 1330 to 1380, scholasticism, far from

---

[58] I tended to take the same attitude in *Heresy in the Later Middle Ages,* but I have since revised my opinion.

being the arid logic-chopping formalism of myth, reached a climax in constructive and fruitful investigation of physical phenomena. Its almost exclusively theoretical orientation should not blind us to the fundamental achievements of a new quantitative methodology that took science to the threshold of a scientific revolution. That it had to wait another two centuries for its consummation was part of the failure of the medieval outlook as whole, to be seen equally in the prevailing attitudes to the church and to temporal society. To seek any correlation between its different facets and the parallel crisis in institutions and economic and political life would, even if it were possible, be beyond the scope of this book. They can together perhaps best be seen as the breakdown of the traditional modes in medieval society as a whole. This engendered an attitude of radical criticism and the search for new ways as well as the increasingly formal repetition of existing ones. The effect on scholasticism was to polarize form and content; the disputations in the schools became largely divorced from the substance of knowledge; and the very revulsion against scholasticism to which this led caused it to be cut off from the humanists. For centuries the humanist caricature of the schoolmen was taken for the true likeness. It is only now that the contribution of later scholasticism to the thinking of the seventeenth century is becoming recognized. If that legacy was not the exclusive creation of scholastic Paris and Oxford, they had a central part in its making.

SELECT BIBLIOGRAPHY

I SOURCES

Abbeville, Gerard of, *Contra adversarium perfectionis christianae,* S. Clasen, ed., *Archivum Franciscanum Historicum* (AFH) 31 (1938), 276–329; 32 (1939), 80–202.

Alexander of Roes, *De translatione imperii,* H. Grundmann, ed. (Leipzig, 1927)

Aquinas, St. Thomas, *Opera omnia* (Venice, 1593).

Aristoteles Latinus, Pars prior, G. Lacombe et al., eds. (Rome, 1939).

Auctarium chartularii Universitatis Pariensis: liber procuratorum nationis Anglicanae, H. Denifle and E. Chatelain, eds., 2 vols. (Paris, 1897–99).

Bacon, Roger, *Fratris Rogeri Bacon compendium studii theologiae,* H. Rashdall, ed. (Aberdeen, British Society for Franciscan Studies, 1911).

Bacon, Roger, *Opus maius,* H. Bridges, ed., 3 vols. (London, 1900).

Bacon, Roger, *Opera quaedam hactenus inedita,* J. S. Brewer, ed., (London, 1859).

Bierbaum, M., *Bettelordern und Weltgeistlichkeit. Franziskanischen Studien Beiheft II* (Münster i. W., 1920).

Bonaventure, Saint, *Opera omnia,* vol. 8 (Quaracchi, 1898).

Bonaventure, Saint, *Collationes in Hexaemeron,* F. Delorme, ed. (Quaracchi, 1934).

Bullarium Franciscanum, S. Sbaralea, ed., III and IV (Rome 1765–8).

Du Boulay, B. (Bulaeus), *Historia Universitatis Parisiensis,* 6 vols. (Paris, 1665–73).

Bradwardine, Thomas, *Tractatus de proportionibus,* H. L. Crosby, Jr., ed. and translator (Madison, Wisconsin, 1961).

Calendar of Close Rolls, Henry III (*1227–72*), 14 vols. (London, 1902–38).

Calendar of Entries in the Papal Registers relating to Great Britain and Ireland: Papal Letters, 1198–1471, W. H. Bliss, ed. (London, 1896–1433).

Calendar of Patent Rolls, Henry III (*1216–72*), 6 vols. (London, 1901–13).

Chartularium Universitatis Parisiensis (*Chart.*), H. Denifle and E. Chatelain, eds., 4 vols. (Paris, 1889–97).

The Constitutions of Canterbury College, vol. I, W. A. Pantin, ed., *Oxford Historical Society* (OHS), (Oxford, 1947).

Davy, M. M., *Les Sermons universitaires parisiens de 1230–1231* (Paris, 1931).

Denifle, H., "Das Evangelium aeternum und die Commission zu Anagni," *Archiv für Literatur und Kirchengeschichte,* I (Berlin, 1885), 49–142.

Eccleston, Thomas of, *De Adventu fratrum minorum in Angliam,* A. G. Little, ed., (Manchester, Manchester University Press, 1951).

Ehrle, F., *I piu antichi statuti della facolta teologica dell' Universita di Bologna* (*Universitatis Bononiensis Monamenta* I, Bologna, 1931).

Emden, A. B., *A Biographical Register of the University of Oxford,* 3 vols. (Oxford, 1957–9).

Faral, E., "Les Responsiones de Guillaume de Saint-Amour," *Archives d'histoire doctrinale et litteraire,* **25–26** (1950–1) 237–88.

Formularies which bear on the History of Oxford c. 1204–1420, (*Oxford Formularies*) H. E. Salter, W. A. Pantin, and H. G. Richardson, eds., 2 vols. (Oxford, OHS, 1942).

Gabriel, A. L., *Student Life in Ave Maria College, Mediaeval Paris* (South Bend, Ind., Notre Dame University Press, 1955).

Garland, John de, *Morale scolarium,* L. J. Paetow, ed., in *Two Mediaeval Satires on the University of Paris,* (Berkeley, 1927).

Giraldus Cambrensis, *Opera,* J. S. Brewer et al., eds., 8 vols. (London, Rolls Series, 1861–91).

Highfield, J. R. L., ed., *The Early Rolls of Merton College* (Oxford, OHS, 1964).

Kingsford, C. L., A. G. Little, and F. Tocco, *Tractatus tres de paupertate,* II (Aberdeen, British Society for Franciscan Studies, 1910).

Le Roux de Lincy, A. J. V., and L. M. Tisserand, *Paris et ses historiens* (Paris, 1867).

Mansi, J. D., *Sacrorum conciliorum nova et amplissima collectio* (*Concilia*), vols. XXI and XXII (Venice, 1776–8).

Matthew Paris, *Chronica majora,* H. R. Luard, ed., 7 vols. (London, Rolls Series, 1872–83).

Mediaeval Archives of the University of Oxford, H. E. Salter, ed., 2 vols. (Oxford, OHS, 1920–1).

Munimenta civitatis Oxonie, H. E. Salter, ed., (Oxford, OHS, 1920).

Munimenta academica Oxoniensis, H. Anstey, ed., 2 vols. (London, Rolls Series, 1868).

Ockham, William of, *Tractatus de successivis,* P. Boehner, ed. (New York, Franciscan Institute, St. Bonaventure, 1955).

Oxford Theology and Theologians, A. G. Little and F. Pelster, eds. (Oxford, OHS, 1934).

Registrum annalium collegii Mertonensis 1483–1521, H. E. Salter, ed. (Oxford, OHS, 1923).

Registrum cancellarii Oxoniensis 1434–1469, H. E. Salter, ed., 2 vols. (Oxford, OHS, 1932).

Reichart, B. M., *Acta capitulorum generalium ordinis praedicatorum,* I, (Rome, 1898).

Rutebeuf, *Poèmes concernant l'Université de Paris,* H. H. Lucas, ed. (Manchester, Manchester University Press, 1952).

Salisbury, John of, *Metalogicon* C. C. J. Webb, ed. (Oxford, 1929).

Shapiro, H., *Medieval Philosophy* (New York, 1964).

Snappe's Formulary, H. E. Salter, ed. (Oxford, OHS, 1924).

Sorbon, Robert de, *De Conscientia et de tribus dietis,* F. Chambon, ed. (Paris, 1902).

Statuta Antiqua Universitatis Oxoniensis, S. Gibson, ed. (Oxford, 1931).

Thorndike, L., *University Records and Life in the Middle Ages* (New York, Columbia University Press, 1949).

Vaux, R. de, *Notes et textes sur L'Avicennisme latin au confins du XIIe et XIIIe siècles* (Paris, 1934).

Weisheipl, J. A., "Curriculum of the Faculty of Arts at Oxford in the Early Fourteenth Century," in *Mediaeval Studies,* 26 (1964), 143–185.

Weisheipl, J. A., "Classification of the Sciences in Medieval Thought," in *Mediaeval Studies,* 27 (1965), 54–90.

Wickersheimer, E., *Commentaires de la faculte dé médecine de l'Université de Paris 1395–1516* (Paris, 1915).

Wilkins, D., *Concilia Magnae Brittaniae,* 3 vols (London, 1737).

II SECONDARY WORKS

Boyce, G. C., *The English-German Nation in the University of Paris* (Bruges, 1927).

Boyle, L., "The Curriculum of the Faculty of Canon Law at Oxford in the First Half of the Fourteenth Century," in *Oxford Studies Presented to Daniel Callus* (Oxford, OHS, 1963), 135–62.

Callebaut, A., Jean Pecham O.F.M. et l'Augustinisme, AFH, 18 (1925), 441–72.

Callus, D. A., "The Introduction of Aristotelian Learning to Oxford," *Proceedings of the British Academy,* 29 (1943), 229–281.

Callus, D. A., ed., *Robert Grosseteste: Scholar and Bishop* (Oxford, Oxford University Press, 1955).

Callus, D. A., "Robert Grosseteste as Scholar" in *Robert Grosseteste: Scholar and Bishop,* D. Callus, ed. (Oxford, 1955).

Chenu, M. D., *Introduction à l'étude de St. Thomas* (Paris, 1954).

Crombie, A. C., *Medieval and Early Modern Science,* 2 vols. (New York, 1959).

Crombie, A. C., *Robert Grosseteste and the Origins of Experimental Science* (Oxford, 1953).

Crombie, A. C., "Grosseteste's Position in the History of Science" in D. Callus, ed., *Robert Grosseteste: Scholar and Bishop* (Oxford, 1955), 98–120.

Davy, M. M., "La Situation juridique des étudiants a l'université de Paris au XIIIe siècle," *Revue de l'histoire de l'église de France,* 17 (1931), 297–311.

Denifle, H., *Die Entstehung der Universitäten des Mittelalters bis 1400* (Berlin, 1885).

Destrez, J., *La Pecia dans les manuscrits universitaires du XIIIe et XIVe siècles* (Paris, 1935).

Douie, D. M., *Archbishop Pecham* (Oxford, 1952).

Duin, J. J., *Le Doctrine de la providence dans les écrits de Siger de Brabant* (Louvain, 1954).

Emden, A. B., *An Oxford Hall in the Middle Ages* (Oxford, Oxford University Press, 1927).

Emden, A. B., "Northerners and Southerners in the Organization of the University [of Oxford] to 1509" in *Oxford Studies Presented to Daniel Callus,* (Oxford, OHS, 1963) 1–30.

Fournier, E., "L'Enseignement des décrétals a l'Université de Paris au moyen âge," *Revue de l'histoire de l'église de France,* 26 (1940), 58–62.

Gabriel, A. L., "The College System in the Fourteenth-Century Universities," in *The Forward Movement of the Fourteenth Century,* F. L. Utley, ed. (Columbus, Ohio, 1961), 70–124.

Gilson, E., *A History of Christian Philosophy in the Middle Ages* (London, 1955).

Glorieux, P., *La Littérature quodlibètique,* 2 vols. (Paris, Vrin, 1925–1935).

Glorieux, P., *Répertoire des mâitres en théologie de Paris au XIIIe siècle,* 2 vols. (Paris, 1933–4). Additions by V. Doucet in AFH, 27 (1935), 531–64.

Glorieux, P., "Le conflit de 1252–1257 à la lumière du mémoire de Guillaume de Saint-Amour," *Recherches de théologie ancienne et mediévale* 24 (1957), 364–72.

Glorieux, P., "La Faculté de théologie de Paris et ses principaux docteurs au XIIIe siècle. *Revue d'histoire de l'église de France,* 32 (1946), 241–64.

Glorieux, P., "Les Années 1242–7 à la faculté de théologie," *Recherches de théologie ancienne et médiévale,* 29 (1962), 234–49.

Glorieux, P., "Les Polémiques contra Geraldinos," *Recherches de théologie ancienne et médiévale,* 6 (1934), 5–41; 7 (1935), 129–55.

Glorieux, P., "Prélats français contre religieux mendiants. Autour de la bulle *Ad fructus uberes*," *Revue de l'histoire de l'église de France* 11 (1925), 309–31, 471–95.

Grabmann, M., *I divieti ecclesiastici di Aristotele sotto Innocenzo III e Gregorio IX,* in *Miscellanea historiae pontificae,* V, No. 7 (Rome, 1941).

Grabmann, M., "Der lateinische Averroismus des 13 Jahrhunderts und seine Stellung zur christlichen Weltanschauung," *Sitzungsberichte der Bayerischen Akademie der Wissenschaften Philos-Hist. Klasse* (Munich, 1931).

Grabmann, M., "Eine für Examinazwecke abgefasste Questionensammlung der Pariser Artistenfakultät aus der ersten Hälfte des 13 Jahrhunderts," *Revue néoscolastique* 36 (1934), 211–29.

Halphen, L. et al., *Aspects de l'Université de Paris* (Paris, 1949).

Haskins, C. H., *The Rise of the Universities* (Cornell, Cornell University Press, Ithaca, 1957).

Haskins, C. H., *Studies in the History of Mediaeval Science* (reprinted New York, Ungar 1960).

Haskins, C. H., *Studies in Mediaeval Culture* (reprinted New York, Ungar, 1960).

Haskins, G. L., "The University of Oxford and the *Ius Ubique Docendi*," *English Historical Review*, 56 (1941), 281–92.

Hinnebusch, W. A., "Foreign Dominican Students and Professors at the Oxford Blackfriars," in Oxford Studies *Presented to Daniel Callus*, (Oxford, OHS, 1963), 101–34.

Hunt, R. W., "Oxford Grammar Masters in the Middle Ages," in *Oxford Studies Presented to Daniel Callus* (Oxford, OHS, 1963), 163–193.

Irsay, S. d', *Histoire des universités françaises et étrangères*, I (Paris, 1935).

Jordan, E., "Joachim de Flore" in *Dictionnaire de théologie catholique*, vol. 8, cols. 1425–58.

Kibre, P., *The Nations in the Mediaeval Universities* (Cambridge, Mass., Mediaeval Academy of America, 1948).

Kibre, P., *Scholarly Privileges in the Middle Ages* (Cambridge, Mass., Mediaeval Academy of America, 1961).

Knowles, D., *The Religious Orders in England*, I (Cambridge, Cambridge University Press, 1948).

Le Bras, G., "La Faculté de droit au moyen âge," in *Aspects de l'université* (Paris, 1949).

Leff, G., *Medieval Thought from St. Augustine to Ockham* (London, 1958).

Leff, G., ed., *Heresy in the Later Middle Ages*, 2 vols. (Manchester, Manchester University Press, 1967).

Leff, G., "The Changing Pattern of Thought in the Earlier Fourteenth Century," *Bulletin of the John Rylands Library*, 43 (1961), 354–72.

Le Goff, J., *Les Intellectuals au moyen âge* (Paris, 1957).

Little, A. G., *Studies in English Franciscan History* (Manchester, Manchester University Press, 1917).

Little, A. G., "The Franciscan School at Oxford in the Thirteenth Century," AFH 19 (1926), 803–74.

Little, A. G., *The Grey Friars in Oxford* (Oxford, OHS, 1892).

Lottin, O., "Psychologie et morale à la faculté des arts aux approches de 1250" *Revue néoscolastique* 42 (1939), 182–212.

McKeon, P. R., "The Status of the University of Paris as *Parens scientiarum*," *Speculum*, 39 (1964), 651–75.

Mallet, C. E., *A History of the University of Oxford*, vol. I (London, 1924).

Mandonnet, P., *Siger de Brabant et l'Averroïsme latin au XIII° siècle*, 2 vols. (Louvain, 1908–11).

Oxford Studies Presented to Daniel Callus (Oxford, OHS, 1963).

Paetow, L. J., *The Arts Course at the Mediaeval Universities with Special Reference to Grammar and Rhetoric* (Champaign, Illinois, 1910).

Pantin, W. A., "The Halls and Schools of Medieval Oxford," in *Oxford Studies Presented to Daniel Callus* (Oxford, OHS, 1963), 31–100.

Pelzer, A., "Les 51 articles de Guillaume d'Ockham censurés en Avignon en 1326," *Revue d'histoire ecclésiastique*, 18 (1922), 240–70.

Post, G., "Alexander III, the *Licentia docendi*, and the Rise of the Universities," in *C. H. Haskins Anniversary Essays in Mediaeval History* (Boston, Houghton-Mifflin, and New York, 1929) 255–77.

Post, G., "Masters' Salaries and Student Fees in the Mediaeval Universities," *Speculum*, 7 (1932), 181–98.

Post, G., "Parisian Masters as a Corporation, 1200–1246," *Speculum*, 9 (1934), 421–45.

Powicke, F. M., "Some Problems in the History of the Universities," *Trans. Royal Historical Society*, 17 (1934), 1–18.

Rashdall, H., "The Friar Preachers and the University," *Collectanea*, II, M. Burows, ed., (Oxford, OHS, 1890) 195–273.

Rashdall, H., *The Universities of Europe in the Middle Ages*, F. M. Powicke and A. B. Emden, eds., 3 vols. (Oxford, 1936).

Reeves, M. E., "The *Liber figurarum* of Joachim of Fiore," *Mediaeval and Renaissance Studies*, II (1950), 57–81.

Salter, H. E., *Medieval Oxford* (Oxford, OHS, 1936).

Smalley, B., "Grosseteste: the Biblical Scholar" in *Robert Grosseteste: Scholar and Bishop*, D. A. Callus, ed. (Oxford, 1953), 70–97.

Smalley, B., *The Study of the Bible in the Middle Ages* (Oxford, Blackwell, 1952).

Steenberghen, F. van, *Siger de Brabart d'après ses oeuvres inédites*, 2 vols (Louvain, Les Philosophes Belges, 1931–42).

Steenberghen, F. van, *Aristotle in the West* (Louvain, 1955).

Stegmüller, F., "Die Zwei Apologien des Jean de Mirecourt," *Recherches de théologie ancienne et médiévale*, 5 (1933), 192–205.

Stelling-Michaud, S., "Les Universités au moyen age et à la renaissance" in *XI Congrès International des Sciences Historiques, Rapports*, I (Stockholm, 1960), 97–143.

Théry, G., *Autour du décret de 1210: 1. David de Dinant, étude sur son panthéisme matérialiste* (Le Saulchoir, 1925).

Thouzellier, C., "La Place du *De periculis* de Guillaume de Saint-Amour dans les polémiques universitaires du XIIIᵉ siècle," *Revue historique*, 156 (1927), 69–83.

Thouzellier, C., "L'Enseignement et les universités," in A. Fliche, C. Thouzellier, and Y. Azais, *La Chrétienté romaine 1198–1274* (Paris, 1950), 341–86.

Vaux, R. de, "La Première entrée d'Averroës chez les Latins," *Revue des sciences philosophiques et théologiques*, 22 (1933), 193–245.

Waddell, H., *Wandering Scholars* (London, 1954).

Watt, D. E. R., "University Clerks and Rolls of Petitions for Benefices," *Speculum*, 34 (1959), 213–29.

REFERENCE ABBREVIATIONS

AFH   *Archivum Franciscanum Historicum*

Chart   *Chartularium Universitatis Parisiensis,* H. Denifle and E. Chatelain, eds., 4 vols. (Paris 1889–1897)

Denifle, *Entstehung*   H. Denifle, *Die Entstehung der Universitaten des Mittelalters bis 1400* (Berlin 1885)

I divieti   M. Grabmann, "I divieti ecclesiastici di Aristotle sotto Innocenzo III e Gregorio IX," in *Miscellanea historiae Pontificae,* V, No. 7 (Rome 1941)

Mansi, *Concilia*   J. D. Mansi, *Sacrorum conciliorum nova et amplissima collectio,* Vols. XXI and XXII (Venice 1776–1778)

Med. Arch.   *Mediaeval Archives of the University of Oxford,* H. E. Salter, ed., 2 vols. (Oxford 1920–1921)

Oxford Formularies   *Formularies Which Bear on the History of Oxford c.1204–1420,* H. E. Salter, W. A. Pantin and H. G. Richardson, eds., 2 vols. (Oxford 1942)

OHS   Oxford Historical Society

Rashdall I and III   *The Universities of Europe in the Middle Ages,* F. M. Powicke and A. B. Emden, eds., 3 vols. (Oxford 1936)

Statuta Antiqua   S. Gibson, *Statuta Antiqua Universitatis Oxoniensis* (Oxford 1931)

ILLUSTRATION CREDITS

INDEX